The *New* KornShell

Command and Programming Language

Morris I. Bolsky, David G. Korn
AT&T Bell Laboratories
Murray Hill, New Jersey

Prentice Hall PTR
Upper Saddle River, New Jersey 07458

Library of Congress Cataloging-in-Publication Data

```
Bolsky, Morris I.
     The new KornShell command and programming language / Morris
  I. Bolsky, David G. Korn. -- 2nd ed.
     Rev. ed. of: The KornShell command and programming language.
  c 1989
     Includes index.
     ISBN 0-13-182700-6 (paper)
     1. KornShell (Computer program language)  I.  Korn, David G.
  II. Bolsky, Morris I.  KornShell command and programming language.
  III. Title.
  QA76.73.K67B64  1995
  005.13'3--dc20                                          95-3380
                                                             CIP
```

Editorial/production supervision: *Harriet Tellem*
Cover design: *Lundgren Graphics, Ltd.*
Cover photo: *Courtesy of New England, Inc.*
Manufacturing buyer: *Alexis R. Heydt*
Acquisitions editor: *Gregory Doench*
Editorial assistant: *Meg Cowen*

Published by Prentice Hall PTR
Prentice-Hall, Inc.
A Simon & Schuster Company
Upper Saddle River, New Jersey 07458

The publisher offers discounts on this book when ordered in bulk quantities. For more information, contact:
Corporate Sales Department
Prentice Hall PTR
1 Lake Street
Upper Saddle River, NJ 07458

Phone: 800-382-3419, Fax: 201-236-7141, e-mail: corpsales@prenhall.com

UNIX is a registered trademark in the United States and other countries, licensed exclusively through X/OPEN Corporation.

Printed in the United States of America

10 9 8 7 6 5 4 3 2 1

ISBN 0-13-182700-6

Prentice-Hall International (UK) Limited, *London*
Prentice-Hall of Australia Pty. Limited, *Sydney*
Prentice-Hall Canada Inc., *Toronto*
Prentice-Hall Hispanoamericana, S.A., *Mexico*
Prentice-Hall of India Private Limited, *New Delhi*
Prentice-Hall of Japan, Inc., *Tokyo*
Simon & Schuster Asia Pte. Ltd., *Singapore*
Editora Prentice-Hall do Brasil, Ltda., *Rio de Janeiro*

CONTENTS

ACKNOWLEDGMENTS

Steven Bourne wrote the Bourne shell, from which the KornShell language is derived, while at Bell Laboratories. Bill Joy wrote the original version of the C shell while at the University of California, Berkeley, California.

Mike Veach of AT&T Bell Laboratories contributed the original code for the **emacs** built-in editor used in the KornShell language. Pat Sullivan, while at AT&T Bell Laboratories, contributed the original code for the **vi** built-in editor used in the KornShell language.

The **emacs** editor was developed by Richard Stallman at the Massachusetts Institute of Technology. The **emacs** program, from which the **emacs** built-in editor used in the KornShell language was adapted, was developed by Warren Montgomery of AT&T Bell Laboratories. The **vi** program, from which the **vi** built-in editor used in the KornShell language was adapted, was developed by Mark Horton and Bill Joy while at the University of California, Berkeley, California.

The Rand Corporation, and the Department of Information and Computer Science at the University of California, Irvine, developed software and documentation for the MH Message Handling System, now in the public domain. Bruce Borden, Stockton Gaines, and Norman Shapiro were the initial designers and developers of MH. (The *Complete Application* chapter uses the MH system as an example of how to write an application in **ksh**.)

We are most grateful to Rosemary Simpson who prepared the index.

We are especially grateful to everyone who has reviewed the drafts of this book, has given us suggestions for improvement, and has helped to debug the examples. In particular, we want to thank Harold Bamford, III, David Beckedorff, Bill Brelsford, Larry Cipriani, Glenn Fowler, Judy Grass, Steve Kennedy, Jeff Korn, Philip Korn, Lisa Kowalski, Steve Lally, Barbara Ling, Doug McIlroy, John Mocenigo, Charlie Northrup, Arnold Robbins, Steve Sommars, Kevin Wall, Robert Wantz, and Elia Weixelbaum.

ABOUT THIS BOOK

This second edition of the KornShell book is the *specification* of the revised KornShell language and a *reference handbook* for **ksh**, the program that implements the KornShell language. The language has undergone major changes and additions since the first edition. The new features of the language have increased the scope of applications that are suitable for writing in **ksh**. In addition, command completion and a key binding mechanism have been added to this version of **ksh**.

This book also contains a *Tutorial* that describes both of the functions of **ksh**: as an interactive command language, and as a programming language. It contains numerous examples illustrating the features of **ksh**, and many chapters have exercises. It also contains a *Quick Reference* summary of the KornShell language, including page references to the book.

The format of this second edition is similar to that of the first edition. This makes it easy for readers familiar with the first edition to use this book. In addition to describing the new features of the language, many reader suggestions have been incorporated.

This book is intended both for new users with little computer or shell experience, and for experienced computer users who are familiar with **ksh** and/or other shells. For new users, it has considerable tutorial material. For all users, it is a comprehensive reference handbook.

What is the KornShell Language?

The KornShell language was designed and developed by David G. Korn at AT&T Bell Laboratories. It is an *interactive command language* that provides access to the UNIX system and to many other systems, on the many different computers and workstations on which it is implemented. The KornShell language is also a complete, powerful, high-level *programming language* for writing applications, often more easily and quickly than with other high-level languages. This makes it especially suitable for prototyping.

There are two other widely used shells, the Bourne shell developed by Steven Bourne at AT&T Bell Laboratories, and the C shell developed by Bill Joy at the University of California. **ksh** has the best features of both, plus many new features of its own. Thus **ksh** can do much to enhance your productivity and the quality of your work, both in interacting with the system, and in programming. **ksh** programs are *easier to write*, and are more *concise* and *readable* than programs written in a lower level language such as C.

The new version of **ksh** has the functionality of other scripting languages such as **awk**, **icon**, **perl**, **rexx**, and **tcl**. For this and many other reasons, **ksh** is a much better scripting language than any of the other popular shells.

The code size for **ksh** is larger than the Bourne shell or C shell programs. The revised version is even larger. In spite of its increased size, **ksh** provides *better performance*. You can write programs to run faster with **ksh** than with either the Bourne shell or the C shell, *sometimes an order of magnitude faster*.

ksh has *evolved* and *matured* with extensive user feedback. It has been used by many thousands of people at AT&T since 1982, and at many other companies and universities. A survey conducted at one of the largest AT&T Bell Laboratories computer centers showed that 80% of their customers, both programmers and non-programmers, use **ksh**.

ksh is *compatible* with the Bourne shell. Virtually all programs written for the Bourne shell run with **ksh**. If you are familiar with the Bourne shell, you can use **ksh** immediately, without retraining. The new version of **ksh** is compatible with earlier versions of **ksh**.

ksh is *readily available*. It is sold (source and binary) by AT&T and Novell, and by other companies under license from AT&T both in the USA and abroad. It has been purchased by dozens of major corporations, and by many individuals for use on home computers.

ksh is *extensible*. The KornShell language uses the same syntax for built-in commands as for non built-in commands. Therefore, system developers can add new commands "transparently" to the KornShell language; that is, with minimum effort and with no differences visible to users other than faster execution. On systems with dynamic linking, it is possible to add new built-in commands at run time. Novell has extended the new version of **ksh** to enable X-windows programming for their desktop **ksh** product, **dtksh**. **dtksh** is a standard part of CDE, the Common Desktop Environment defined by COSE (Common Operating System Environment), supported by most major UNIX system hardware vendors.

ksh is intended to conform to the Shell Language Standard developed by the IEEE POSIX 1003.2 Shell and Utilities Language Committee. At the time the manuscript of this book was sent to the publisher, 1992 was the current version of the POSIX Standard. To the best of our knowledge, the description of **ksh** in this book is consistent with the 1992 standard.

Organization of this Book

Part I, Introduction, tells what a shell is and lists the benefits of the KornShell language. It tells how to obtain **ksh** and explains about different versions of **ksh**. It also specifies the notation used in this book.

Part II, Tutorial, has chapters on *Operating System Concepts* and on the use of the KornShell language as a *Command Language* and a *Programming Language*. The *Operating System Concepts* chapter covers *files, processes, strings* and *patterns* that provides background information to help you understand the KornShell language. You do not have to understand everything in it to read the remaining chapters.

The *Command Language* chapter is intended as a guide through the language by giving step-by-step instructions for some of the typical uses of **ksh**. It is not intended to explain in detail all of the features of **ksh**, or all of the possible uses of the features that are discussed in this chapter. All of the features of the KornShell language are covered in detail elsewhere in this book.

The *Programming Language* chapter is intended as an introduction to the features of the KornShell that are used primarily for writing scripts or applications in the shell language.

Part II, Tutorial, also has a chapter on *Customizing Your Environment*, which describes how to set up your profile and environment files. It also suggests ways for optimizing the performance of shell scripts.

Part III, The Built-In Editors, is a detailed manual for the **emacs** and **vi** built-in line editors that are part of **ksh**. Each of these is a subset of the corresponding editor. A major benefit of using **ksh** is that you can use **emacs** or **vi** directives to edit your current command line, or to edit and reenter previous commands.

Part IV, Programming Language, is both a specification for the KornShell language and a detailed guide to using it. It contains chapters on *Syntax, Command Processing, Compound Commands, Parameters, Built-in Commands*, and *Invocation and Environment*. It also contains a chapter, *Other Commands*, which documents programs that are not part of **ksh**, but which are used in the examples in this book and may prove useful to many users. UNIX systems and many other systems have these programs.

Part V, Application Programming, has a chapter on *Shell Functions and Programs*, with several functions and programs written in the KornShell language. They are included primarily for illustrative purposes. However, you may find some of these functions and/or programs useful. It also has the chapter, *A Complete Application*, with an example of how to use **ksh** as a high-level programming language, to program an application. The example that we use is a slightly modified version of the MH (Message Handling) system.

Part VI, *Appendix*, contains a *Glossary*. It also has a *Quick Reference*, with the formats, options, and page references for all **ksh** built-in, non-built-in, and editor commands, parameters, and other details.

The *Portability* chapter contains information to help you write portable scripts. There are sections listing features of **ksh** not in the Bourne Shell, features of **ksh** not in the System V Release 4 Shell, and features of **ksh** not in the POSIX shell. This chapter also lists **ksh** features that are in the POSIX shell but not in the System V Release 4 shell. In addition it discusses incompatibilities between **ksh** and the System V Release 4 Bourne Shell, and how **ksh** meets the POSIX requirements. A summary of all the new features in the 12/28/93 version of **ksh**, obsolescent features, and possible extensions to **ksh** are presented. Because of the large number of **csh** users migrating to **ksh**, we have included a section of helpful hints for making this task easier.

The *Character Set* chapter defines the character representation for ASCII encoding, and the character classes that each character belongs to in the C and POSIX locales.

There is also a detailed *Index*. The outside back cover has page references to all commands and parameters, and a brief summary of key **emacs** and **vi** directives.

Obtaining Examples in this Book in Electronic Form

The code for many of the examples in this book is available on the Internet via anonymous ftp to ftp.research.att.com. The programs are in the directory dist/ksh/examples.

PART I

INTRODUCTION

1 ABOUT THE KornShell LANGUAGE

WHAT IS A SHELL?

Much of the excitement when the UNIX shell emerged from AT&T Bell Laboratories nearly twenty years ago was over the fact that this new command interpreter was also a programming language. Two major consequences of this development changed the landscape at the time and continue to influence the way we think and work today. First, overnight the power of programming was placed in the hands of non-programmers, that is, of users. In fact, this new language was called the *shell* to suggest an outer layer that pointed to operating system services, called a kernel, underneath the shell. Second, because the command interpreter mediated between all the other commands, the shell became a kind of "glue language" that could combine languages, tools, and utilities into still other tools.

A shell enables the user to interact with resources of the computer such as programs, files, and devices. An *interactive* shell acts as a command interpreter. In its role as a command interpreter, the shell is the interface between the user and the system. The user types commands to the shell and the shell carries them out, usually by running programs. This is the primary function of the shell for many users. Some interactive shells contain a built-in command line editor facility to make it easy and fast to repeat or edit the current and previous commands.

Most shells can also be used as programming languages. Users can combine command sequences to create new programs. These programs are known as shell scripts. Shell scripts automate use of the shell as a command interpreter. For instance, if you frequently use the same sequence of, say, five shell commands, you could write and execute a file with these five commands to avoid having to retype them each time. When you reference this file, the shell will interpret the lines in it as though they were typed from a terminal.

Some shells, such as the KornShell, are, in effect, a complete high-level programming language. The KornShell language includes variables, functions, built-in commands, and control flow commands (for instance, conditional and iteration commands). Thus, KornShell scripts can be application programs just like those written in other medium and high-level languages such as Basic, Fortran, or the C language (not to be confused with the C shell!).

The new version of **ksh** has the functionality of other scripting languages such as **awk**, **icon**, **perl**, **rexx**, and **tcl**. For this and many other reasons (see *Benefits of Using* ksh, below), **ksh** is a much better scripting language than any of the other popular shells.

The KornShell language is described in *About This Book*. Because of the ease of programming in the KornShell language, it is especially useful for prototyping. A prototype for an application system may be written first in the KornShell language. Parts of the application can then be rewritten in a lower level language as the need arises.

Today the dominant glue language at AT&T and many other corporations and universities is the KornShell, or **ksh**. It has evolved to serve today's needs by placing far more programming power into users' hands than does any other shell.

BENEFITS OF USING ksh

There is just one KornShell language, but you can use it as a command language and/or as a programming language. We use the term *commands* to indicate what you type at your terminal for immediate execution. We use the term *scripts* to indicate programs that you write in the KornShell language and place into a file for later execution.

ksh is very portable and runs on many different systems. This enables programs written for one system to be run without change on other systems. It also enables programmers who are familiar with **ksh** to use new systems without going through time-consuming learning periods, and to use several systems at the same time without the confusion caused when each system has a different interface.

Compared to other shells, **ksh** has benefits for use as a command language and benefits for use as a programming language. These benefits are summarized below.

Improvements as a Command Language

Command line editing. Retyping a command is tedious, time-consuming, and error-prone, especially if changes need to be made several times. A major benefit of **ksh** is that it has an **emacs**-like and a **vi**-like interface with which to edit the current command line. Thus with **ksh** it is not necessary to backspace to the point where a change is needed, or to start over. Users of **ksh** tend to form the habit of editing their current command before pressing RETURN . The same interface can also be used to make changes to previous commands, which **ksh** keeps in a history file.

Command history mechanism. ksh keeps a history file that stores the commands you enter. The history file can be accessed via **emacs** or **vi** editor directives, or via the built-in command **hist**. The history file is maintained across login sessions, and can be shared by several simultaneous instances of **ksh**. Thus a previous command can be modified and reentered with minimal effort.

Command name completion. You can have **ksh** complete the name of a command or a file name after entering part of it. You can either request a list of alternatives or request that **ksh** fill in as many of the remaining characters as it can.

Command name aliasing. Command name and option combinations can be customized by defining shorthand names, called aliases, for commands that you use frequently.

Job control. ksh provides a facility for managing multiple jobs simultaneously. On most systems, jobs can be stopped and moved to and from the background.

New cd capabilities. You can return to the previous directory without having to type the name of the directory. The working directory can be changed to a similarly named directory without having to type the complete name. **ksh** allows you to extend the functionality of the **cd** command by replacing it with a user-defined function.

Tilde expansion. The home directory of any user, and the last directory that you were in, can be referred to symbolically. It is not necessary to type, or even to know, the name of the directory.

Improvements as a Programming Language

More general I/O mechanism. More than one file can be simultaneously opened and read. The number of columns printed for each item of information can be specified in a program. The new version of **ksh** has the same formatting capability as ANSI C.

Menu selection primitive. ksh provides a structured way to write programs that query the user via menus. **ksh** adjusts the menu display to the size of the terminal screen display.

Built-in arithmetic. ksh can perform arithmetic using the C language expression syntax. The new version of **ksh** performs floating point calculations and supports the standard math library, while the previous version was restricted to integer arithmetic.

Substring operators. ksh can generate substrings from the values of shell variables. The new version of **ksh** supports new operators and allows operations to be applied to aggregates.

Array variables and attributes. Strings can be converted to uppercase or lowercase. One-dimensional arrays of strings or numbers can be used. The new version of **ksh** also supports associative arrays (arrays whose subscripts are strings), in addition to indexed arrays (arrays whose subscripts are integers).

Enlarged name space and reference variables. The name space for variables is a hierarchy of identifiers with . (dot) as a delimiter, allowing data aggregates to be defined. Reference variables provide a way of referring to data aggregates without the need of copying.

More general function facility. Local variables within functions can be defined and, therefore, recursive procedures can be written. Code can be specified to be executed whenever the function terminates. Functions can be loaded dynamically.

Active variables. Each variable can have functions defined that are invoked when the variable is referenced, set, or unset. These are called discipline functions.

Co-process facility. ksh provides the capability to run one or more programs in the background, and to send and receive queries from it. This makes it easy to use shell scripts as a front end to a database management system, an Internet server, or another system.

Easier to debug. ksh displays better error diagnostics when it encounters an error. Thus the cause of the error can be located more easily. The execution of each function can be traced separately.

Better performance. ksh scripts can often be written to run an order of magnitude faster than comparable Bourne shell or C shell scripts.

Better security. ksh allows a system administrator to log and/or disable all privileged scripts. On current UNIX systems, users need read permission on a script in order to execute a script. With **ksh**, a system administrator can allow **ksh** to read and execute a script without giving a user permission to read it.

International. ksh has full 8-bit transparency so that it can be used with extended character sets. **ksh** can be compiled to support multibyte and multiwidth character sets as found in several Asian languages. The new version of **ksh** also supports locale-specific pattern matching, collation, and string translation.

Extensible. On systems with dynamic linking, **ksh** built-in commands can be added at run time. These built-in commands can customize parts of the variable name space by adding additional discipline functions.

VERSION TO WHICH THIS BOOK APPLIES

ksh has evolved and matured with extensive user feedback. Thus there are several versions of **ksh**. This book specifies the version of **ksh** dated 12/28/93. New features in this version are listed in the ***Appendix*** on page 359. This book also describes the older version dated 11/16/88, commonly available on many systems.

New features or changes in the 12/28/93 version are noted in this book by the word "***Version***," followed by a statement such as, "This feature is available only on versions of **ksh** newer than the 11/16/88 version." Note that most examples do not use the 12/28/93 features, except where indicated.

You can find the date of the version of **ksh** you are using by:
- Using the CONTROL v directive of the **vi** or **emacs** built-in editor.
- Looking in your system documentation.
- Using the **what** command with the appropriate pathname. (However, your system may not have the **what** command.)
  Example
  ```
  what /bin/ksh | grep Version
          Version 12/28/93b
  ```
- Displaying the variable **.sh.version** variable. ***Version***: The **.sh.version** variable is only available on versions of **ksh** newer than the 11/16/88 version.
  Example
  ```
  print ${.sh.version}
  Version 12/28/93b
  ```

A suffix (b in the above example) following a date indicates minor and/or local modifications to the code. However, the features are nearly the same for all releases of **ksh** with the same date, regardless of the suffix. *Note*: The last release for the 1988 version was 11/16/88i.

As with many other programs, **ksh** is implemented on many different systems, and on many different multiuser and single user (personal) computers. There inevitably are differences between implementations, usually minor, and presumably documented by the supplier of the program. Features of **ksh** that are most likely to vary on different implementations are noted in this book by the words "***Implementation-dependent***," followed by an explanation.

On some systems, the organization that built or installed **ksh** may have replaced the original date by another means of indicating the version, such as numbers and/or letters, or even by a date that has no relation to the dates mentioned above. In this case, you have to determine what you have from the documentation, by experimenting, and/or by asking others. However, the fact remains that most, if not quite all, of the information in this book will almost certainly be applicable to the implementation of **ksh** that you have.

For those readers who are familiar with the Bourne shell, subtle differences between the Bourne shell and **ksh** are noted in this book by the words, "*Bourne shell*," followed by an explanation of the differences. Also, the chapter on *Portability* lists differences.

HOW TO OBTAIN ksh

The 1988 version of **ksh** is included in UNIX System V Release 4, and also with other operating systems. Some specific examples are: AT&T Global Information Solutions (GIS) UNIX systems; Hewlett-Packard running HP-UX; IBM RS/6000 running AIX; Apple Computer running A/UX; Sun Microsystems running Solaris 2.x; DEC running OSF/1; and Intel 386 running SCO UNIX.

Other vendors sell the binary of the 1988 version of **ksh** as add-ons to their systems or for other systems. For instance, an MS-DOS version of the 1988 KornShell language is available from Mortice Kern Systems, Inc. of Waterloo, Ontario, Canada.

The 1993 version of **ksh** will be included with the Common Desktop Environment, CDE, that was defined by COSE, the Common Operating System Environment supported by most major UNIX system hardware vendors.

Other vendors can obtain binary distribution licenses for the 1993 version of **ksh** from the AT&T Software Solutions Group, 800-462-8146; or by writing to AT&T Software Solutions Group, 10 Independence Blvd., Warren, NJ 07059 USA. For instance, the Congruent Corp., 110 Greene Street, New York, NY 10012 USA, 212-431-5100, sells binaries for several operating systems, including Microsoft Windows NT.

Source code for the 1988 and 1993 versions of **ksh** is available from the AT&T Toolchest. For further information, phone or write the AT&T Software Solutions Group, as shown above. Individuals within AT&T who wish to get the 1993 version of **ksh** for any system should send e-mail to ksh@mozart.att.com.

Caution: Some programs that may be somewhat similar to **ksh**, such as **pdksh** and **bash**, unfortunately do not presently conform to either the 1988 or 1993 versions of **ksh**. They lack many of the features of **ksh** documented in this book and cannot run many of the examples.

2 NOTATION USED IN THIS BOOK

GENERAL

For conciseness, we refer to:
- The program that implements the KornShell language, as **ksh**.
- The **emacs** and **vi** built-in editors, as **emacs** and **vi**. When we mean the complete programs, we say the **emacs** program or the **vi** program.
- Commands, just by their names. The names are in **bold** type, for instance, **alias** and **date**.
- The person providing input to **ksh**, as "you." Depending on the context, this would mean the person using **ksh** as an interactive command language, or as a programming language.

Usual pronunciation:
- **emacs**. *ee-macks* (*ee* as in *beet*).
- **ksh**. Pronounce each letter separately.
- MH. Pronounce each letter separately.
- POSIX. *pahz-icks*.
- UNIX. *u-nix* (*u* pronounced like *you*).
- **vi**. Pronounce each letter separately.

KEYS ON TERMINAL

Special keys that you press, such as `CONTROL`, are in uppercase Helvetica bold type in a box. Individual letter or symbol keys that you press, such as **h** or **]**, are also in **bold** type but are in Times font and are not in a box. Uppercase and lowercase characters are equivalent when you use the `CONTROL` key; for instance, `CONTROL` **h** or `CONTROL` **H**.

Some of these special keys may be labeled differently on different terminals. Some possible alternate labels are shown below. If your keyboard doesn't have any of these alternate labels, you can try the `CONTROL` key plus the individual letter or symbol key shown below. If necessary, see the **Character Set** for further clarification, plus the documentation for your keyboard.

`BACKSPACE`   Press the key labeled BACKSPACE, or else `CONTROL` **h**.

`CONTROL`   Always use this key in conjunction with an individual letter or symbol key. While holding down the key labeled CONTROL or CTRL, press whatever individual letter or symbol key is appropriate.

`DELETE`   Press the key labeled DEL or DELETE, or RUB or RUBOUT, or `CONTROL` **?**, or else `CONTROL` `BACKSPACE`.

`ESCAPE`   Press the key labeled ESCAPE or ESC, or else `CONTROL` **[**.

`RETURN`   Press the key labeled RETURN or NEWLINE or ENTER, or else `CONTROL` **m**.

`SPACE`   Press the space bar.

`TAB`   Press TAB, or else `CONTROL` **i**.

TYPE FONTS USED IN THIS BOOK

Bold type indicates anything that you type exactly as shown, such as command and option names.

Lowercase *italics* are used for generic terms that represent values, including:

file   A pathname for a file.

string   One or more characters.

c   Any single character (letter, digit, or special character), as specified. For instance, on page 119, **f***c* means that you can type **f** followed by any character to move the cursor right to the next occurrence of the character defined by *c*.

n   Any single- or multi-digit number.

motion   A text region from the current cursor position to the cursor position defined by the **vi** built-in editor **Moving the Cursor** or **Moving To Character** directives.

Italics with Initial Caps is used for terminal control characters that you can define if you don't want to use the following defaults:

End-of-file   `CONTROL` **d**

Erase   **#** or `CONTROL` **h** or `DELETE`

Interrupt   `DELETE` or `CONTROL` **c**

Kill   **@** or `CONTROL` **u** or `CONTROL` **x**

Lnext	CONTROL v
Quit	CONTROL \
Restart	CONTROL q
Stop	CONTROL s
Suspend	CONTROL z
Werase	CONTROL w

Courier Font Used in Examples. Most of this book is in the Times font. However, examples are in the Courier font to distinguish the examples from the rest of the text, and because Courier is a constant width font, which is closer to most computer displays than is the proportionally spaced Times font.

The following Courier typefaces are used:

Bold   What you have in your **ksh** script.

Oblique   What you type to **ksh**.·

Plain   Output to you.

_(underline) In examples in the chapters on **emacs** and **vi**, we indicate the current cursor position by an underline.

Example

abcde̲fg

SYMBOLIC NAMES FOR CONSTANTS

Symbolic names are in Helvetica font with initial caps. If any of these names is followed by the letter s in Times font, it means that one or more are allowed. For instance, Spaces means that one or more spaces are allowed.

True   Return value of 0 (zero). This means that a command has completed successfully.

False   Non-zero return value. This means that a command has not completed successfully. A number enclosed in parentheses after False indicates the value.

Null   Empty string; that is, a string with no characters.

Space   ASCII character decimal 32.

Tab   ASCII character decimal 9.

Newline   ASCII character decimal 10.

Return   ASCII character decimal 13.

Bell   ASCII character decimal 7.

COMMAND SYNTAX NOTATION

[ ] (brackets) indicate an optional argument. For instance,

[a] means **a** or no argument

a[b] means **a** or **ab**

[a [b]] means **a**, **ab**, or no argument

[a] [b] means **a**, **b**, **ab**, or no argument

... (ellipsis) indicates that you can repeat the preceding argument, separating repetitions by either of:

• Spaces or Tabs.

• Newlines, as indicated in the format by the ellipsis appearing alone on a line. If the ellipsis follows a closing bracket, you can repeat everything within the bracket.

PART II

TUTORIAL

3   OPERATING SYSTEM CONCEPTS

ksh is a command and programming language that provides you with a method for communicating with your operating system. To make the best use of **ksh,** you need to understand two basic operating system concepts – *files* and *processes*. In addition, to use **ksh** effectively, it is necessary to understand the concepts of *strings* and *patterns*.

This chapter describes what you should know about files, processes, strings, and patterns to use **ksh** to its fullest extent. It gives you background information that will help you to understand the following two chapters on the KornShell, **Command Language** and **Programming Language**.

New users may find this chapter difficult because it introduces many unfamiliar concepts. However, there is no need to master these concepts in order to move to the next chapter. Refer to the **Glossary** in the Appendix for terms that you do not understand. If you have difficulty with this chapter, return to it later. Experienced KornShell users may want to just skim over this chapter.

FILES

For the most part, a file is a named set of data that resides on a permanent storage device, usually a disk. The data contained in a file can range from program instructions to a word processor document. A special type of file called a *directory* contains the names of other files. It may be useful to think of the permanent storage device as a file cabinet, directories as file folders, and files as files within the folders. Note that a folder may contain other folders (i.e., a directory may contain other directories).

A system of organizing files on disk such as the one described above is known as a *file system*. In addition, a file system usually dictates how files are named and how *permissions* on files are set, as well as several other properties of files and their organization.

ksh uses the UNIX file system model which is described throughout this chapter. If you are using **ksh** on a non-UNIX system, your operating system will probably use a different file system. In this case, there are two possibilities. If your operating system provides a method for "imitating" the UNIX file system, known as emulation, **ksh** will not be affected and will behave as described in this chapter. If not, some of the features of **ksh** will not work. You should refer to the documentation for **ksh** on your system for differences between your version and the UNIX version.

Naming Conventions

The overall structure of the UNIX file system is that of a tree as shown in the diagram below.

The tree is composed of directories (shown as ovals) and files (shown as rectangles). The name of the root directory is /. All other directory names and filenames can be a sequence of characters other than /. Uppercase and lowercase characters are distinct. Some systems limit a filename to 14 characters, and some systems limit the set of characters that can be used in a filename. Filenames which begin with a . (dot) are sometimes called *hidden files* because they are not listed unless specifically requested.

A sample file tree. Directories are ovals, files are rectangles.

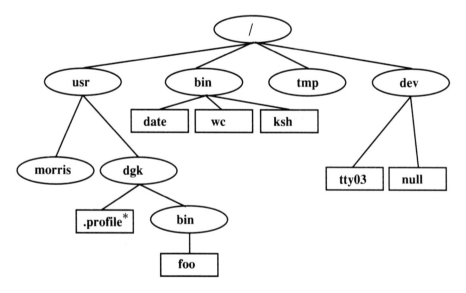

* Pathname for .profile is /usr/dgk/.profile

A *pathname* is more specific than a single directory name or filename. A pathname prefixes the directory name or filename with a *path*, a route from one directory to another. A pathname can also be referred to as a *link* to the file. A path is named by a series of directory names separated from each other by the / character. For instance, in the sample above, a pathname from the directory **dgk** to the file **foo** would be **bin/foo**. A pathname from the root directory to the file **tty03** would be **/dev/tty03**.

A pathname beginning with a / starts at the root and is called an *absolute pathname*. If the pathname does not begin with a /, it is called a *relative pathname*. Relative pathnames begin at the current directory, or *working directory*, rather than the root directory. The working directory is automatically maintained by **ksh** and is initially set to the directory you were in when you invoked **ksh**, or to your home directory. In addition, the *parent directory* of a directory X is the directory that contains X. In this case, X may also be referred to as a *subdirectory* of its parent.

The working directory and the parent directory can also be referred to using the special directory names **.** (dot) and **..** (dot-dot), respectively. Every directory on your system automatically contains a **.** directory which refers to itself, and a **..** directory which refers to the parent directory. The parent of the root directory (/) is itself. These two directories serve many purposes as will be seen later.

File Permissions

Each file has an owner id and a group id, which regulate access to the file. The owner id of a new file depends on the process that creates it. The group id of a new file may depend either on the process that creates it or the group id of the directory in which the file is created, depending on your system. See **Process Permissions** on page 20 for details.

Files and directories have three types of permissions, named read, write, and execute. The names read and write are self-explanatory for files. Execute permission on a file permits running the program contained in the file. For a directory, read permission permits reading the list of filenames contained in that directory. Write permission on a directory gives permission to add new filenames or delete existing filenames. Execute permission on a directory gives permission to search for a specified filename in that directory so that files in the directory can be accessed.

A file or directory can have three sets of permissions, each consisting of any combination of read, write, and execute. The three permission sets are:
• Permissions for the owner of the file.
• Permissions for members of the group corresponding to the group id of the file.
• Permissions that apply to all other users.

In addition, on some systems an executable file can have setuid permission and/or setgid permission. These permissions are explained in **Process Permissions** on page 20.

Some systems have additional finer granularity control called access lists that control access on a per user basis. A discussion of access permissions is beyond the scope of this book.

Special Files and Directories

By convention, several directories serve special purposes. For example, the **/bin** directory usually contains frequently used system programs. Users often create a subdirectory of their home directory named **bin** to store their own programs. Temporary files are usually stored in a directory named **/tmp** by convention.

The **/dev** directory is usually reserved for *device files*. Device files are special files that are used only to refer to input and output devices such as terminals, tape drives, speakers, etc. The device file called **/dev/null** is a special file which is always empty.

A pipe is a special file that is designed to pass data from one process to another. See **Interprocess Communication** on page 22.

Some systems have a special file type called a symbolic link. The contents of a symbolic link file is a pathname. When a filename is referenced and the system determines that it is a symbolic link, the system replaces the filename or pathname by the pathname defined by the symbolic link. When the pathname defined by the link begins with a **/**, the pathname is replaced; otherwise, the filename is replaced. We refer to the original pathname as the logical name, and the name that is obtained by replacing all filenames with the symbolic link pathnames as the physical name. For instance, if **/bin** is a symbolic link to **/usr/bin,** then the physical pathname for **/bin/date** is **/usr/bin/date**.

PROCESSES

ksh uses the UNIX system model of processes. If you are using **ksh** with an operating system other than the UNIX system, and if the operating system has a different computing model than does the UNIX system, then the operating system must have special code to make it appear as if it has processes with the properties described below. If it has this special code, all of the features of **ksh** should work. Otherwise, some of the features of **ksh** will not work as documented in this chapter. As an example, the MS-DOS system does not allow multitasking; thus it cannot run programs in the background as described on page 45.

You can think of a process as a program that has been launched but has not yet completed. It is an object created and controlled by the UNIX system and other similar systems. It consists of a program to execute, and of resources allocated to it by the operating system (such as memory and files) that it can read and/or write.

Each process has a single thread of control. In theory, several processes can be running at the same time, even the same program. On a computer that has many processors, this might actually be possible. However, on a computer with only one processor, processes take turns sharing the processor. This is called time-sharing. Time-sharing is also possible on a system with multiple processors. Even when the computer has as many processors as processes, the processes may not all be running at the same time because some of them might be waiting for data from a terminal or from another process.

Creating and Destroying Processes

The operating system that **ksh** runs on must provide a means of creating and destroying processes. **ksh** provides you with a simplified interface to the system for creating, destroying, and managing processes.

When a process is created, it is allocated resources such as a memory area and open files. When a process finishes executing, the system destroys the process and recovers its resources, so they may be reallocated to other processes.

Each process has a unique number associated with it called the process id. This number distinguishes the process from all other processes that have been created but have not yet been destroyed.

The system assigns a priority to each process. When there are more processes to execute than there are processors, those processes with a higher priority are given preference over those with a lower priority. A program such as **ksh** can influence process priority.

Each process belongs to a group identified by the process group id. Only one process group can be associated with your terminal at a time; this group is called the foreground process group. Any process of yours that is not in the foreground process group is called a background process.

Process Relationships

A process that creates another process is called the parent process. The created process is called the child process.

In the UNIX system, a process creates a child process by making a copy of itself. Except for the process id, these processes are initially identical. To run a new program, the child process overwrites itself with the code and initial data of the new program and then begins to execute the new program. A property of this method is that the child process has a copy of all the resources of the one that created it. **ksh** can use, but does not require, the UNIX system method of process creation.

The term process environment refers to all the information associated with a process that affects how it will behave (see page 22). When a child process is created, it inherits a copy of most of the environment of the parent. As a process runs, it may modify its copy of the environment. The parent process environment is not affected by changes made by the child, except by side effects through shared files. Similarly, the child environment is not affected by subsequent changes made by the parent process.

A parent process can suspend its execution until one or more of its child processes complete. For example, **ksh** normally runs programs by creating a child process and waiting for it to complete before prompting you for the next command. When a child process completes it returns a number (the "return value") to its parent that indicates whether it encountered any errors; by convention, processes that run successfully have a zero return value.

Process Permissions

Each process has a real user id and one or more real group ids. These are set when you log in, and are inherited by all processes you create.

Each process also has an effective user id and an effective group id that determine what permissions that process has to read, write, and/or execute files. These ids are set to the real user id and real group id when you log in, and are inherited from the parent process.

The effective user id and effective group id are used to determine which files the process can access. The owner id of any file created by a process is determined by the effective user id of the process. The group id of any file created by a process is determined either by the effective group id of the process, or else the group id of the directory it is created in, depending on the system. On some systems, the setgid permission on a directory causes files created in that directory to belong to the same group that the directory belongs to. On other systems the group of the file is determined by the effective group id of the process.

If a file that contains a program has setuid and/or setgid permission, then when the system runs that program, the system sets the effective user and/or group id of the process to the owner and/or group of the file. *Caution*: There are important security issues associated with setuid and setgid programs. Do not specify either of these permissions unless you understand the ramifications. Some systems remove these permissions whenever you write to a file as a security precaution.

Signals

A signal is a message (a number represented by a symbolic name) that can be sent to a process or a process group by either the system or another process. Also, pressing certain keys on your terminal causes a signal to be sent to all processes in the foreground process group.

Different systems support different.signals. For each of these signals, a process must either explicitly ignore the signal or must specify the action to be taken when it receives the signal; otherwise, a default action takes place. Unless stated otherwise, the default action for the signals listed below is to terminate the process. **ksh** requires that the system support at least these signals:

HUP   Hangup. This signal is sent by the system to the foreground process group when you disconnect from the system. Some systems also send **HUP** to background process groups associated with your terminal when you log out.

INT   Interrupt. This signal is sent to the foreground process group by pressing the *Interrupt* key. Depending on the system, the default *Interrupt* key is usually `DELETE` or `CONTROL` c.

KILL   Kill. This signal is sent by a process to one or more processes owned by the same user to cause them to terminate. This signal cannot be ignored by the receiving process; also, the receiving process cannot specify any action to take when it receives this signal. Therefore, the process will terminate. *Caution*: Do not confuse the **KILL** signal with the *Kill* character described later.

TERM   Termination. This signal is sent by a process to one or more processes owned by the same user, to request termination. A process can specify an action to take when it receives this signal, or it can ignore it.

The job control feature described in the ***Command Language*** chapter requires these signals:

CONT   Continue. This signal causes a stopped process to resume execution.

STOP   Stop. This signal causes the receiving process to stop. A stopped process continues when it receives the **CONT** signal. This signal cannot be ignored by the receiving process.

TSTP   Keyboard stop. This signal is sent to the foreground process group
           when you press the *Suspend* character, normally ⌐CONTROL¬ Z.
           By default, a process stops if it receives this signal.
TTIN   Terminal (tty) input. This signal is sent to each process in the
           background process group that tries to read from the terminal.
           By default, a process stops if it receives this signal.

Keys that cause the foreground process group to receive a signal can be altered by
any process that has access to the terminal. However, these settings are associated
with the terminal (not the process environment), so that all processes sharing the
terminal are affected.

A process can send a signal to another process only if it has appropriate
permission. For most signals, this means that the receiving process must have the
same effective user id as the sending process. Some systems are less restrictive on
sending signals.

Interprocess Communication

In addition to sending signals, processes communicate with another process by
reading from and writing to an ordinary disk file, or by using a special file called a
pipe. A pipe is designed to be shared by more than one process. When a process
tries to read from a pipe, the process performs one of these actions:
• Returns the data if a process has written to the pipe.
• Returns with an end of file indication if no other process has the pipe open for
  writing.
• Suspends execution until a process writes data to it.

In another form of interprocess communication, a child process uses the return
value when it exits, to communicate to its parent process.

Process Environment

The environment of a process consists of all information within a process that
affects the process. This includes:
• Process and process group ids.
• Open files.
• Working directory.
• File creation mask. (This is commonly referred to as the user mask or umask.)
• Real and effective user and group ids.
• Resource limits such as the size of the largest file that the process can create,
  and the maximum amount of memory that it can use.
• Signal action settings.
• A set of named variables.

Each process has a separate environment that is initialized from its parent.
A process can change its environment by using several of the **ksh** commands.
However, changes made in the environment of programs that **ksh** runs do not
change the environment of **ksh**.

Open files are inherited by child processes unless they are specified close-on-exec.

File Descriptors

A process associates a number with each file that it has opened. This number is
called the file descriptor. When you log in, your first process has the following
three open files connected to your terminal:
- Standard input: File descriptor 0 is open for reading.
- Standard output: File descriptor 1 is open for writing.
- Standard error: File descriptor 2 is open for reading and writing.

A file descriptor can be duplicated, giving another number that refers to the same
file. Each file descriptor corresponding to a regular file has a current byte offset
that is shared by all duplicates of the file. Thus, reading from or writing to a file
affects the current byte of all duplicates of the file.

Each file descriptor can have a bit set (known as the close-on-exec bit) that will
cause the file descriptor to close when you execute a new program. If this bit is off
the child process inherits a duplicate of the file descriptor.

STRINGS AND PATTERNS

This section introduces concepts and definitions that are used throughout the book.

Characters and Strings

A character is a set of one or more bytes that represent a graphic symbol (also
known as a *glyph*). The set of valid characters, and the number of bytes that
comprise a character, are defined by the current *locale*. In most American and
European locales a character is a single byte. The character set for the default
POSIX locale using the ASCII encoding is listed in the table on page 368; each
character consists of a single byte. All locales must contain the characters marked
with a √ in that table. However, the characters can use a character encoding other
than ASCII.

Each character can be a member of one or more of the classes whose names
appear on page 133. For example, the **alpha** class normally contains all characters
that are used to form a word in the current locale. The table on page 368 lists the
character classes to which each character in the POSIX locale belongs.

A string is a sequence of zero or more characters. The length of a string is the number of characters in the string. By convention, the characters of a string are numbered starting at 0. A string consisting of zero characters is called a Null string. The process of adding one string to the end of another string is called concatenation. A sequence of one or more contiguous characters of a string is called a substring.

There is no limit to the length of a string in the **ksh** language. Unlike many other programming languages, strings in **ksh** do not need to be quoted unless they contain characters that have special meaning in the language. **ksh** quoting rules on page 141 describe how to quote a character or a string of characters.

Collation Ordering of Strings

Strings can be ordered or collated based on the given locale. To perform the ordering, a string is broken down to a sequence of collating elements.
For example, in Spanish the character sequence **ch** is a collating element.
Each collating element is assigned one or more weights that are used for ordering strings. The first weight is called the primary weight and all characters that have the same primary weight form an equivalence class. The rules for collation, which depend on the current locale, may be very complex and are beyond the scope of this book. In the default POSIX locale, each character is a collating element and the weight of each character is the numerical value of the character as shown in the table on page 368. In the POSIX locale, strings are ordered from left to right.

Patterns

One of the major features of **ksh** is its pattern-matching capability. A pattern is a notation used to represent a set of strings. Since a pattern is represented by a sequence of characters, it is itself also a string. In any situation where a string or a pattern can be used, and a string is intended, it is necessary to quote characters that would otherwise be special pattern-matching characters.

There are three common notations for patterns. You may already be familiar with the two pattern-matching notations, called basic regular expressions and extended regular expressions, used in some UNIX system utilities such as **ed**, **sed**, **grep**, and **egrep**. **ksh** pattern matching constructs differ in notation from these, yet offer similar functionality.

One use of patterns is to specify sets of filenames. For example, the pattern *, which is a wildcard for a string of any length composed of any characters, can be used to expand to a list of all the filenames in the current directory that do not begin with . (dot), which are hidden by default.

Patterns are used to extract strings with particular features from a list of strings. For example, the pattern ***.c** can be used to represent all C programming language files in the current directory that do not begin with **.** (dot). Pathnames that begin with **.** (dot) are hidden files.

Patterns are also used for substring operations, whereby a substring of a string can be deleted from that string, can be extracted from the string, or can be replaced by another string.

EXERCISES

1. When do path **bar** and path **/foo/bar** refer to the same file?

2. Can standard error and standard output be the same file? What file descriptor number is standard error? What number is standard input?

3. What is the absolute pathname for file **foo** in the sample file tree on page 16?

4. Which of the following are legal filenames on your system? Which are legal pathnames?

   a. `foo`
   b. `foo/bar`
   c. `foo*`
   d. `/foo/bar`
   e. `//foo///bar`
   f. `*/*`
   g. `foo.@#( )bar`
   h. `.profile`

5. What is the physical pathname corresponding to **/home/dgk/bin**, if **/home** is a symbolic link to **/n1/usr** and **/home/dgk/bin** is a symbolic link to **oldbin**?

6. Under what circumstances can two processes have the same:
   a. Process id?
   b. Parent process id?
   c. Process group id?

7. Why should you never specify setuid permission and write permission for others on the same file?

8. Can a file have more than one owner id? Can a file have more than one group id?

9. In what ways can the actions of a child process affect its parent?

10. What is the purpose of **/bin**, **/tmp**, and **/dev**?

11. Can you execute a program that is in a directory for which you do not have read permission?

12. What is the resulting string when you concatenate the strings **foo** and **bar**? What is the length of the resulting string?

13. What is the substring of the string **language** from characters 2 through 4?

4 COMMAND LANGUAGE

This chapter is a tutorial for the KornShell command language. It is intended to guide you through the language by giving you step-by-step instructions for some of the typical uses of **ksh**. It is not intended to explain in detail all of the features of **ksh**, or all of the possible uses of the features that are discussed in this chapter. All of the features of the KornShell language are covered in detail in *Part IV* of this book.

This chapter is intended both for new users with relatively little computer or shell experience, and for experienced computer users who are familiar with other shells. For this reason, some material may appear too detailed to new users, while other material may appear not detailed enough to experienced users. New users who are not familiar with these commands may want to practice using them as they are introduced. However, new users should note that the intent of this chapter is to help you learn how to use **ksh** as a whole, not how to use each command in detail. Experienced KornShell users may want to skim over or skip this chapter.

There is only one KornShell language. The division between command language and programming language into separate chapters is for tutorial purposes only. We use the term *commands* to indicate what you type at your terminal for immediate execution. We use the term *scripts* to indicate what you put into a file for later execution. Scripts are programs that are written in the KornShell programming language. Learning **ksh** as a command language is one of the best ways of easing your way into writing scripts. On the other hand, you can use the features described in the *Programming Language* chapter when you are using **ksh** as a command language.

If you are not familiar with the **emacs** editor or the **vi** editor, and your terminal does not have local line editing, you will benefit by learning one of these editors before using **ksh**. You should first read the *Built-in Editors* part of this book.

The examples in this chapter use **ksh** built-in commands, which are described in the *Built-in Commands* chapter; they are a part of **ksh**. The examples also use programs, described in the *Other Commands* chapter, which are common UNIX system commands. These programs may behave differently than documented in this book, or may not be on your system at all.

The back cover of this book is a quick index to more detail about each of the commands in the examples, and all the other commands in this book as well. Use it to locate more complete descriptions of a command if you have difficulty with any of the examples. In addition, the **Quick Reference** chapter has detailed information on the commands and other aspects of **ksh**, as well as page references. Also see the **Glossary** starting on page 323 for terms with which you are not familiar.

Run **ksh** by typing its name, **ksh** (on some systems it may be **sh**), and then pressing RETURN . To make it even easier, on most systems your system administrator can arrange to have **ksh** be your default shell when you turn on your computer or when you log in. On some systems you can make **ksh** your default shell by typing **chsh** RETURN . You will be prompted for the name of the new shell that you want; type the pathname of **ksh** on your system, usually **/bin/ksh**.

ksh displays a prompt when it is ready to read a command. This prompt is called the primary prompt. The default primary prompt string is **$** (dollar followed by Space).

To see the commands numbered as in this tutorial, type **PS1='!$ '**. Numbering commands in your prompt is explained on page 88.

EXECUTING SIMPLE COMMANDS

Enter a **ksh** command by typing a sequence of words. The first word in the line is the command name*. The following word(s) are mandatory or optional items of information used by the command, called command arguments. Press SPACE and/or TAB one or more times to separate the command name word from the command argument word(s), and to separate each of the command argument words. Uppercase and lowercase characters, such as **A** and **a**, are distinct. By convention, most command names and arguments are in lowercase.

ksh does not begin to process the command until you press RETURN . If the command refers to a program, then **ksh** creates a child process to run the program and waits for the child process to complete. Otherwise, **ksh** itself executes the command; commands executed by **ksh** are called built-ins.

To continue a command onto another line, type \ as the last character of the line before pressing RETURN . **ksh** then displays a secondary prompt, normally > . The \ and the RETURN are discarded by **ksh**.

---

* This description is an oversimplification. The words you type are processed as described in the **Command Processing** chapter to yield the command name and arguments.

ksh redisplays the primary prompt if you press RETURN without entering a command. **ksh** displays the next primary prompt when it completes processing your preceding command. On most systems you can start typing your next command as soon as you press RETURN, without waiting for the prompt. This is useful for commands that take several seconds to complete. Output from the command may be intermixed with the keys that you type, but this does not interfere with your input.

To abort a program before it completes, press the *Interrupt* key. This causes the process to receive an **INT** signal, which causes most programs to terminate. This also causes any typeahead characters to be discarded. On some systems, the BREAK key may also cause the process to receive an **INT** signal. A few commands ignore the **INT** signal; in this case, use the *Quit* key, normally CONTROL \, to send the **QUIT** signal if your system supports this.

On systems that support stopping output (flow control), press the *Stop* key, usually CONTROL s, to stop the display of output to your terminal. Resume the output by pressing the *Restart* key, usually CONTROL q. On some systems, you can resume output by pressing any key.

The examples below use the following commands:
date   To display the date and time.
print   To display its arguments.
cat   To display the contents of the files you specify as arguments.

Examples
```
1$ date
Sat Aug 28 09:57:08 1993
2$ print hello world
hello world
3$ cat file1 file2
This is what is in file1.
You are now reading the second line.
This is the last line.
This is what is in file2.
You are now reading the second line.
This is the last line.
```

You can specify options to many commands. By convention, command arguments that represent options follow the command name; they consist of a single letter preceded by a – (minus sign). The –? option will display the list of available options for almost all built-in commands, and many other commands, that allow options. *Version*: The –? option only works with built-in commands on versions of **ksh** newer than the 11/16/88 version.

Some options have a value associated with them. The value is given by the argument that follows the option. Most commands allow you to group options without associated values, into a single word preceded by a –. For example, the options **–x** **–v** can be written as **–xv**. Arguments such as pathnames for files usually come last. A – – by itself is often used to signify that there are no more options. This allows you to enter other command arguments that begin with –, without **ksh** mistaking them for options.

However, not all commands use the – convention. Some use a + in addition to a –, often to reverse the normal meaning of the option.

If you enter a command incorrectly by providing unknown options, or too many or too few arguments, an error message is usually displayed. Error messages often display the correct usage for the program.

The **ls** command displays the names of files in your working directory. The **–l** option of **ls** causes a long listing for each file containing the:
- Access permission string (see page 34).
- Number of names that refer to the same file.
- Owner.
- Group.*
- Size in bytes.
- Time it was last modified.
- Filename.

Example
```
4$ ls -l
drwxr-xr-x   2 dgk    user      128 May   8 23:41 bin
-rw-rw-r--   1 dgk    user       86 Apr  14 10:04 file1
-rw-r--r--   1 dgk    user       86 Apr  14 10:11 file2
-rwxr-xr-x   1 dgk    user     4786 Apr  30 20:32 prog
-rw-r--r--   1 dgk    user      674 Apr  30 20:31 prog.c
-rw-r--r--   1 dgk    user      526 May   9 09:13 todo
-rw-rw-r--   1 dgk    user    29386 May   4 15:48 wishlist
```

SETTING AND DISPLAYING OPTIONS

ksh is itself a program. Thus **ksh** has several options that you can specify either when you invoke **ksh**, or with the **set** command. This tutorial describes many of these options. All of the options and their meanings are defined starting on page 216.

---

* On some systems **–g** is needed to display the group. Use **–lg** to get indicated behavior.

Several options affect how **ksh** processes commands. **ksh** turns on some options automatically, and you can specify some options. For instance, **ksh** automatically turns on the **interactive** option when you invoke **ksh** interactively. **ksh** issues prompts only when this option is on. **ksh** assigns default values to options, but you can change most of them. Use **set** to turn on, turn off, and display options.

You usually specify default options in your profile file (see page 87), which **ksh** executes when you log in, and/or in your environment file, which **ksh** executes when it begins execution. These files are described in more detail in the *Customizing Your Environment* chapter. For example, the **ignoreeof** option is customarily set in your profile file. It prevents you from being logged off if you inadvertently press the *End-of-file* character which is typically ⌐CONTROL⌐ d. With **ignoreeof** set, you must type the command **exit** to log out. The examples below use **set** to turn on the **ignoreeof** option and to display all the option settings. Note that you turn on an option with **–o**, and you turn off an option with **+o**.

Examples
```
5$ set -o ignoreeof
6$ set -o
Current option settings
allexport        off
bgnice           off
emacs            off
errexit          off
gmacs            off
ignoreeof        on
interactive      on
keyword          off
markdirs         off
monitor          on
noclobber        off
noexec           off
noglob           off
nohup            off
nolog            off
notify           off
nounset          off
privileged       off
restricted       off
trackall         on
verbose          off
vi               on
viraw            off
xtrace           off
```

Version: The **notify** option is available only on versions of **ksh** newer than the 11/16/88 version.

CORRECTING YOUR TYPING

The **stty** command defines terminal control settings. In particular, you can use it to set the backspace character (referred to as the *Erase* character), and the line erase character (referred to as the *Kill* character). The default for *Erase* on some systems is #, and for *Kill* it is often @. You can change the *Erase* and *Kill* characters so that you can use the # and @ keys normally. Use **stty** as shown in the following example to set the *Erase* character to BACKSPACE and the *Kill* character to CONTROL x. **stty** affects the terminal settings for all processes that access your terminal. **stty** interprets the ^ in front of a character as meaning CONTROL . **stty** is normally placed in your profile file.

Example
```
7$ stty erase ^h kill ^x
```

On many systems you can enter a terminal control character as a regular character by preceding it with a \.

If you make an error before typing RETURN , there are several ways that you can make corrections:

- Press the *Erase* character to back up to the error, and correct the line from that point on.
- Press the *Kill* character to erase the entire line, and then type it over.
- If the **emacs**, **gmacs**, or **vi** option is on, you can move to earlier parts of the command line and correct mistakes by issuing editing commands (called directives to distinguish them from shell commands). Issuing editing directives is referred to as command editing. A list of available editing directives for each of the edit options is in the *Built-in Editors* part of this book. You can also use command editing to make corrections to commands that you previously entered, and then to reenter them.

USING ALIASES AS SHORTHAND

An alias is a name that you can use as a shorthand for a command. As an example of how to use aliases, suppose that you always want to see long listings with the **ls** command. By defining an alias for **ls -l**, you do not have to type the **-l** each time that you list the contents of a directory.

You define an alias with the **alias** command, followed by a word of the form *name=value* where *name* is shorthand for *value*. Do not press SPACE or TAB before or after the =; if you do, **ksh** will read what you typed as two or three words, not as the one word that it should be. If *value* has any Spaces or Tabs in it, then you must quote them using any of the mechanisms described briefly in this chapter on page 42, and in detail on page 141. *Note*: You can use the name of the alias inside its value. For instance, in the example below, the alias for **ls** will be set to **ls -l**. The **ls** within the quotes will not be replaced again by **ls -l**.

To display the value of one or more aliases, specify the names of these aliases as arguments to the **alias** command. To display the complete list of aliases, run **alias** without arguments. Several aliases have been preset; they are listed on page 156.

ksh checks each command name to see if you have defined an alias for it. If you have, **ksh** replaces the command with the value of the alias.

Examples
```
8$ alias ls='ls -l'
9$ alias ls
'ls -l'
10$ ls
drwxr-xr-x    2 dgk      user      128 May  8 23:41 bin
-rw-rw-r--    1 dgk      user       86 Apr 14 10:04 file1
-rw-r--r--    1 dgk      user       86 Apr 14 10:11 file2
-rwxr-xr-x    1 dgk      user     4786 Apr 30 20:32 prog
-rw-r--r--    1 dgk      user      674 Apr 30 20:31 prog.c
-rw-r--r--    1 dgk      user      526 May  9 09:13 todo
-rw-rw-r--    1 dgk      user    29386 May  4 15:48 wishlist
```

REENTERING PREVIOUS COMMANDS

ksh keeps a log of commands that you enter from your terminal in a history file. Type **history** to display the most recent commands that you typed. **history** by itself displays at most 16 commands. However, you can specify, for instance:

    history −11 to limit the display to the last 11 commands.

    history 3 7 to display commands 3 through 7.

    history 11 to display commands starting at 11.

The indicated commands must still be accessible in the history file.

To reenter the previous **ksh** command, run the **r** command with no arguments. **ksh** displays the command, and then executes it. To reexecute command 4, type **r 4**. To reexecute the last command that starts with **d**, type **r d**.

Examples
```
11$ r d
date
Sat Aug 28 10:03:13 1993
12$ history
1        date
2        print hello world
3        cat file1
4        ls -l
5        set -o ignoreeof
6        set -o
7        stty erase ^h kill ^x
8        alias ls='ls -l'
```

```
9       alias ls
10      ls
11      date
12      history
```

Use **emacs, gmacs,** or **vi** directives to access and edit commands in the history file. Any editor directive that would move you to a previous line if you were using the editor program, causes that previous line of the history file to be copied onto the line with your cursor so that you can edit and reenter the command.

EXERCISES

1. Practice the basics by doing each of the following in order:
   a. Press ⬚RETURN⬚ without entering a command.
   b. Turn on the **ignoreeof** option.
   c. Use the **stty** command to set the *Erase* character and the *Kill* character to whatever you choose.
   d. Display the options of the **print** command.
   e. Use the **print** command to display your first and last name. Practice using the *Erase* character and the *Kill* character as you type your name.
   f. Repeat this command using the **r** command.
   g. Define an alias named **d** that displays the date.
   h. Use **d** to display the date and time.
   i. Use **r** to reexecute the **print** command.
   j. Display your option settings.
   k. Display the last six commands that you entered.
   l. Display the value of the aliases **d** and **r**.
   m Display names and values of all the aliases.
   n. List the filenames in your working directory.
   o. Use the **print** command to enter a command and continue it onto another line.
   p. Use one of the built-in editors to fetch the command that printed your name. Delete your last name and enter the command.
   q. Practice using one of the built-in editors to change the arguments to the preceding command and then to reenter it. Do this until you feel comfortable with using the built-in editor to make corrections to the previous command.

2. Which of these input lines adhere to the normal command syntax conventions:
   a. `print`   b. `PRINT`
   c. `date=time`   d. `c128 is a computer`
   e. `ls foobar -l`   f. `-c foobar`
   g. `foobar -option`   h. `print -- -`

CHANGING FILE PERMISSIONS

File permissions are specified in one of two possible formats.

You can specify permissions with a 3- or a 4-digit octal number:
- 1st: Setuid and/or setgid permissions. Use this digit only if you wish to give a program special permissions. Setuid and setgid permissions often do not exist on non-UNIX systems.
- 2nd: Owner.
- 3rd: Group.
- 4th: Others.

Each octal digit, except the first, is the sum of all of the values corresponding to the permissions of the owner, group, and/or others. Thus, for instance, if the owner has read and write permissions, then the 2nd digit would be the sum of 4 and 2, which is 6. The values are:
- Read: 4
- Write: 2
- Execute or Search: 1

As a complete example, the permission **4751** means:
- Setuid
- Read, write, and execute for owner
- Read and execute for group
- Execute for others

Or you can specify permissions with a symbolic permission expression.
The format of the expression is one or more of [*who*] *op* [*permission*] separated by a comma, where:
- *who* is a combination of the letters:
    - **u**   Owner permissions. (**u** stands for user)
    - **g**   Group permissions.
    - **o**   Other permissions.
    - **a**   Default if you do not specify *who*. Specifies owner, group, and other permissions.
- *op* is one of the following:
    - **+**   Add *permission*.
    - **–**   Delete *permission*.
    - **=**   Assign *permission*.
- *permission* can be any or all of:
    - **r**   Read.
    - **w**   Write.
    - **x**   Execute or Search.
    - **s**   Set owner id and/or group id when used with **u** and/or **g**.

The permission mask **4751** in the previous example can be represented with the symbolic permission expression **u=rwxs,g=rx,o=x**.

Access permissions are sometimes displayed as a permission string of 10 characters (as in **ls –l** above). The first character is **d** for a directory, **c** for character devices such as terminals, or – for a file. The other nine characters, in groups of three, represent the owner, group, and other permissions. An **r** indicates read permission, and a **w** indicates write permission. An **x** indicates execute permission for a file and search permission for a directory. A – in any location indicates that it lacks the corresponding permission. An **s** in place of an **x** indicates setuid or setgid permission. As an example, **–rwsr–x– –x** represents the file permission **4751** described above.

Each process has a file creation mask to disable permissions whenever a file is created. The file creation mask can be represented as a 3-digit octal number, or as a symbolic permission. Its digits represent the permissions to be disabled when a file is created. For instance, a file creation mask value of **022** disables write permission by group and others. Alternatively, the symbolic permission expression **go–w** represents the same file creation mask.

Use the **umask** command to set and/or display the file creation mask. Use the **chmod** command if it is necessary to change the access permissions.

Examples
```
13$ umask
002
14$ umask -S
=rx,ug+w
15$ umask 022
16$ umask -S
=rx,u+w
17$ chmod g+w prog.c
18$ ls -l prog.c
-rw-rw-r--   1 dgk    user    674 Apr 30 20:31 prog.c
```

REDIRECTING INPUT AND OUTPUT

By convention, most commands write their normal output to standard output (file descriptor 1), and error messages to standard error (file descriptor 2). By default, **ksh** directs both standard output and standard error to be displayed on your terminal.

You can redirect the standard output of a command to a file instead of to your terminal by typing the redirection operator, >, followed by the name of the file.

You can put the > anywhere on the line; by convention, the > is normally placed at the end of the command after its arguments. Spaces and/or Tabs before and after the > are optional, unless the argument that precedes the > is a single digit. *Note*: This paragraph applies to all redirection operators, not just to >.

If the file already exists, and if the **noclobber** option is on, then **ksh** displays an error message. However, you can use >| instead of > to redirect to a file that already exists even if **noclobber** is on. If **noclobber** is off, or if you specify >|, then **ksh** deletes the contents of the old file.

Examples
```
19$ date > savedate
20$ cat savedate
Sat Aug 28 10:07:34 1993
```

If the file does not already exist, then **ksh** creates it. **ksh** sets permissions to read and write by everyone, minus any permissions specified by the value of the file creation mask. The file creation mask was set by **umask** in command 15 above.

Use > without specifying a command to create an empty file. Use **rm** to remove a file that you have created.

Examples
```
21$ > tempfile
22$ ls -l tempfile
-rw-r--r--   1 dgk     user       0 Aug 28 10:08 tempfile
23$ rm tempfile
```

If you want to discard the standard output from a command, you can do so by redirecting it to the special file, **/dev/null**. Any characters written to this file will be thrown away.

You can append the standard output of a command to a file by typing the redirection operator **>>** followed by the name of the file. If the file does not already exist, then **ksh** creates it for you.

Example
```
24$ date >> savedate
25$ cat savedate
Sat Aug 28 10:07:34 1993
Sat Aug 28 10:08:57 1993
```

You can also redirect the standard input of a command so that it reads from a file instead of from your terminal. Type the redirection operator < followed by the name of the file.

Example
```
26$ mail morris < savedate
```

The **cat** command reads from standard input if you do not specify any file. Therefore, both **cat savedate** and **cat < savedate** yield the same result. However, in the former, **savedate** is an argument to **cat**, and in the latter, **cat** reads from standard input where **ksh** has opened **savedate** for use by **cat**. If **savedate** does not exist, you will get different error messages depending on whether you typed **cat savedate** or **cat < savedate**. This is because the error message is originated by **cat** in the former case, and by **ksh** in the latter.

You can redirect any file descriptor from **0** through **9** by specifying the file descriptor number immediately before the redirection operators **<**, **>**, and **>>**. For instance, to redirect standard error, specify **2>**. You can discard the output on both standard output and standard error by redirecting them both to **/dev/null**.

Example
```
27$ date > /dev/null 2> /dev/null
```

You can also specify that a file descriptor be redirected to the same place as another file descriptor. To cause file descriptor 2 to be redirected to the same file as file descriptor 1, specify **2>&1**. You can think of **>&** as meaning "redirect to the same file as".

The order in which you specify redirection is important because the redirection operators are processed from left to right. In the following example, standard output is first redirected to **/dev/null** and then standard error is redirected there also so that both will be discarded. If the order of redirection were reversed, standard error would be redirected to wherever standard output is currently directed, and then standard output would be redirected to **/dev/null**.

Example
```
28$ date > /dev/null 2>&1
```

PIPELINES AND FILTERS

You can connect the standard output of one command with the standard input of another command by using the pipeline operator | between the commands. This is nearly equivalent to running the first command with its output redirected to a temporary file, then running the second command with its input redirected from the temporary file, and then removing the temporary file. However, **ksh** uses the pipe special file on systems that have it, rather than creating an intermediate file. By using a pipe special file, **ksh** will work even if the first command produces more output than the largest permissible file size. Also, **ksh** won't wait for the first command to complete before starting the second command. Pipes are typically faster than temporary files since the data is kept in memory.

You can connect a sequence of commands together with | to create a pipeline. The number of commands you can connect may be limited by the number of processes the system allows you to create. You can continue pipelines onto more than one line by typing RETURN after the |.

A command that reads from its standard input and writes on its standard output is called a filter. You can use the | operator to connect one or more filters to preprocess and/or postprocess the output of any command.

As with many commands that process files, **grep** reads from standard input if you do not specify the name of a file as an argument. Therefore, **grep** can be used as a filter. **grep** displays the lines in one or more files that contain a specified sequence of characters. Use **grep** when you want to limit the output to only those lines that you need to see. The example below displays only those lines from the output of **set –o** that contain **ignoreeof**.

Example
```
29$ set -o | grep ignoreeof
ignoreeof        on
```

ksh redirects standard output to the pipe before any I/O redirections for the individual commands. Therefore you can use **2>&1** to direct standard error into the pipeline.

Use **tee** to capture, in a file, the data passing through any pipe in a pipeline. **tee** does not alter the data that passes through it. In the example below, the file **users** will contain the list of users logged onto your system as generated by the **who** command. In the example, both standard output and standard error are written to the pipe.

The **wc** command displays the number of lines, words, and characters in the specified file(s). The **–l** option limits the output to the number of lines. If no files are specified, **wc** uses its standard input.

Example
```
30$ who 2>&1 | tee users | wc -l
159
```

On some terminals you cannot scroll back to earlier pages of output to the display. In this case you may want the output to stop whenever the screen fills up, until you indicate that you are ready to view the next page. A program that does this is called a pager, and **more** is a commonly used pager program. You can cause the output of any command to be paged by running **more** as the last command in a pipeline. Systems that do not have **more** often have a command named **pg** to perform this function. One difference between **pg** and **more** is that **more** uses `SPACE` to show you the next page, whereas **pg** uses `RETURN`.

TILDE EXPANSION

You can reduce your typing effort by using ~ at the start of certain words. **ksh** checks for expansion of each word you type that begins with a ~. Use the tilde expansion mechanism as an abbreviation for:
• Your home directory. Use ~ by itself.

- The home directory of any user on the system. Follow ~ by the login name of the desired user (yourself or anyone else).
- The absolute pathname of your working directory. Use ~+.
- The previous working directory. Use ~–.

Tilde expansion characters extend up to the first /, if any. If there is no /, **ksh** processes the entire word. **ksh** leaves the word you typed as is, if the ~ is not followed by one of the above.

Example
```
31$ print ~morris/reminders
/usr/morris/reminders
```

VARIABLES

Variables allow you to store and manipulate information within **ksh**. Variables are used primarily within the **ksh** programming language, and are therefore described in more detail in the next chapter. However, a brief introduction to variables is appropriate before continuing.

A variable has a name, called a *varname,* and a value. A value is a string of any length. A variable can be assigned a value in two ways – either by the user, or by **ksh**. A user explicitly sets the value of a variable using an *assignment* command. This is commonly done in your profile and environment files (see page 87) and while programming with **ksh**, and is described in detail on page 132. In other cases, **ksh** assigns the value of a variable, usually as the result of a command. Some variables are initialized or inherited by **ksh** when you log in. For instance, the value of **HOME** is set to the absolute pathname of your login directory.

You access the value of a variable by preceding its name with a $ and surrounding the name with { }. You can think of the $ as meaning, "the value of." For instance, ${**PWD**} means "the value of the **PWD** variable." The { and } are required only if the variable name contains a . (dot), or the character following the { is a letter, digit, or _ (underscore).

Example
```
32$ d=$HOME/.profile s=~morris
33$ print ${d}_file $s/bin
/usr/dgk/.profile_file /usr/morris/bin
```

PATHNAME EXPANSION

Many commands take a list of files as arguments. You can cause **ksh** to generate a list of arguments that are pathnames by typing a word that consists of a pattern rather than typing each individual name. Patterns are used in other contexts by **ksh**, and are described more fully on page 133. If you use any of the following characters unquoted in a command word (see page 42 about quoting), then **ksh** processes that word as a pattern and expands it as follows:

*   Matches any string of characters, including Null.
?   Matches any single character.
[...]   Matches any character(s) specified between the brackets.
(...)   When preceded by a *, ?, **@**, +, or !, patterns inside the parentheses are matched using the pattern matching rules on page 135.

When you specify a pattern as a command word, **ksh** expands the pattern to the complete list of pathnames that match this pattern. If there are no matching pathnames, then **ksh** leaves the pattern unchanged.

When patterns are used to match pathnames, a . (dot) as the first character of each filename must match explicitly. Each filename must be matched. If the **FIGNORE** variable is set, then filenames matching the pattern defined by the value of the **FIGNORE** variable are excluded from the match rather than filenames that contain a leading . (dot). *Version*: **FIGNORE** is only available on versions of **ksh** newer than the 11/16/88 version.

If the **markdirs** option is on, then a trailing / is added to each directory name that matches the pattern.

The pathnames that match the pattern become arguments to the command. Because the matching is done by **ksh**, pathname expansion applies to all commands.

If you specify a pattern as the pathname associated with an I/O redirection operator, **ksh** expands the pattern only if it matches a single pathname.

Examples
```
34$ print *
file1 file2 foobar prog prog.c todo users wishlist
35$ ls file?
-rw-rw-r--   1 dgk    user     86 Apr 14 10:04 file1
-rw-r--r--   1 dgk    user     86 Apr 14 10:11 file2
```

TIMING COMMANDS

You can find out how long it takes to process a command or a pipeline, as with the example below, by using the **time** command. **time** is a reserved word in **ksh** and is processed specially. It applies to complete pipelines, not just to single commands.

After the command or pipeline completes, **ksh** displays on standard error three lines that specify in minutes and seconds:
- The clock time that has elapsed.
- The processor time used by the program.
- The processor time used by the system in running the command or pipeline.

I/O redirections apply to the command that you time, not to **time** itself. Enclose the **time** command in one of the grouping commands described on page 173, and redirect standard error for the grouping command to redirect the output from **time**.

Example
```
36$ time ls -l /bin | wc
98        875       5715

real  0m4.31s
user  0m0.80s
sys   0m1.36s
```

The **sleep** command in the following example suspends execution for the number of seconds specified by its arguments. It is usually used within one of the compound commands described in the ***Programming Language*** chapter. ***Version***: On versions of **ksh** newer than the 11/16/88 version, **sleep** is a built-in command, and the number of seconds does not have to be an integer. Fractions of seconds can be specified.

Example
```
37$ time sleep 10

real  0m10.01s
user  0m0.01s
sys   0m0.00s
```

EXERCISES

1. Explain what each of the following commands does. Assume that they are run in the order shown.
   a. `umask =rx,u+w`
   b. `print Keep track of everything > file1.out`
   c. `print Be careful >> file1.out`
   d. `set -o | tee tee.out | grep ignoreeof`
   e. `cat tee.out | grep monitor`
   f. `grep monitor < tee.out`
   g. `print ~joe | grep joe | cat >> file1.out`
   h. `print *.out`
   i. `grep track *.out  | wc`
   j. `grep track < f*out | wc`
   k. `time sleep 20 > /dev/null 2>&1`

2. Write a command to do each of the following:
   a. Display the names of files in your directory ending in **out**.
   b. Display all the lines in files in the directory **/usr/include** that contain the string **FILE**.
   c. Display the time it takes to sleep for 5 seconds.
   d. Display the contents of your home directory.
   e. Create a file named **junk** that contains the date and time.
   f. Append to **junk** the lines from all files in your working directory that contain the word **bar**.
   g. Count the number of lines in **junk**.
   h. Remove the file **junk**.

3. Answer the following file permission questions:
   a. What does a file creation mask of 024 mean?
   b. What does symbolic permission expression **g–r**, **g–x**, **o–r** mean?
   c. What does the file permission 751 mean? Represent this permission as a permission string. Represent this permission as a symbolic permission expression.

QUOTING SPECIAL CHARACTERS

Suppose that you want to display the character I. If you type **print** I, then **ksh** will prompt you with the secondary prompt **PS2** (normally >), indicating that it is waiting for you to type the remainder of the pipeline.

To remove the normal meaning that **ksh** places on I, or on any other special character, you must quote it. You can quote a single character by preceding it with a \. You can quote a string of characters by enclosing them in:

• Literal (single) quotes, '...', to remove the special meaning of all characters except '.

• ANSI C strings, $'...', to remove the special meaning of all characters except the ANSI C escape sequences on page 226. For example, $'\t\n\'\\' represents the four-character string Tab, Newline, ', and \. *Version*: ANSI C strings are only available on versions of **ksh** newer than the 11/16/88 version,

• Grouping (double) quotes, "...", to remove the special meaning of all characters except $, \, and `. If the $ is not quoted, then variable substitution is done inside double quotes.

ksh normally splits the results of parameter expansion and command substitution (see page 159) of command words into fields, by using as field delimiters the characters in the value of a variable named **IFS**. By default, the value of **IFS** is Space, Tab, and Newline. **ksh** generates the actual arguments by performing pathname expansion on the fields. Use grouping (double) quotes to prevent both field splitting and pathname expansion. The quoting characters are removed after each command word is expanded.

In the following example we use the **–r** option to prevent the character \ from being processed specially by **print**.

Example
```
38$ print -r \\foo \~ '<$HOME>' "<$HOME>"
\foo ~ <$HOME> </usr/dgk>
```

WORKING DIRECTORY

Whenever a command uses a pathname that does not begin with a **/**, the system looks for the file relative to your current working directory.

To find the name of the working directory, use **pwd**. By default, **pwd** displays the logical name for the directory. Use **pwd –P** to display the physical name of the directory, the name of the directory with all symbolic links resolved (see page 18). To change the working directory, use **cd** followed by the pathname of the new directory. The **–P** option to **cd** causes the name you specify to be converted to a physical name. You can use the **CDPATH** variable to specify a list of directories for **cd** to search through when you specify a pathname not beginning with a **/**. **cd** displays the name of the new working directory when it uses the **CDPATH** variable to find it, and the new directory is not a subdirectory of the working directory.

To return to the previous working directory that you were in, use **cd –**. **ksh** displays the name of the new working directory.

ksh sets the **PWD** variable to the working directory whenever you use **cd**. **ksh** also sets the **OLDPWD** variable to your previous working directory.

If you want to change to a directory whose pathname differs slightly from that of your working directory, you can do so by using **cd** with two arguments. The first specifies the part of the pathname that you want to change, and the second specifies what you want to change it to. **ksh** displays the new working directory.

Examples
```
39$ pwd
/usr/dgk
40$ pwd -P
/n/toucan/u6/dgk
41$ cd /usr/morris
42$ cd -
/usr/dgk
43$ cd -
/usr/morris
44$ cd morris dgk
/usr/dgk
```

HOW ksh *FINDS A COMMAND*

If the command name is an alias, **ksh** replaces the command name with the value of the alias and begins the search again.

If the command name contains a /, then, if possible, **ksh** executes the program whose pathname is the command name.

If the command name does not contain a /, then **ksh** checks the command name for one of the following, in the order shown:

- Reserved word (see page 130). If the reserved word begins a compound command, then **ksh** reads as many lines as necessary until it reads the complete command or it encounters an error, or until you press the *Interrupt* key. If the reserved word is invalid as the first word of the command, then **ksh** displays a message on standard error.
- Special built-in command (see page 209). **ksh** executes the special built-in command in the current environment.
- Function. **ksh** executes the function in the current environment.
- Regular built-in utility. **ksh** executes the regular built-in utility in the current environment.
- Otherwise. **ksh** uses the value of the **PATH** variable followed by the value of the **FPATH** variable to construct a list of directories to search for the command name. The **PATH** and **FPATH** variables each contain a colon-separated list of directories. The search occurs in the order that the directories are listed in the **PATH** variable. If the command name is found in a directory, **ksh** will do one of the following:
  - If that directory is also in the list of directories defined by the **FPATH** variable, then **ksh** reads and executes the file in the current environment and then executes a function of the given name.
  - Or else, if **ksh** contains a built-in version of the command corresponding to the absolute pathname of the command, this built-in command is executed.
  - Otherwise, **ksh** executes the given command as a program in a separate environment.

Version: With the 11/16/88 version of **ksh**, directories in the **PATH** variable could not contain function directories and there were no built-in commands that corresponded to absolute pathnames. Also, all built-in commands were found before functions of the same name, so it was necessary to define an alias and a function to override the name of a built-in command with a function.

ksh displays a message on standard error if it cannot find the command, or if you do not have execute permission for the file.

Use the **type** preset alias to find out what a given name refers to. **type** tells you what type of item the specified name refers to. If the name corresponds to a program, **type** displays a pathname for the program. **whence** is similar to **type** except that **whence** displays only the absolute pathname for the command, if any.

Examples
```
45$ type ls date print r
ls is an alias for 'ls -l''
date is a tracked alias for /bin/date
print is a builtin
r is an alias for 'hist -s'
46$ whence date
/bin/date
```

COMMAND SUBSTITUTION

You may want the output of a command to become the value of a variable. Or you may want the argument(s) to a command to be generated by another command. You can tell **ksh** to do either of these things by putting the command whose output you want inside $(...). In addition, $(< *file*) expands to the contents of *file*.

Bourne shell: The Bourne shell syntax `...`, defined on page 143, is recognized by **ksh** but is considered obsolescent. All the examples in this book use $(...) instead of `...`. $(...) has simpler quoting rules and it nests easily.

Examples
```
47$ print dgk > foobar
48$ foo=$(< foobar)
49$ print $foo: "$(date)"
dgk: Sat Aug 28 11:02:28 1993
50$ d=$(whence date)
51$ print $d
/bin/date
```

RUNNING COMMANDS IN BACKGROUND

By default, **ksh** waits for commands to finish executing before it issues the next prompt. The command for which **ksh** waits is called a foreground command.

Some commands take a long time to execute. You can type an **&** at the end of a command or a pipeline just before you press RETURN , to cause it to execute in the background.

Before **ksh** starts a background command, it displays a message with a job number inside brackets, [ ], followed by the process id. If you did not redirect the output of the background command, then the output of the background command is displayed at your terminal.

The **find** command performs specified actions on every file in one or more specified directories and subdirectories that satisfy specified conditions. It often takes a long time to complete. In the next example, the **/usr** directory is specified, and the action is to display the pathnames of all files with filename **foobar** as their last component. No conditions are specified, so all such pathnames will be displayed.

Example
```
52$ find /usr -name foobar -print &
[1] 2345
```

ksh dissociates background commands from your terminal. Therefore, you cannot use the *Interrupt* key to terminate a background command. You can use the **kill** command to send the job a **TERM** signal or any other signal.

If the **monitor** option is on, **ksh** runs each background command as a job in a separate process group that is not associated with your terminal. Otherwise, if you have not redirected the standard input, **ksh** sets the standard input for the command to the empty file **/dev/null**, preventing it from trying to read from the terminal at the same time that the shell does.

If the **monitor** option is on, **ksh** displays a completion message for each background command that has completed before displaying the prompt. If the **notify** option is set, the completion message will be displayed as soon as the background command completes. *Version*: The **notify** option is available only on versions of **ksh** newer than the 11/16/88 version.

If the **bgnice** option is on, then **ksh** runs background jobs at a lower priority. The **bgnice** option is on by default for interactive shells.

When you log out, **ksh** sends a **HUP** signal to each background job. Use the **disown** command to prevent **ksh** from sending the **HUP** signal to the given background jobs when you log out. *Version*: The **disown** command is available only on versions of **ksh** newer than the 11/16/88 version.

Use the **nohup** command to cause a job to ignore any **HUP** signal that it receives so that it can continue running even after you log out. The standard output and standard error are redirected to be appended to the file named **nohup.out** in the working directory. **nohup** takes as its arguments the command name and arguments of the command you wish to run.

Examples
```
53$ find /usr/morris -name foobar -print > saveout 2>&1 &
[2] 2347
54$ disown %2
55$ nohup find /usr/morris -name foobar -print &
[3] 2348
```

Use **tail –f nohup.out** to keep track of the progress of a command run in the background with **nohup**. **tail** displays the last few lines of the specified file. The **–f** option causes **tail** to keep checking for additional output when it reaches the end of the **nohup.out** file. Use the *Interrupt* key to cause **tail –f** to terminate. This will not affect the **nohup** command since it is running in the background. The following example reports on the progress of the preceding example.

Example
```
56$ alias ckhup='tail -f nohup.out'
57$ ckhup
/usr/morris/shell/book/foobar
```

JOB CONTROL

Job control allows you to manage the execution of foreground and background jobs. **ksh** provides only a subset of the job control features on some systems due to operating system limitations; typical limitations involve the lack of the **bg** and **fg** commands, and CONTROL **z** to stop a job.

The **monitor** option must be set for job control to be active.
Implementation-dependent:
- On systems that allow complete job control, the **monitor** option is implicitly turned on for interactive invocations of **ksh**.
- On other systems, you must specify this option with **set –o monitor**. You would normally do this in your environment file.

Each pipeline that you run is called a job. **ksh** assigns each job a small number. If the **monitor** option is on, then **ksh** displays the job number enclosed in [ ] when each background job is started. Before issuing a prompt, **ksh** displays a status message for each background job that completes whenever the **monitor** option is on.

You can refer to a job by process id, by job number, or by job name with **bg**, **disown**, **fg**, **jobs**, **kill**, and **wait**. The job name is the command you entered to run the job. To refer to a job by number or name, use:

%number	To refer to the job by *number*.
%string	To refer to the job whose name begins with *string*.
%?string	To refer to the job whose name contains *string*.
%+ or *%%*	To refer to the current job.
%–	To refer to the previous job.

Use **jobs** to display the list of background jobs and their status.

You can cause **ksh** to wait for a specific background job to complete, or to wait for all background jobs to complete, with **wait**.

You can cause a foreground job to receive an interrupt signal, **INT**, by pressing *Interrupt*. Most programs terminate when they receive this signal. On systems that support the **QUIT** signal, you can cause a foreground job to receive the **QUIT** signal by pressing *Quit*. Some systems generate a core dump when you do this. You may be able to use the core dump for debugging.

You can terminate a background job or process by sending it a **TERM** signal with the **kill** command.

Systems that have full job control allow you to stop a process and to reestablish the association with your terminal. On these systems, you can use **ksh** to stop jobs and to move commands to and from the background. The following three paragraphs and the examples apply to systems that have this capability.

Press *Suspend*, normally ⌷CONTROL⌷ z, to stop the job that is running in the foreground. **ksh** displays a message when the job stops, and issues a prompt.

A background job will stop whenever it tries to read from your terminal. Use **stty tostop** to specify that a background job is to stop whenever it tries to output to your terminal. Use **kill** to send a **STOP** signal to stop a background job. The alias **stop='kill –STOP'** is useful if you frequently stop background jobs.

Use **fg** to move a background job into the foreground or to restart a job that you have stopped and run it in the foreground. Use **bg** to restart a job that you stopped and to run it in the background.

Examples

```
58$ sleep 60
CONTROL z
^Z[1] + Stopped          sleep 60
59$ bg
sleep 60&
60$ jobs
[1] + Running            sleep 60
61$ kill %s
[1] + Terminated         sleep 60
```

COMPOUND COMMANDS

Compound commands are described in the *Programming Language* chapter that follows and are presented in more detail in the *Compound Commands* chapter. You ordinarily use compound commands such as **if**, **while**, **select**, and **for** when writing scripts. However, once you become familiar with these commands, you can enter any compound command interactively as well.

Most compound commands are normally entered on more than one line. Type
RETURN following any command within a compound command to cause the
command to be continued onto another line; in this case, **ksh** displays the
secondary prompt (the value of the **PS2** variable). *Note*: **ksh** does not begin
execution until you enter the entire command.

The following example uses the **for** compound command (described in the next
chapter). The string *[0–9] is a pattern that matches all filenames in the current
directory ending in a digit. For each file, this example creates a new file whose
name is the same as the old name but with **.new** appended. The **tr** command, as
specified, converts lowercase characters from the original file to uppercase in the
new file.

Example
```
62$ for i in *[0-9]
>  do  print -- "$i"
>      tr "[a-z]" "[A-Z]" < $i > $i.new¹
>  done
file1
file2
```

SHELL SCRIPTS

Use any editor to put a group of **ksh** commands into a file to create a new
command. A file that contains **ksh** commands is called a shell script, or just a
script. A script behaves like any other program that you can invoke. Run a script
by typing its name followed by its arguments, separated by Spaces or Tabs, as
you do for any other command. This is referred to as invoking a script by name.
You can also run a script by running **ksh** with the name of the script, and the
arguments to the script, as arguments to **ksh**.

Special scripts are also processed by **ksh** when you log in or invoke **ksh**
interactively. These scripts enable you to customize your environment. Even if
you do not intend to write programs, you need to know something about shell
scripts to customize your environment.

You do not have to compile your script after you write it, but you do have to make
the file executable with **chmod +x** to run the command by name. If you write
scripts frequently, you could define an alias such as **cx='chmod +x'**.

Use the **#** comment syntax defined on page 129 to make your script easier to read.
Caution: Some systems process **#!** specially (as described on page 262) when
they are used as the first two characters of the first line of a script.

---

¹ The [and] are not needed with some versions of **tr**.

Also, indent the code in your script to make it easier to read. See the examples in the **Application Programming** chapter for a suggested indentation style.

ksh reads, expands, and runs the commands in your script sequentially until requested to terminate or until there are no more commands. See **Command Processing** for a description of how commands are read and expanded. See page 263 for a list of conditions that cause a script to terminate.

Example

```
63$ alias cx='chmod +x'
64$ print 'print hello world' > world
65$ cx world
66$ world
hello world
67$ ksh world
hello world
```

EXERCISES

1. Explain what each of the following commands does. Assume that they are run in the order shown.
    a. `type type time print cat whence`
    b. `d=/dev b=/bin h=~ s=$PWD`
    c. `print $d \$d '$d' '$'d "$d" $PWD/bin`
    d. `cd $h`
    e. `type date`
    f. `x=$(whence date)`
    g. `ls $d | grep tty > ~/foo`
    h. `rm ~/foo`
    i. `cd -`
    j. `cd ~-`
    k. `> bar`
    l. `rm ~/bar ~-/foo`
    m. `nohup ls -l /bin &`

2. Write a command line to do each of the following:
    a. Display all the directories named **bin** on your system.
    b. Run a job in the background.
    c. Wait for the last **nohup** command to complete.
    d. Assign the number of users logged into your system to a variable named **nusers**.
    e. Display the absolute pathname of the **grep** command.
    f. Remove a file that has a * in its name.
    g. Change directory to the last directory that you were in.
    h. Change directory from **/usr/src/cmd/shell** to **/usr/home/src/cmd/shell**.

5 PROGRAMMING LANGUAGE

This chapter is a tutorial for the KornShell programming language. Full details of the KornShell programming language are in Part IV of this book, *Programming Language*.

As stated earlier, there is only one KornShell language. The division of command language and programming language into separate chapters is for tutorial purposes. Use **ksh** as a programming language by grouping commands together into programs that are called scripts. Scripts can consist of a sequential list of commands. Also, you can write **ksh** scripts using control flow commands to perform tasks usually written in a more traditional programming language such as the C language or the BASIC language.

INTRODUCTION TO PARAMETERS

Shell variables were introduced in the preceding chapter. A variable is one of three types of parameters that **ksh** understands. Since variables are used primarily when writing scripts, many aspects of their use were not discussed there and are discussed here instead. The *Parameters* chapter describes in detail each parameter and variable that **ksh** uses.

A parameter is used to store and manipulate information. A parameter can be one of the following:

- Variable. A variable name consists of one or more identifiers separated by . (dot) and is called a *varname*. Variables were introduced briefly on page 39 of the previous chapter. Assign values to variables with variable assignment commands. Variable assignment commands are of the form *name=value* ... . You cannot put any Spaces or Tabs before or after the =. *Version*: Variable names were restricted to a single identifier in the 11/16/88 version of **ksh**.
- Positional parameter. The name for a positional parameter is a number. Positional parameters are used mainly in scripts.

- Special parameter. The name of a special parameter is one of the following characters: ∗ @ # ? − $!. Special parameters are described in detail on page 190. Special parameters are set by **ksh**. For example, the parameter **$** expands to the process id of the current shell environment, and the parameter **!** expands to the process id of the most recently created background process.

You access the value of a parameter by preceding its name with a **$** and surrounding the name with { }. You can think of the **$** as meaning, "the value of." The { } are optional when the name is a single digit or if the name is a single identifier or a special parameter, unless the parameter is followed by characters that could be considered part of the parameter name. For instance, **$$** means "the value of the $ special parameter."

You can specify a parameter to be expanded anywhere, even as part of a word, for instance **${foo}.c**.

POSITIONAL PARAMETERS

Parameters denoted by numbers are called positional parameters.

When you invoke a script, **ksh** stores the arguments to the script as positional parameters. **ksh** sets positional parameter **0** to the name of the script and sets the other positional parameters, from **1** on, to the other arguments that you supply.

Reference positional parameters with any of the following:

$4 The fourth argument. Braces around the parameter number are required with a positional parameter greater than **9**, for example, **${20}**.

$# The number of positional parameters, not counting **0**.

"$∗" One argument consisting of all positional parameters from **1** on.

"$@"** **$# arguments consisting of all positional parameters from **1** on. The double quotes prevent parameter values with Spaces, Tabs, or Newlines from being split up into separate arguments, and prevent Null positional parameters from being removed. This has the effect of expanding to **"$1" "$2" "$3"** … for as many parameters as exist.

"${@:3}" All positional parameters from **3** on.

"${@:3:7}" **7** or fewer positional parameters starting from **3**.

Version: The last two forms are available only on versions of **ksh** newer than the 11/16/88 version.

Examples
```
68$ print 'print hello $1' > hi
69$ cx hi
70$ hi there world
hello there
```

```
71$ print 'print hello "${@:2:3}"' > hi
72$ hi there how are you feeling
hello how are you
```

Use **set** to assign new values to the positional parameters beginning with **1**. You cannot assign values to positional parameters individually. You can only replace one set of positional parameters with another.

Use **set – –** without arguments to unset the positional parameters.

Use **set –s** to sort the positional parameters based on the collation weights in the current locale. In the default locale, the position in the ASCII character set (see **Character Set** in the Appendix) is used to determine the sort order.

Use **shift** to shift positional parameter(s) to the left. **ksh** discards as many parameter(s) as it shifts, beginning with parameter **1**.

Examples

```
73$ set -- foo bar bam
74$ print "$@"
foo bar bam
75$ set -s
76$ print "$@"
bam bar foo
77$ shift 2
78$ print "$@"
foo
```

MORE ABOUT PARAMETERS

ksh does not limit the length of a variable name or its value. Choose names for variables that make your script easier to read. We recommend using lowercase for variables that are local to your script. To concatenate the value of two or more parameters together, reference them one after the other, for instance, **foo1**.

When you reference a parameter, you can modify the value of its expansion by following the parameter inside the braces with one of the following modifiers and a word (see **Parameters** for a complete list). If the word following the parameter modifier is needed to complete the parameter expansion, **ksh** performs command substitution and parameter expansion on it before using it. Use the parameter modifier to specify:

–   A value to be used if the parameter is not set; for example, **${1–***default***}**. Use a **:** in front of the **–**, if *default* is to be used if the parameter is Null or is not set.

?   A message to be displayed on standard error if the parameter is not set. Use a **:** in front of the **?**, to cause the message to be displayed if the parameter is Null or is not set. Non-interactive shells exit after printing this message.

\#   That the smallest leading portion of the value matching the pattern following #, be discarded.

\#\#   That the largest leading portion of the value matching the pattern following ##, be discarded.

%   That the smallest trailing portion of the value matching the pattern following %, be discarded.

%%   That the largest trailing portion of the value matching the pattern following %%, be discarded.

:   That only the substring that starts at the arithmetic character position specified after : be expanded. The first character position is 0. A second : and a length can also be specified.

/   A pattern to be matched and a replacement string. Only the first occurrence of the pattern is replaced.

//   A pattern to be matched and a replacement string. All occurrences of the pattern are replaced.

Version: The last three forms are available only on versions of **ksh** newer than the 11/16/88 version.

Examples

```
${foo%??}   # Expands foo and deletes last two characters.
${0##*/}    # Expands pathname of script to a filename.
${d-$(date)} # Expands to value of d if set;
            # otherwise expands to output of date.
${d:3}      # Expands to value of d starting at 4th
            # character.
${d:3:2}    # Expands to 4th and 5th character of d.
${d/x/foo}  # Expands to value of d replacing first x with
            # foo.
${d//x/foo} # Expands to value of d replacing each x with
            # foo.
```

Caution: Unless a reference to a parameter is inside double quotes, leading and trailing Spaces are discarded when the parameter is used as a command argument.

The value of **${#*parameter*}** is the number of characters in the value of *parameter*.

Each variable can be given one or more of the attributes listed beginning on pages 177. Some attributes affect the value of the variable. Use **typeset** to assign or change any attribute of a variable. Some attributes are used to specify how much space variables will occupy when they are displayed. This is useful for formatting reports. To control the width and justification of its value, use:

typeset –L [*width*]

To specify a left-justified fixed-width variable. When you assign a value that is wider than the width, **ksh** discards excess trailing characters from the end of the value. If the value is narrower than the width, **ksh** adds Spaces at the end.

typeset –R [*width*]

To specify a right-justified fixed-width variable. When you assign a value that is wider than the width, **ksh** discards excess leading characters from the beginning of the value. If the value is narrower than the width, **ksh** inserts Spaces at the beginning.

typeset –Z [*width*]

To specify a fixed-width field that behaves like the right-justified attribute, except that if you assign a value beginning with a digit that is narrower than the width, zero(s) are inserted at the beginning to fill up the field.

Examples
```
typeset -L4 x  # x is 4 characters, left-justified.
typeset -R5 y=7 # y is 5 characters, right-justified.
typeset -L1 z  # z will be the first character only.
typeset -Z3 n=7 # n will be 007.
```

To specify the case of alphabetic characters in variables, use:

typeset –u

To cause all lowercase characters to be changed to uppercase.

typeset –l

To cause all uppercase characters to be changed to lowercase.

Examples
```
typeset -u x=abc       # x will have value ABC.
typeset -L2 -l y=ABC   # y will have value ab.
print x=$x y=$y
x=ABC y=ab
```

RETURN VALUES

Each command has a return value. The return value of a command is used with conditional commands and iteration commands discussed later in this chapter. The return value of a command that does not terminate due to a signal is a number from 0 to 255. A value indicates:

- 0   Normal exit. When used in a conditional or iteration command, this value represents True. Any other value means that the command returns False.
- 1-125   Failure.
- 126   A command was found but cannot be executed.
- 127   A command could not be found.
- 128-255   Failure.
- 256 and above

A command has exited because of the receipt of a signal. Use the **–l** option of **kill** to determine the name of the signal that caused the command to exit, or subtract 256 to get the number.

Version: With the 11/16/88 version of **ksh**, 129-160 indicated that a command had exited because of the receipt of a signal. Subtracting 128 determined the number of the signal that caused the command to exit. A command that could not be found or could not execute had a return value of 1.

ksh sets the parameter **?** to the return value of the last command. The return value is documented with each command in this book.

Make sure that each script or function you write has sensible return values. The return value should be **0** (True) if it ran successfully. The return value of a script or function is the return value of the last command it executes – either set explicitly by an **exit** or **return** command, or set implicitly by any other command.

Use **exit** within a script to cause the script to exit with the return value that you specify.

MORE ON QUOTING

Quoting restores the literal meaning to characters that are processed specially by **ksh**. Literal (single) quotes, '...', cause all the characters between them to retain their literal meaning. The literal quotes are not passed on to the command.

ANSI C strings, $'...', cause all the characters between them to retain their literal meaning except for escape sequences, which are introduced by an escape character (\ ) and are interpreted as the ANSI C escape sequences as described on page 226. The $ is discarded. *Version*: This quoting mechanism is available only on versions of **ksh** newer than the 11/16/88 version.

Grouping (double) quotes, "...", allow parameter expansion, arithmetic expansion, and command substitution to take place, but processes the rest of the characters literally. Only the characters $, `, and \ are special with "...". When you use "...", **ksh**:
- Expands parameters and commands contained within the double quotes.
- Treats literally the characters in the resulting expansion.
- Removes the grouping (double) quotes.

A double quoted string preceded by a $ represents a string that needs to be translated to the local language when not in the C or POSIX locale. The $ is discarded. *Version*: This feature is only available with versions of **ksh** newer than the 11/16/88 version.

Use the escape character, \, to quote the next character. Inside a double quoted string, \ retains its literal meaning except when followed by a $, `, ", or \.

Caution: Use double quotes around command words that contain parameter references to prevent the value from being split into separate arguments and to prevent pathname expansion on the value. Also, if a command word expands to Null and it is not enclosed in "...", **ksh** does not create a command argument. Therefore, use "..." to specify a mandatory command argument as a parameter that might expand to Null. The double quotes are not needed for parameter references within the value of variable assignments because, as noted in the table on 157, field splitting and pathname expansion are not performed there.

Examples

```
x='foo bar'     # Variable x has a space in its value.
"|$x|"          # Expands to single argument, |foo bar|.
*foo\ bar\**    # Matches anything containing foo bar*.
y=              # Sets y to null string.
set -- $y "$y"  # Expands to one null argument.  The first $y
                # is discarded.
x=$'\E]a\'\n'   # Assigns string consisting of characters
                # ESC ] a ' Newline to x.
x=$"hello"      # Assigns hello to x in C or POSIX locale.
                # Otherwise, looks up and replaces hello.
```

PATTERN MATCHING

Except for the syntax, patterns are similar to regular expressions as used by **grep** and **ed**. In fact, the **%P** format conversion of **printf** will convert an extended regular expression into a shell pattern so that it can be used within a shell script. *Version*: The **%P** format conversion is available only on versions of **ksh** newer than the 11/16/88 version.

Patterns were introduced briefly in connection with pathname expansion on page 40. In addition to pathname expansion, **ksh** uses patterns in **case** and [[...]] compound commands, and for substring expansions. The complete rules for forming patterns can be found starting on page 133.

In addition to *, ?, and [, patterns can be formed with any of the following:

?(*pattern* [|*pattern*]...)   To match zero or one of the given patterns.
*(*pattern* [|*pattern*]...)   To match zero or more of the given patterns.
+(*pattern* [|*pattern*]...)   To match one or more of the given patterns.
@(*pattern* [|*pattern*]...)   To match exactly one of the given patterns.
!(*pattern* [|*pattern*]...)   To match anything except the given patterns.

Patterns can be formed by using any combination of these pattern expressions and regular characters. The parenthesized pattern groups are called sub-patterns. The portion of the string that matches a sub-pattern can be referred to later in the pattern by using a backreference. A backreference is indicated by *digit*, where *digit* is the number of the left parenthesis of the sub-pattern starting from the left. *Version*: Backreferences are available only on versions of **ksh** newer than the 11/16/88 version.

Examples
```
@(foo|bar|bam)      # Matches foo, bar, or bam.
?(foo|bar|bam)      # Matches foo, bar, bam, or null.
+([0-9])?(.)*([0-9]) # Matches one or more digits,
                    # optionally followed by a decimal
                    # point and any number of digits.
!(*.o)              # Matches any string not ending in .o.
@(?)*\1*\1          # Matches string beginning and ending
                    # in same character and containing the
                    # same character somewhere in-between.
```

OPENING AND CLOSING FILES

Use **exec** without arguments to open and close files in the current environment. Use the I/O redirection syntax defined on page 145 to specify the files that you want to open or close. You can open and/or close file descriptors from **0** to **9**. **ksh** sets the close-on-exec bit on file descriptors from **3** to **9**.

Use I/O redirection without a command name to create a file or to remove the contents of an existing file. **ksh** opens or creates the file and then closes it.

The parameter $ expands to the process id, which is a number that is unique to all scripts running at the same time. Use $$, the value of parameter $, within a pathname to generate the name of a temporary file to ensure that the temporary file name is unique.

Examples
```
exec 3< foo    # Opens foo for reading, as file descriptor 3.
exec 3<&-      # Closes file descriptor 3.
>/tmp/foo$$     # Creates a temporary file.
exec 3<> foo   # Opens foo for reading and writing,
               # as file descriptor 3.
```

ksh processes certain file names specially when specified after a redirection operator. A file name of the form **/dev/fd/***number* is treated as meaning use file descriptor *number*.

File names of the form **/dev/tcp/***hostid***/***portid* and **/dev/udp/***hostid***/***portid* are treated as socket connections using **tcp** and **udp** protocol, respectively. *hostid* is an address of the form *n.n.n.n*, where each *n* represents any number. The *hostid* **0.0.0.0** can be used to refer to services on your machine. The *portid* is the number of the service, for example 13 is the date and time server. This makes it easy to connect to Internet services directly from the shell. The means to obtain the *hostid* of a machine, and the *portid* for a particular service are system dependent and beyond the scope of this book. *Version*: This feature is available on versions of **ksh** newer than the 11/16/88 version and some versions of the 11/16/88 version.

Examples
```
exec 3< /dev/fd/5        # Equivalent to exec 3<&5.
cat < /dev/tcp/0.0.0.0/13 # cat the date/time server
Sat Aug 28 12:39:42 1993
```

READING FROM TERMINALS AND FILES

By default, data input to **ksh** is line oriented. **ksh** does not process its input until it reads the Newline character. Use:
- **read** to read from any open file. **read** reads one line at a time.
- **read −u***n* to specify file descriptor *n*. If you omit **−u**, the default is **0** (standard input).

You normally specify **read −r** when reading from files. If you do not specify **−r** and the character preceding the Newline character is \, then **ksh** discards the \ and joins the current line with a **read** of the next line.

read reads a line and assigns the characters to the variable(s) that you specify as arguments. If you specify:
- No variable, **ksh** assigns the characters it reads to the **REPLY** variable.
- One variable, **ksh** assigns the characters it reads to the variable that you specify.
- More than one variable, **ksh** splits the line it reads into fields using the characters contained in the **IFS** variable as follows:
  - Each **IFS** character terminates a field. Each field is assigned to the next variable.
  - Two adjacent **IFS** characters in the line, neither of which belongs to the **space** character class, indicate a field whose value is Null; for example, if **IFS** is **:**, then **a::b** will be split into three fields, **a**, Null , and **b**.
  - **ksh** assigns leftover characters to the last variable.
  - **ksh** sets excess variables to Null if you specify more variables than needed.

To specify a prompt that is displayed when you read from a terminal, follow the first variable with a **?** and the prompt.

If the input to **read** comes from a terminal and an editor option is on, then editor directives can be used when entering lines. The **–s** option causes each line that is read to be saved into the history file (see page 86).

You can cause **ksh** to read up to a given character, *c*, rather than terminating at a Newline by using the **–d** *c* option.

When reading from a terminal or from a pipe, you can use the **–t** *timeout* option in order to limit the wait for input to *timeout* seconds. The return value will be False if the **read** command times out.

Version: The **–d** and **–t** options are available only on versions of **ksh** newer than the 11/16/88 version.

Examples
```
read -r               # Reads a line into variable REPLY.
read -rs              # Also copies line into history file.
read -r line          # Reads a line into variable line.
read -u3 line         # Reads from file descriptor 3.
read -r line?"Enter foo "
                      # First displays "Enter foo ".
read -d : field       # Reads up to : into variable field.
read -t 15 line       # Waits up to 15 seconds to read a line
                      # into variable named line.
IFS=: read -r a b c # Reads a line into variables a, b, and
                      # c, using a single : to delimit fields.
```

WRITING TO TERMINALS AND FILES

Use **print** or **echo** to display lines on a terminal and to write lines to a file. *Caution*: The behavior of **echo** is system dependent and is provided for compatibility with the Bourne shell. We use **print** in all the programs and examples in this book.

Ordinarily **ksh** replaces certain sequences beginning with \, as described on page 226, and then displays each of the arguments to **print** on standard output followed by a Newline. *Caution*: You must quote escape sequences to prevent **ksh** from removing the \ when it expands the arguments to **print**.

Specify:

–r   To prevent escape sequences from being replaced. Use **–r** to display a parameter whose value can contain an escape sequence.

–u *n*   To direct the output to file descriptor *n*. If omitted, **ksh** uses file descriptor **1**.

–n   To prevent a Newline from being appended.

–s   To direct the output to be appended to the history file as a command.

−− To indicate that subsequent arguments are not **print** options.
Use −− to display anything that might begin with a −. The examples in
this book use − − whenever the next argument is a parameter reference,
to avoid problems that arise when the parameter expands to a string
beginning with −.

−f *format*

To print the arguments as specified by the ANSI C format specification.
A Newline is not appended. If there are more arguments than field
specifications, the format is reused. The command **printf** is equivalent to
print −f . *Version*: This formatting mechanism is available only on
versions of **ksh** newer than the 11/16/88 version.

Examples
```
print -r -- "$foo"       # Displays line with value of foo.
print -u2 -r -- "$foo"   # As above, except file descriptor 2.
print -rs -- "$foo"      # Appends line with value of foo
                         # to the history file.
print -n "\t\t"          # Displays two tabs and stays on the
                         # line.
print -f '%s\t%s\n' *    # Displays files in the current
                         # directory two files per line.
```

HERE-DOCUMENTS

You can specify that one or more commands in your script read input from lines
within your script, rather than from your terminal or a file. Use the I/O redirection
operator <<, followed by an arbitrary delimiter-word. The lines starting after the
next Newline and continuing until a line containing only the delimiter-word, are
called a here-document. A here-document is also sometimes referred to as in-line
data.

Ordinarily, **ksh** performs parameter expansions, arithmetic expansions, and
command substitutions on the here-document before the contents are passed to the
specified command. The characters $, `, and \ are special and should always be
preceded by a \ if you want them to have their literal meaning. However, if you
quote any character of the delimiter-word in any way, then the here-document is
passed to the command without any expansions.

If you specify the operator <<− instead of <<, then **ksh** deletes leading Tabs from
each line of the here-document before passing it on to the command.
As illustrated in the next example, Tabs that precede the delimiter-word are also
ignored. Tabs can make your script easier to read.

You can use a here-document as the basis for a form letter generator or program
generator. Specify **cat** with the template for the form or program you want to
generate. Use parameter expansion and/or command substitution to generate the
variable information in the form or program.

Example
```
name=Morris
cat <<- EOF    # Deletes leading tabs, quits at EOF.
        Dear $name,

        I am writing this on $(date).
        Remember to go to the dentist at two-thirty.
        EOF
Dear Morris,

I am writing this on Wed May 19 12:03:13 1993.
Remember to go to the dentist at two-thirty.
```

CO-PROCESSES

From within a script, you can run a command or a pipeline in the background that can communicate with your program. This is particularly useful when you want to provide a new interface to an existing program, or to write a program that interfaces with a transaction-oriented program such as a database manager.

To run a co-process in the background, put the operator **|&** after the command. The standard input and the standard output of the command will each be connected to your script with a pipe.

Use **print –p** to write to the co-process, and use **read –p** to read from the co-process.

Caution: The co-process must:
• Send each output message to standard output.
• Have a Newline at the end of each message.
• Flush its standard output whenever it writes a message.
A shell script has all of these properties; thus it is possible to write a co-process as a shell script.

Example
```
ed - foobar |&
print -p /morris/
read -r -p line
print -r -- "$line"
This line in file foobar contains morris.
```

Use I/O redirection to move the input and/or output pipes of the co-process to a numbered file descriptor. Use **exec 3>&p** to move the input of the co-process to file descriptor **3**. Once you connect the input of a co-process to a numbered descriptor, you can redirect the output of any command to the co-process with the usual redirection syntax. For instance, **date >&3** directs the output of **date** to the co-process that has been moved to file descriptor **3**. You can invoke another co-process once you move the co-process input to a numbered descriptor. The output of both co-processes will be connected to the same pipe. Use **read –p** to read from this pipe. Use **exec 3<&–** to close the connection to the first co-process.

Use **exec 4<&p** to move the connection from the output of the co-process to file descriptor **4**. Use **read –u4** to read from the co-process after you move the connection to file descriptor **4**.

Example
```
(read; print -r "$REPLY") |&     # Begin co-process 1.
[1]   258
exec 5>&p                        # Move to descriptor 5.
(read; print -r "$REPLY") |&     # Begin co-process 2.
[2]   261
exec 6>&p                        # Move to descriptor 6.
date >&6                         # Date to co-process 2.
print -u5 foobar                 # Print to co-process 1.
exec 3<&p                        # Move input of both
                                 # co-processes to 3.
read -ru3 line                   # Read from co-process.
print -r "$line"                 # Display the line.
Sat Aug 28 12:13:05 1993
read -ru3 line                   # Read another line.
print -r "$line"                 # Display it.
foobar
```

GROUPING COMMANDS

A Newline terminates commands. However, you can put several commands on the same line by separating them with a ;. Since ; is an operator, you do not need Spaces or Tabs before or after it.

Example
```
print -n '\t'; print -r -- "$HOME"
        /usr/dgk
```

Use braces { } to group several commands together. For historical reasons, { and } are reserved words (see page 130), not operators. A Space, Tab, Newline, or control operator (see page 130) is required before and after the { and }. Otherwise **ksh** will read them as part of the next word. Because { and } are reserved words, they must appear as the first word of a command. The ; (or a Newline) just before the } in the example below is required; if you omit the ;, the } would be processed as a command argument rather than a reserved word. However, to avoid potential conflicts with future changes to the language, each { or } which represents itself should be quoted. You can specify I/O redirection after the }. Any redirection you specify applies to all commands within the group except those that are otherwise explicitly redirected. The next example reads the first two lines of file **foobar** into variables **line1** and **line2** and then displays the rest of the file on standard output.

Example
```
{ read -r line1; read -r line2; cat;} < foobar
```

You can also use ( ) to group several commands together. Since (and) are operators, you do not have to separate them with Spaces or Tabs; however, the (must appear as the first word of the command. ( ) creates a subshell environment (see page 263) to run the enclosed commands. Therefore, there can be no side effects, except on files. Because it runs in a subshell environment, it may be slower than { }, unless the group of commands would run in a subshell environment anyway; for example, a brace group followed by **&**. You can specify I/O redirection after the). Any redirection that you specify applies to each command within the group, unless it is explicitly redirected.

Example
```
( date; who ) | wc
```

ARITHMETIC

Arithmetic is denoted by enclosing an arithmetic expression inside ((...)). Arithmetic expressions use the ANSI C language operators, precedences, and math library functions. See *Arithmetic Expressions* on page 136 for a list of operators, precedences, and math library functions.

Arithmetic computations are performed using C double precision floating point arithmetic. Whenever **ksh** encounters a variable name within an expression, it replaces the variable name with the value of the variable. Thus, a $ preceding a variable name is unnecessary and may be a little slower. **ksh** can also do integer arithmetic in any arithmetic base from 2 through 64. Use the format *base#number* for constants in any base other than 10.

A command of the form ((*expression*)) is called an arithmetic command. The return value of an arithmetic command is True when the value of the enclosed expression is non-zero, and is False when *expression* evaluates to zero.

The construct $((expression))$ can be used as a word or part of a word; it is replaced by the value of *expression*.

The construct **let** "*expression*" is equivalent to $((expression))$. *Caution*: Each argument to **let** is a string that it evaluates as an arithmetic expression. Therefore you cannot use Spaces or Tabs without using quotes. Many of the arithmetic operators have special meaning to **ksh**, and must be quoted.

You can specify the integer attribute and an arithmetic base for any variable with **typeset –i**, or with the preset alias **integer**. You can specify the floating point attribute or the scientific notation attribute for any variable with **typeset –F** or **typeset –E**, respectively. **float** is a preset alias for **typeset –E**. The value of an integer or floating point variable is evaluated when you specify a value with a variable assignment command. You do not need to use **let**.

Use the **RANDOM** variable to generate a uniformly distributed sequence of random numbers in the range 0-32767. Each time **RANDOM** is referenced, it expands to a different random number.

Version: Floating point arithmetic and bases greater than 36 are available only on versions of **ksh** newer than the 11/16/88 version. Previous versions had integer arithmetic only.

Example
```
float r a=1 b=1.5 c=-1
(( r=sqrt(b*b-4*a*c) ))
print r1=$(( (-b+r)/2 )) r2=$(( (-b-r)/2 ))
r1=.5 r2=-2
```

TESTING FILES AND STRINGS

ksh has conditional expressions to check for the existence of a file, its access permissions, and/or its type; to test whether two pathnames refer to the same file; and/or to test whether one file is older than another. Conditional expressions can also be used to compare two strings or to compare two arithmetic expressions. See *Conditional Expression Primitives* on page 139 for a list of conditions to test.

Use the compound command [[...]] to specify conditional expressions.
Since words inside [[...]] do not undergo field splitting and pathname expansion, many of the errors associated with **test** and [are eliminated. Also, since **ksh** determines the operators within [[...]] before the words are expanded, no problem arises when a parameter expands to a value that starts with –. Finally, **&&** and | | are used as logical connective operators, and unquoted parentheses can be used for grouping.

Use [[**–z** $*parameter*]] or [[$*parameter* == ""]] to test whether *parameter* is Null. You need:
- Spaces and/or Tabs after the [[and before the]].

- Spaces and/or Tabs before and after the **–z** or **==**, since **–z** and **==** are separate arguments to the [[...]] command.

Version: The **==** conditional expression primitive is available on versions of **ksh** newer than the 11/16/88 version and on some 11/16/88 versions. You must use **=** on earlier versions.

To specify more complex tests, use the logical connective operators (listed here in decreasing order of precedence):

!   Not
&&   And
|| Or

Use parentheses to override normal precedence. For [[...]], parentheses are part of the grammar and must not be quoted. For **test** and [, parentheses are separate arguments and must be quoted.

Note: Each operator and operand must be a separate argument.

Examples
```
[[ -x file && ! -d file ]]        # True if file is executable
                                  # but is not a directory.
[[ $1 == abc ]]                   # True if $1 expands to abc.
[ "X$1" = Xabc ]                  # Same as above.
test "X$1" = Xabc                 # Same as above.
[[ $1 -ef . ]]                    # True if $1 is the working
                                  # directory.
[[ foo -nt bar ]]                 # True if foo is newer than
                                  # bar.
[[ ! (-w file || -x file) ]]      # True if file is neither
                                  # writable nor executable.
test ! \( -w file -o -x file \)   # Same as above.
```

COMPOUND COMMANDS

A compound command is a command that begins with one of the reserved words listed on page 130, or a grouping command, or a sequence of two or more commands separated by an operator. The pipeline command described earlier is an example of a compound command. See the **Compound Commands** chapter for a more detailed description of each of the compound commands described here.

Use pipelines to perform complex programming tasks. Each element of a pipeline can be any command, including any of the compound commands. The pipeline in the following example reads its input and displays on standard output each word in alphabetical order, preceded by a count of the number of times it appears in its input. It does this with a sequence of filters, which performs each of the following steps in order:

- Creates a list of all words in the input, one per line. The **-c** (complement) option of **tr**, combined with the character class **[A-Za-z]**, cause all characters that are not alphabetic to be replaced by the Newline character. The **-s** option causes multiple Newlines to be squeezed into a single Newline.
- Makes all characters lowercase.
- Sorts the lines.
- Displays each distinct line preceded by a count of how many times it occurs in descending order of occurrence

Example
```
tr -cs '[A-Za-z]' '\n' < file  |  tr '[A-Z]' '[a-z]' |
     sort -r | uniq -c
```

ksh does not recognize words such as **if** as reserved words, unless they appear as the first word of a command. It is customary to put most reserved words as the first word on a line. Use indentation to improve readability.

Use **if** to cause conditional execution. **ksh** executes the **then** command part only if the return value of the conditional command is True. **ksh** executes the **else** command part only if the return value of the conditional command is False. The **if** command ends with the reserved word **fi**. The conditional command can itself be a compound command. In the example below, note that **read** returns True if it has successfully read a line of data. The **:** (colon) built-in command has no effect. It is needed because the **then** reserved word must be followed by a command.

Example
```
if    print 'Please enter your name: \c'
      read -r name
then if    mail "$name" < mailfile
      then  :
      else  print "Cannot mail to $name"
      fi
else print 'end-of-file'
      exit 1
fi
```

ksh provides two other operators for combining commands more compactly than with the **if** command. The binary operator:

| | Runs the command following the | | only if the command preceding the | | returns False.

&& Runs the command following the **&&** only if the command preceding the **&&** returns True.

Examples
```
read -r line || exit
cd foobar && echo $PWD
```

Use **case** for a multiway branch. **case** finds which specified pattern, if any, matches a given word, and executes the command list associated with that pattern. Use **;;** or **;&** to terminate each command list. If **;&** is used in place of **;;**, then **ksh** will fall through to the next command list if this list is selected. You can specify a list of patterns for the same command sequence by separating them with **|**.
The following example tries to match the value of positional parameter **1** with strings beginning with **–d** or **–D**, strings beginning with **–e**, strings beginning with **–f**, or anything else, in that order. If **–e** is matched then both **eflag** and **fflag** will be set to 1. It is not necessary to use double quotes around **$1** because **ksh** does not perform field splitting or pathname expansion in this context.

Example
```
case  $1 in
-[dD]*)  dflag=1;;
-e*)     eflag=1;&
-f*)     fflag=1;;
*)       print -u2 'You must specify -d, -D, or -e or -f'
         exit 1;;
esac
```

Parameters in **case** pattern words are expanded to form the pattern. This makes it easy to construct patterns within a script. *Version*: Words that expanded to patterns containing parentheses did not work with the 11/16/88 version of **ksh**.

The following example reads a line and checks if the line begins with any character found in the value of positional parameter **1**.

Example
```
read -r line
case  $line in
[$1]*)  ;; # ok
*)      print -u2 "Line must begin with one of: $1"
        exit 1;;
esac
```

Use **while** to execute a group of commands repeatedly as long as the conditional command has a True return value.

Example
```
while read -r line        # read a line
do   print -r -- "$line"  # print the line
done
```

until is like **while**, except that the body of the loop is executed until the conditional command has a return value of True. The example below uses the return value of a pipeline command. The return value of a pipeline is the return value of the last command in the pipeline.

Example
```
until who | grep morris   # until morris logs in
do   sleep 60             # try again in 60 seconds
done
```

Use **for** to repeat a sequence of commands once for each item in a specified list. Before the loop begins, **ksh** expands the list of words that you specify following the reserved word **in**. These words are expanded just as **ksh** expands command words. The body of the **for** command is executed once for each argument in the expanded list. **ksh** assigns the loop index variable, **i** in the following example, the value of each argument in turn.

Example
```
for i in *  # For each file in the working directory.
do  if    [[ -d $i ]]
    then  print -r -- "$i"  # Print subdirectory names.
    fi
done
```

Use the arithmetic **for** command described on page 171 to execute a sequence of commands until some arithmetic condition is satisfied. The arithmetic **for** command is similar to the C language **for** statement. *Version*: The arithmetic **for** is available only on versions of **ksh** newer than the 11/16/88 version.

Example
```
integer even=0 odd=0 count
for ((count=0; count < 100; count++))
do    if    ((RANDOM%2==0))
      then  even=even+1
      else  odd=odd+1
      fi
done
print even=$even odd=$odd
even=47 odd=53
```

ARRAYS

An array is a variable that can store multiple values, where each value is associated with a subscript. There are two types of arrays – indexed arrays and associative arrays. The subscript for an indexed array is an arithmetic expression; the subscript for an associative array is an arbitrary string. You do not have to declare that a variable is an indexed array. Use **typeset –A** to declare that a variable is an associative array.

You can specify a subscript with any variable using the array syntax notation, *varname*[*subscript*]. The subscript for an indexed array can be any arithmetic expression that evaluates between 0 and some implementation-defined value that is at least 4095. The subscript for an associative array can be any string.

Each attribute that you specify applies to all elements of an array.

You can assign values to array elements individually with variable assignment commands. You can assign values to indexed array elements sequentially, starting at index 0, using the compound assignment *name*=(*value* ...). Alternatively, you can use **set –A** *name* to assign a list of values to an array sequentially. Use the compound assignment name=([*subscript*]=*word* ...) to assign multiple elements to an associative array.

Use braces around the array name and subscript when referencing an indexed or associative array element, for instance **${foo[bar]}**. If you omit the braces, **ksh** would expand **$foo**, concatenate it with the pattern **[bar]**, and replace it with pathnames that match this pattern. When you reference an array variable without specifying a subscript, then **ksh** uses element **0**. Use subscript **@** or ∗ to refer to all the elements of an array.

Use the name operator **!** to expand the list of subscripts in an array. For example, **${!foo[@]}** expands to the list of array subscripts for variable **foo**. The size operator **#** can be used in place of **!** to obtain the number of elements in the array.

Version: Associative arrays, compound assignments, and the name operator **!** are available only on versions of **ksh** newer than the 11/16/88 version. Previous versions only have indexed arrays, and some implementations limit the subscript to a maximum of 1023.

Examples
```
# The following prints a random card from a card deck.
integer i=0
typeset -u card  # Upper case.
for suit in clubs diamonds hearts spades
do   for n in ace 2 3 4 5 6 7 8 9 10 jack queen king
     do   card[i]="$n of $suit"
          i=i+1  # The let command is not required with
                 # integer variables.
     done
done
print -- ${card[RANDOM%52]}
QUEEN OF DIAMONDS

# The following illustrates indexed array assignment.
files=(*)  # versions newer than 11/16/88
print -r -- "${#files[@]}: ${files[@]}"
7: file1 file2 foobar prog prog.c todo wishlist

# The following example demonstrates associative arrays.
typeset -A color
color=( [apple]=red [grape]=purple [banana]=yellow )
print -- ${!color[@]}    # print list of subscripts
grape apple banana
print -- ${color[@]}     # print list of elements
purple red yellow
```

CREATING AND USING MENUS

Use **select** to display a list of alternatives for a user to select from. **select** displays the list of items you specify in rows and columns, with each item preceded by a number and a right parenthesis. **select** uses the variables **COLUMNS** and **LINES** to help format the menu selections.

select displays the **PS3** variable as a prompt when it is ready to read the user selection. The user's reply is saved in the **REPLY** variable. If the user enters a number corresponding to one of the choices, the **select** index variable is assigned the corresponding value. Otherwise, the **select** index variable is set to Null. If the user enters RETURN by itself, **ksh** redisplays the choices and the **PS3** prompt and reads the selection again.

Version: On versions of **ksh** newer than the 11/16/88 version, if the **TMOUT** variable contains a value greater than 0, **select** will time out after the number of seconds defined by **TMOUT** and the return value will be False.

You usually use a **case** command within the body of **select** to specify the appropriate action to take.

Example
```
PS3='Pick one of the above: '
TMOUT=10
select i in list edit quit
do    case $i in
      list)    cat "$foo";;
      edit)    ${EDITOR-vi} "$foo";;
      quit)    break;;
      "")      print -u2 you must select one of the above;;
      esac
done
1) list
2) edit
3) quit
Pick one of the above: 3
```

USING eval

A shell script is itself a sequence of characters that can be stored in a variable. The **eval** command can be used to process its arguments as if it (the **eval** command) were a shell script. Because **eval** is a command, its arguments are expanded before **eval** is run. **eval** creates a script by concatenating its arguments, each separated by an unquoted space, and then running the resulting string as if it were a shell script.

The *Command Processing* chapter explains the order in which **ksh** processes a command to construct the command name and arguments. Use **eval** when you want results from expansions to be applied to earlier stages of the expansion, or when you want a stage of the processing repeated again. **ksh** expands the arguments to **eval** with the normal processing rules. **ksh** then forms a string by concatenating the arguments of **eval**, separating each by a Space. **ksh** reads and processes the resulting string as a command.

Use **eval** to:
- Process the result of an expansion or substitution by a step that precedes it during command processing.
- Find the value of a parameter whose name is the value of another parameter.
- Execute a line you read.

The return value of **eval** is the return value of the command formed by its arguments.

Examples
```
eval last='$'{$#}       # Last positional parameter.
eval print '$'$name     # Displays variable named $name.

cmd='date | wc'
eval $cmd               # Causes | to mean pipeline.

read -r line
eval "$line"            # Processes line as a command line.

if    eval [ ! -d \${$#} ]
then  print -r -- "${0}: Last argument is not a directory."
      exit 1
fi
```

EXERCISES

1. Explain what each of the following commands does. Assume that they are run in the order shown.
   a. `typeset -L1 x; typeset -R1 y`
   b. `x=foobar y=foobar`
   c. `print x=$x y=$y ${#x}`
   d. `{ integer i=3 j=2; i=i*2; print $i+$j ; }`
   e. `( i=i+j; print $i )`
   f. `a[1]=foo a[3]=bar; print "${a[@]}"`
   g. `((i>j)) && i=j`
   h. `eval eval print hello world`
   i. `PS3= ; select i in * ; do : ; done < /dev/null`
   j. `x=(*.c); print ${#x[@]}`

2. Write a command to do each of the following:
   a. Assign the value **foo** to a variable whose name is stored in variable **bar**.
   b. Open a here-document on file descriptor 3.
   c. Read 50 lines of a file (or until the end of the file, if the file is less than 50 lines), looking for a line containing the string **foobar**. Output the line number and the contents of the line.
   d. Display the sum of two random numbers in the range 1 to 6, 100 times.
   e. Read a line and execute:
      date if user types **d**
      who if user types **w**
      exit if user types **e**

PROCESSING ARGUMENTS

It is a good practice to follow the command argument conventions described on page 28 when designing shell programs.

All arguments, both option and non-option, are stored as positional parameters when the script begins. Process options by reading each of the option arguments and creating variables for each of the specified options. Shift the positional parameters so that after option processing is complete, they contain only non-option arguments.

The **getopts** command makes it easy to process the command line arguments in a way that follows the standard command line conventions described on page 28. With **getopts** you specify which options are permitted, and which options are allowed to take arguments. Options that require arguments are followed with a : (colon). Enclose information in [...] following a : or after a Space to have it included in automatically generated usage messages. A : (colon) at the beginning of the option string causes errors to be returned in the option variable rather than be displayed automatically by **ksh**. In this case, an option that requires an argument is returned as a : (colon), and unknown options are returned as a ?. You also specify the name of a variable that is used to store the option that **getopts** finds. **getopts** processes the argument list one option at a time. To process all the arguments, **getopts** needs to be called from within a compound command. Normally a **while** command is used to process the complete set of options, and a **case** command is used inside the **while** to process each option.

The variables **OPTARG** and **OPTIND** are set by **getopts**. After processing an option that takes an argument, **OPTARG** will contain the value of the option argument. The **OPTIND** variable will contain the index of the positional parameter that will be processed by the next **getopts** call. You would normally shift the positional parameters by **OPTIND–1** after processing all options, so that the positional parameters contain only the non-option arguments.

The return value for **getopts** is True as long as there are more options to be processed, so that all errors can easily be detected and reported. A – – in the option list signifies the end of options.

Version: On versions of **ksh** newer than the 11/16/88 version, a *Usage* message will be generated with the **–?** option.

Example
```
prog=${0##*/}  # use only the filename, not the pathname
while getopts :abo: c
do  case $c in
    a)  aflag=1;;
    b)  bflag=1;;
    o)  oflag=$OPTARG;;
    :)  print -u2 "$prog: $OPTARG requires a value"
        exit 2;;
   \?)  print -u2 "$prog: unknown option $OPTARG"
        print -u2 "Usage: $prog [-a -b -o value] file ..."
        exit 2;;
    esac
done
shift $((OPTIND-1))
```

BUILT-IN COMMANDS

Built-in commands look like programs and scripts, but are processed by the shell rather than by a separate process. This makes it possible for built-in commands to do things that cannot be done as separate programs. For example, the **cd** command changes the directory for the current process. If **cd** were written as a separate program, then the directory would be back at the original location when **cd** completed.

Built-ins start up much faster than do separate programs. On some systems, the startup time for programs is more than one hundred times as long as that of a built-in command. Commands that are built-in solely to improve performance can be associated with an absolute pathname. These built-ins will only execute after doing a path search and finding the executable program of that name. Otherwise, built-ins are found before searching for programs.

The **builtin** command without arguments lists the current set of built-ins, including the pathname for those built-ins that have an associated pathname. It is possible to change the pathname for a built-in or to delete a built-in with **builtin**. If the code for a built-in command is already loaded in the shell, then you can make it a built-in by giving the name of the command as an argument to **builtin**. You can delete a built-in command with the **–d** option to **builtin**.

In addition, on systems that have the ability to link in code at runtime, the **builtin** command can be used to add code libraries and built-in commands. The description of how to create these commands is outside the scope of this book.

Version: The **builtin** command is available only on versions of **ksh** newer than 11/16/88.

Example
```
type wc test
wc is a tracked alias for /bin/wc
test is a shell builtin
builtin wc
builtin -d test
type wc test
wc is a shell builtin
test is a tracked alias for /bin/test
```

DOT SCRIPTS

ksh runs a script in a separate environment whether you invoke a script by name, or by running **ksh** with the name of the script as an argument. In either case, changes made to the environment of the script, such as changing the value of any variable, will not affect the environment of the calling program.

Use the **.** (dot) command to cause the script to execute in the current environment. The arguments to the **.** command are the name of the script and its arguments. If arguments are given, they replace the positional parameters within the script. *Version*: With the 11/16/88 version of **ksh**, if arguments to the script were specified, the positional parameters were not restored when the script completed.

The first argument to the **.** (dot) command can be a function defined with the **function** *name* syntax described on page 77. In this case the function is executed in the current environment.

A script invoked by the **.** command is called a dot script. A dot script is normally used to initialize the environment of a program. An application can read a **.** (dot) script to create a default environment prior to processing command arguments.

Use **return** to terminate the dot script. Use **exit** to terminate the current shell or shell script.

Examples
```
cat foo.init
# This file sets default values.
Logfile=$HOME/foo.log
Tmpdir=/usr/tmp
Prompt='feed me! '
```

```
. foo.init
# The following example doesn't work in the 11/16/88 version
# of ksh because of the lack of quoting of the set output.
set > /tmp/save$$  # Save variables in a temporary file.
. /tmp/save$$      # Restore variables from temporary file.
```

DEFINING AND USING FUNCTIONS

Functions provide an efficient vehicle for writing relatively simple commands that execute in the current environment. They also provide a means of breaking a script into smaller, well-defined pieces that are easier to write. A function differs from a script in that it can run in the current environment and, therefore, can share variables and other side effects with the script that invokes it. A function executes faster than a dot script because **ksh** reads a function just once when it is defined, rather than reading it each time that it is referenced.

Because of deficiencies in the POSIX shell standard, there are two types of functions in **ksh** that differ slightly in syntax and semantics. POSIX functions are defined with the syntax *name*( ){*body*;}, and do not provide any scoping of variables or traps. This makes it hard to write functions that don't have side effects.

The other way to define functions in **ksh** is with the **function** compound command which uses the syntax **function** *name* {*body*;}. Use **typeset**, with or without options, within such a function definition to declare local variables. The names for local variables must be identifiers. Changing the value of a local variable has no effect on a variable of the same name in the script that calls the function. If you do not declare a variable to be local, then any change that you make to the variable remains in effect after the function returns to the calling script.

Use **return** to return to the calling script. If you do not use **return**, the function returns after **ksh** processes the last command in it. Do not use **exit** unless you really want to terminate the current script.

Invoke a function by name in the same way that you invoke a built-in command, a script, or a program. A function must be defined, or found in a directory named by the **FPATH** variable before it is referenced. Specify the function name followed by its arguments, if any. These arguments become the positional parameters inside the function, but do not change the current positional parameters for the invoking script. The value of positional parameter **0** is set to the name of the function, only when the function has been defined with the **function** compound command. When a POSIX function is invoked, **$0** is not changed.

A function defined with the **function** compound command can be given as an argument to the **.** (dot) command, instead of the name of a file. In this case the function executes without separate scope, and without resetting parameter **0**, as if it had been defined with the POSIX syntax. *Version*: This feature is only available with versions of **ksh** newer than the 11/16/88 version of **ksh**.

After expanding all the words of a command, **ksh** first checks the command name using the search order defined on page 44. Therefore, it is meaningless to define a function whose name is the same as that of a special built-in command.
The **command** built-in command can be used within a function to invoke a built-in command or a program that has the same name as the function, rather than invoking the function recursively.

When you write functions, try to avoid producing side effects with each of the following:
- Variables. Alter global variables only when it is essential to do so. Do not change their values or their attributes.
- Functions. Create or delete only when it is essential to do so.
- Aliases. Create or delete only when it is essential to do so.
- Working directory. Because functions execute as part of the same process, it is possible to change the working directory. The calling script should not unexpectedly be left in another directory.
- Temporary files. Before it returns to its caller, a function should remove any temporary files that are created for its exclusive use. Take special care when creating temporary pathnames formed using the $ parameter, which evaluates to the current process id, because both the function and its caller run in the same process. Use the function name, or an abbreviation, as part of the pathname.

Function names and definitions are not inherited by scripts or across separate invocations of **ksh**. You should put function definitions in a file whose name is the name of the function, in a directory defined in the **FPATH** variable. Additionally, you can put function definitions in your environment file if you want them to be defined whenever **ksh** is invoked interactively.

When functions are read by **ksh**, they are copied into the history file unless the **nolog** option is on so that they can be listed. Use the preset alias, **functions**, to display the definition of one or more functions. To remove a function, use **unset −f** followed by the name of the function.

Version: With the 11/16/88 version of **ksh**, functions defined with either syntax behaved like functions defined with the **function** command. In addition, a built-in command was found before a function of the same name; thus it was necessary to use a combination of aliases and functions to write a function to override a built-in command. Also, the built-in **command** was not available.

Example
```
# isnum returns True if its argument is a valid number.
# The first pattern requires a digit before the decimal
# point, and the second after the decimal point.
function isnum # string
{
    case $1 in
    ?([-+])+([0-9])?(.)*([0-9])?([Ee]?([-+])+([0-9])) )
        return 0;;
    ?([-+])*([0-9])?(.)+([0-9])?([Ee]?([-+])+([0-9])) )
        return 0;;
    *) return 1;;
    esac
    # Not reached.
}
```

AUTO-LOAD FUNCTIONS

A function that becomes defined the first time it is referenced is called an auto-loaded function. Its primary advantage is better performance, since **ksh** does not have to read the function definition if you never reference the function.

You can specify that a function auto-load with the **autoload** preset alias. When **ksh** first encounters an auto-loaded function, it uses the **FPATH** variable to search for a filename whose name matches that of the function. This file must contain the definition of this function. **ksh** reads and executes this file in the current environment and then executes the function.

Version: With versions of **ksh** newer than the 11/16/88 version, functions are also auto-loaded when a command is found in a directory that is listed in both the **PATH** variable and the **FPATH** variable.

Example
```
FPATH=$HOME/funlib
                # Directories to search for functions.
autoload foobar # Specifies that foobar be auto-loaded.
foobar *.c      # Executes foobar with files ending
                # in .c.
```

Note: You can load a library of related functions with the first reference to any of its members, by putting them all in one file. For each function defined, you can use **ln** to create a filename with the name of the function that refers to this file.

DISCIPLINE FUNCTIONS

Version: The features described in this section are available only on versions of **ksh** newer than 11/16/88.

In addition to functions whose names are identifiers, each variable can have one or more functions associated with it. These functions have names of the form *varname.action*, where *varname* is the name of a variable and *action* is an identifier that can be applied to that variable. These functions are called discipline functions for the given variable. Each variable can define a discipline function for each of the following actions:

get   Called when the variable is referenced. If the variable **.sh.value** is given a value within this discipline function, then this will be the value of the variable that was referenced.

set   Called when the variable is assigned a value. The variable **.sh.value** is set to the value that would be assigned. The value after the discipline function returns will be used in the assignment. If **.sh.value** is unset inside the discipline function, then no assignment will be performed.

unset   Called when the variable is unset. The variable will not be unset unless it is unset inside the discipline function.

Whenever a discipline function is invoked, the variable **.sh.name** is set to the name of the variable, and **.sh.subscript** is set to the value of the subscript.

These discipline functions can be used to make variables active rather than passive storage cells. For instance, if you define variable **foo** to be an associative array, and you define a **get** discipline for **foo**, then ${**foo**[*subscript*]} behaves like a function whose argument is *subscript*.

Additional disciplines can be created for variables created by built-in commands that are added to the shell.

Examples
```
function date.get
{
        .sh.value=$(date)
}
print -r -- "$date"
Sat Aug 28 12:48:25 1993
typeset -A linecount
function linecount.get
{
        .sh.value=$(wc -l < ${.sh.subscript} 2>/dev/null)
}
print -r -- $((linecount[file1] + linecount[file2]))
19
```

NAME REFERENCES

Version: The features described in this section are available only on versions of **ksh** newer than the 11/16/88 version.

It is often desirable to pass the name of a variable rather than the value of the variable, as an argument to a function. A reference variable provides a mechanism for providing a local name for this variable. A reference variable is created with **typeset –n**, or with the preset alias **nameref**. The name of a reference variable must be an identifier. The value of the variable at the time the **typeset –n** attribute is specified, defines the variable that will be referenced by the reference variable. All subsequent uses (except **typeset +n**) of the reference variable cause the operation to occur on the variable that is being referenced by the reference variable. For instance, if the variable **foo** is assigned the value **bar**, and **foo** is given the name reference attribute, **–n**, then each assignment to **foo** will be an assignment to **bar**.

Example
```
function reverse  # array name
{
    nameref foo=$1
    typeset temp
    integer i n=${#foo[@]} # number of elements in the array
    for ((i=0; i < n/2; i++))
    do   temp=${foo[i]}
         foo[i]=${foo[n-1-i]}
         foo[n-1-i]=$temp
    done
}
```

COMPOUND VARIABLES

Version: The features described in this section are available only on versions of **ksh** newer than the 11/16/88 version.

A compound variable is a variable whose name consists of more than one identifier. A compound assignment is an assignment of the form *name=(word ...)* which is used for array assignment as described earlier, or *name=(assignment ...)*, where *assignment* can be a simple assignment or a compound assignment.
For each *assignment* in the list, the variable *name.assignment* is assigned to.
In addition, the value of *name*, $*name*, consists of a list of assignments enclosed in parentheses that is equivalent to an assignment for all compound variables whose names begin with *name*.

Once the compound variable *name* has been created, you can operate on each member independently. Variables of the form *name.* created or deleted, will be created or deleted from the compound variable *name*. Individual members of a compound variable cannot be given the export attribute, because the export attribute cannot be given to any variable whose name contains a **..**

Examples
```
picture=(
        bitmap=$PICTDIR/fruit
        color=([apple]=red [grape]=purple [banana]=yellow)
        size=( typeset -E x=8.5  y=11.0 )
)
print -r -- "$picture"
(
     size=(
           typeset -E x=8.5
           typeset -E y=11
     )
     bitmap=/usr/local/pictures/fruit
     color=(
           [grape]=purple
           [apple]=red
           [banana]=yellow
     )
)
print -r -- "${picture.size.x}"
8.5
unset picture.color
typeset -F2 picture.cost=22.50
print -r -- "${picture}"
(
     typeset -F 2 cost=22.50
     size=(
           typeset -E x=8.5
           typeset -E y=11
     )
     bitmap=/usr/local/pictures/fruit
)
```

The name of a compound variable is often passed as a name reference to a function. The function can then use, modify, add, or delete individual members.

Example
```
function rotate # point angle
{
        nameref point=$1
        float temp c=$((cos($2))) s=$((sin($2)))
        (( temp = c*point.x - s*point.y ))
        (( point.y = s*point.x + c*point.y ))
        (( point.x=temp ))
}
p=(x=1.0 y=0.0)
rotate p $(( 2*atan(1.0) ))
print p=$p
p=( y=1 x=0.000000000005 )
```

SETTING TRAPS TO CATCH INTERRUPTS

Use **trap** to specify actions to be executed when any one of a specified set of asynchronous conditions arises. A condition arises when your script receives a signal.

The action you specify is expanded when **trap** is processed, and again just before **ksh** executes the action. Therefore, use literal (single) quotes rather than grouping (double) quotes to avoid expansion when you specify the action.

A trap on **EXIT** is executed when the script or **ksh** function completes. Use this trap to specify cleanup actions such as removing temporary files.

If you specify a trap on **EXIT** within a non-POSIX function, then the trap executes right after the function completes. A trap on **DEBUG** is executed after each command is expanded but before it executes. Use this trap to aid debugging functions and/or scripts.

Version: A trap on **DEBUG** was executed *after* each command executed with the 11/16/88 version of **ksh**.

Examples
```
trap 'rm -f /tmp/file$$' EXIT   # Remove /tmp files before
                                # exiting.
trap 'mail morris <<\!
The program aborted
!
'  HUP TERM
```

DEBUGGING

You can check the syntax of a script without actually executing it by invoking **ksh** with the **noexec** or **–n** option. We strongly recommend that you run each script you write with this option. You can often catch errors that you would not find when running the script, because certain portions of a script may be skipped when you run it without **noexec**. In addition, warnings about obsolete features and likely errors will also be produced.

You can cause **ksh** to display its input as it reads it, with the **verbose** option.

A simple method to debug a script is to have **ksh** display an execution trace. An execution trace is a listing of each command after **ksh** has expanded it, but before it has run the command. To cause **ksh** to display an execution trace of each command in a:
- Script. Invoke **ksh** with the **xtrace** option, or turn on the **xtrace** option with **set –x** (or **set –o xtrace**) within the script.
- Function. If the function is defined with type **function** *name* syntax, specify **typeset –ft** and the name of the function you wish to trace. Otherwise, the function shares the **xtrace** option with the caller.

The **PS4** prompt is evaluated for parameter expansion, arithmetic expansion, and command substitution and displayed in front of each line of an execution trace. Use the **LINENO** variable within the **PS4** prompt to identify the line number in the script or function that corresponds to the line **ksh** displays. For instance, **PS4='[$LINENO]+ '** will display the line number inside [...]+ before each command in the trace.

When **ksh** detects a syntax error while reading a script, it displays the name of the script, the line number within the script it was reading when it encountered the error, and the cause of the error. The line number that **ksh** displays for a mismatched quote is often not the line that caused the error, because quoted strings can legally extend over any number of lines. Work your way back through the script or function until you find the quote you omitted, or the extra quote you inserted. Also, **ksh −n** may help to find the missing quote.

Examples
```
# line 1 -- This is the file bar.
function badquote
{
    print "This is line 1  # This is the culprit.
    for i in *
    do    foo
    done
    print "Last line"
}
bar: syntax error at line 8 : `"' unmatched
ksh -n bar
bar: warning: line 4 : " quote may be missing
bar: syntax error at line 8 : `"' unmatched
```

When **ksh** detects an error while executing a function or script, it displays an error message preceded by the function name or script name, and the line number of the error enclosed in [ ]. Line numbers are relative to the beginning of the file for a script, and relative to the first line of the function when inside a function.

Sometimes it is helpful to comment out portions of the code to locate an error. Insert a # at the beginning of each line that you want commented out.

You can insert a call to a function, such as the function defined in the following example, at any point in a script or function that allows you to interactively examine the environment at that point.

Example
```
function breakpoint
{
    while read -r line?">> "
    do    eval "$line"
    done
}
```

You can use the **DEBUG** trap to specify a command to execute after **ksh** executes each command. A full breakpoint debugger for **ksh** has been written by Bill Rosenblatt and is available via anonymous ftp through the Internet at ftp.uu.net as the file /published/oreilly/nutshell/ksh/ksh.tar.Z.

INTERNATIONALIZATION

Version: The features described in this section are available only on versions of **ksh** newer than the 11/16/88 version.

It is possible to write scripts whose behavior depends on the country or locale in which it is run. Different locales may use different character sets, classify character types differently, collate characters differently, and use a different character to represent the decimal point for numbers. In addition, strings and error messages may need to be displayed in the language defined by the current locale.

ksh uses the variables **LANG, LC_ALL, LC_COLLATE, LC_CTYPE**, and **LC_NUMERIC** to provide support for internationalized applications. The value of these variables is the name of the locale that will be used. If **LC_ALL** is set, it overrides the value of all the other variables. Otherwise, each of the **LC_** variables overrides the value of the **LANG** variable.

Strings and error messages are translated into the current locale by looking up the message or string in a dictionary that is defined for the current locale. Some error messages are generated by **ksh** itself. You can put a **$** in front of each double quoted string to denote strings that need to be translated to a string in the current locale. You can invoke **ksh** with the **–D** option and the name of the script to generate the list of strings that need translation. You can then make a translation dictionary for these strings. The procedure for making language dictionaries is beyond the scope of this book.

EXERCISES

1. Write a function to do each of the following:
   a. Display its arguments on standard error and exit.
   b. Return True if its first argument is a number.
   c. Given an argument that is a number representing dollars and cents, display the value in words as you would write it on a check.
   d. Read lines from the terminal and execute only commands whose names do not contain a /. The function should prompt the user with the **PS1** prompt when it is ready to read a command. Each command should be entered into the history file.

2. Write a script named **behead** that displays a file without the first few lines. You should be able to specify the number of lines to behead as an option –*n*.

3. Write a script named **bundle** that takes a list of pathnames, and creates a shell program that will restore the files if they are deleted. You do this by creating a here-document for each file whose pathname is the contents of the file. The script should also preserve the file permissions.

4. What is the output of the following program when called with an argument of 2, and when called with an argument of 3?

```
function hanoi # n from to spare
{
    integer nm1=$1-1
    ((nm1>0)) && hanoi $mn1 $2 $4 $3
    print "Move disc $2 to $3"
    ((nm1>0)) && hanoi $nm1 $4 $3 $2
}
case $1 in
[1-9])
      hanoi $1 1 2 3;;
*)    print -u2 "Argument must be from 1 to 9"
      exit 1;;
esac
```

5. Write a program that draws a histogram of an array of integers. Each row of the histogram should represent the number in that array element. Scale using **COLUMNS** if necessary, so that the histogram fits across the page.

6. Write a program that takes a positive integer and does the following:
   a. If the number is 1, stops.
   b. If the number is even, divides by two and starts over.
   c. If the number is odd, displays the number in base 10 and in base 2. Then multiplies the number by 3, adds 1, and starts over.

7. Write a command to compute the number of times each word appears in a file similar to the example on page 67, using associative arrays rather than the **tr** command.

8. Write a function named **optparse** that takes as arguments an option string in the format used by **getopts**, the command name, and the command arguments, and finds all option arguments. The **optparse** function should create an associative array named **.option** whose subscripts are the options that have been specified by the command arguments. If there are invalid options, the **optparse** function should display error and usage messages and exit. Otherwise, the positional parameters of the caller should be shifted by the number of option arguments when control is returned to the caller.

---

6 CUSTOMIZING YOUR ENVIRONMENT

This chapter describes some files that **ksh** uses, and explains how you can customize your environment based on your own preferences.

You can specify actions for **ksh** to perform each time you log onto the system and run **ksh** interactively.

You can specify functions and aliases that will be defined whenever you run **ksh** interactively.

This chapter also gives you advice on how to decrease the time it takes **ksh** to start up. It also tells you how to write scripts that run faster.

HISTORY FILE

ksh uses a file to store the commands that you enter from your terminal. This file is called the history file. Both the **emacs** and **vi** built-in editors have editing directives that allow you to retrieve commands from the history file to edit them and reenter them. Use **history** to display commands in your history file.

If you do not specify the **nolog** option, then **ksh** also uses the history file to store function definitions.

ksh opens the history file as soon as it encounters a function definition and the **nolog** option is off, or after it finishes reading the environment file, whichever is first. The name of the history file will be the value of the **HISTFILE** variable at the time that **ksh** opens it. If the history file does not exist, or if **ksh** cannot open it for reading and appending, then **ksh** creates a new history file in a temporary directory and sets its permissions so that only you can read and write it. *Caution*: Changing **HISTFILE** after the history file has been opened will not affect the current **ksh**. It will only affect subsequent **ksh** invocations.

ksh always appends commands to the history file. You can also use **read –s** and **print –s** to add commands to the history file. For example, to change the value of the **PATH** variable, run **print –s "PATH=$PATH"** and then use one of the built-in editors to edit the previous command. *Caution*: It is possible for the length of this command to be larger than the line length limit imposed by the inline editors. With the **vi** edit mode you can use the **v** directive to invoke the **vi** command on this line. Otherwise, you can use the **hist** command to edit the command.

ksh imposes no limit to the size of the history file. However, the value of the **HISTSIZE** variable at the time that the history file is opened specifies a limit to the number of previous commands that **ksh** can access.

ksh does not delete the history file at the end of a login session. When **ksh** is invoked and it determines that no other instance of **ksh** has the history file open, and the history file hasn't been modified for 15 minutes or more, **ksh** deletes commands from your history file older than the last **HISTSIZE** commands. *Caution*: On some systems, **ksh** does not delete old commands from the history file when you log in, and the history file may continue to grow. This causes **ksh** to take longer to begin execution and uses space on the file system. On some systems you can avoid this problem by specifying **ksh** as your login shell. On other systems you have to remove your history file periodically.

Separate invocations of **ksh** share the history file between all instances that specify the same name and have appropriate permission. Commands typed from one invocation are accessible by all the interactive instances of **ksh** that are running concurrently and sharing the same history file. The **HISTSIZE** variable in each **ksh** instance determines the number of commands accessible in each instance. On a terminal with multiple windows, you can type a command in one window and access it through another window.

LOGIN ENVIRONMENT (PROFILE)

Whenever you use **ksh** as your login shell, **ksh** executes the script **/etc/profile** if it exists, and then executes the file with the pathname that results from parameter expansion on **${HOME:–.}/.profile**. You can use this file to:
- Set and export values of variables that you want to have set for all the programs that you run, such as the **TERM** variable to specify the type of terminal that you are using.
- Set options such as **ignoreeof** that you want to apply to your login shell only.
- Specify a script to execute when you log out. Use **trap** on the **EXIT** condition.

Caution: For security reasons, your profile file is not processed when the **privileged** option is on.

The *Shell Functions and Programs* chapter contains a sample **.profile** suitable for most UNIX systems.

ENVIRONMENT FILE

Whenever **ksh** begins an interactive execution, it expands the **ENV** variable, and executes a script by this name if it exists. This file is called your environment file. Use this file to:
- Define aliases and functions that apply for interactive use only.
- Set default options that you want to apply to all interactive **ksh** invocations.
- Set variables that you want to apply to the current **ksh** invocation.

Version: The file defined by the **ENV** variable was also executed for non-interactive shell invocations with the 11/16/88 version of **ksh**.

Caution: For security reasons, your environment file is not processed when the **privileged** option is on.

The *Shell Functions and Programs* chapter contains a sample environment file suitable for most UNIX systems.

CUSTOMIZING YOUR PROMPT

ksh displays the primary prompt whenever the **interactive** option is on and **ksh** is ready to read a command.

The **PS1** variable determines your primary prompt. **ksh** performs parameter expansion, arithmetic expansion, and command substitution on the value of **PS1** each time before displaying the prompt. After **PS1** is expanded, the character **!** is replaced by the current command number. Use **!!** if you want the prompt to contain **!**.

Use the parameter expansion **'${PWD#$HOME/}'** or **'${PWD/$HOME/\~/}'** within your prompt to display your working directory relative to your home directory.

Use the **SECONDS** variable to put the time of day in your prompt.
Use arithmetic substitution to generate the hour and minute of the day from the **SECONDS** variable. Put the following lines in your profile file:
```
# Set SECONDS to number of seconds since midnight.
export SECONDS="$(date '+3600*%H+60*%M+%S')"
# The following variables store hours and minutes.
typeset -Z2 _h _m        # Two columns, leading zeros.
# The following expression reformats SECONDS.
_time='$((_h=SECONDS/3600)%24)):$((_m=(SECONDS/60)%60))'
# Use _time within PS1 to get the time of day.
PS1="($_time)"'!$ '
# Note that $_time gets replaced by above expression.
# Expression gets evaluated when PS1 is displayed.
```

CHANGING DIRECTORIES

ksh always remembers your previous working directory. Use **cd –** to return to the previous working directory.

You can set the **CDPATH** variable to a list of directory prefixes that **ksh** searches whenever you type a pathname that does not begin with a **/**. **ksh** displays the pathname of the new working directory when the new directory is not a subdirectory of your current working directory.

When you run interactively, you may want **ksh** to keep track of the directories you visit so that you can go back to a directory without typing its name again. You can write functions and put them in your environment file to do this. The *Shell Functions and Programs* chapter has the code for two different interfaces for directory manipulation. Refer to that chapter for details.

IMPROVING PERFORMANCE

ksh reads the history file whenever you begin an interactive execution. Therefore, you should:
- Remove the history file if it gets large.
- Use **set –o nolog** to keep function definitions from being stored in the history file.

To improve the interactive performance of **ksh**:
- Minimize the amount of information that you put into your environment file.
- Put functions that you use infrequently in a directory named by **FPATH**, instead of putting the definitions in your environment file.
- Follow the guidelines in the next paragraph for writing efficient scripts, when writing your environment file.
- Specify the **trackall** option in your environment file. This will reduce the time it takes to find some commands.
- Do not use command substitution in the value of the **PS1** prompt variable.
- On a multi-user system, if you use the **vi** built-in editor, do not use the **viraw** option unless you need to.
- Do not set the **MAILCHECK** variable to a value lower than its default.

To decrease the time it takes **ksh** to execute a script or function:
- Use built-in commands whenever possible. Built-in commands usually run more than an order of magnitude faster than do programs.
- Functions are slower than built-in commands but are still much faster than programs.
- Avoid command substitution altogether whenever you can use parameter expansion, arithmetic evaluation, or pattern matching to achieve the same result.
- Move loop invariants, especially command substitutions, to before the loop.
- Use the construct **$(** < *file*), rather than **$(cat** *file*) or `**cat** *file*`.

- Avoid using **read** from standard input when standard input is a pipe. On some systems, **ksh** may have to read a byte at a time to ensure correct positioning of standard input.
- Use **set –f** (**set –o noglob**) when you don't want pathname expansion.
- Set **IFS** to Null if you do not require field splitting.
- Use { } rather than ( ) to group commands. ( ) may create a process for the new subshell environment, whereas { } does not create a subshell environment.
- It is faster to specify redirection for a complete **for**, **while**, or **until** loop, rather than redirecting commands within the loop.
- Use the **–u** option to **read** and **print** rather than redirecting these commands.
- Specify the integer or floating point attribute on numeric variables. If **foo** is an integer or floating point variable, it is faster to use **foo** rather than **$foo** within an arithmetic expression.
- Do not use the **exec** command to keep **ksh** from creating extra processes. **ksh** has been optimized to reduce the number of processes it creates. Using **exec** should never help and in some cases could cause scripts to run slower.
- It is faster to perform several variable assignments, alias definitions, attribute declarations, or arithmetic evaluations by using multiple arguments to one command, than by using individual commands for each assignment, etc.

You can use the line count profiler script on page 279 to see how many times each line is executed. You can see the execution time of each command by including **SECONDS** as part of the **PS4** execution trace prompt and running the script with the **xtrace** option turned on. For example, **PS4='[$LINENO.$SECONDS] +'** displays the line number and the time each command begins execution before each command. *Version*: The granularity of **SECONDS** is one second with the 11/16/88 version of **ksh** so that this will not supply much useful information.

EXERCISES

1. Is it possible to display more than **HISTSIZE** history commands? How?

2. How can you cause **ksh** to use a separate history file for each interactive invocation?

3. Time how long it takes to run a builtin command, function, and program 100 times.

4. For each of the following, which one is likely to execute faster, a or b:

a. `print foo >&2`	b. `print -u2 foo`
a. `/bin/echo`	b. `echo`
a. `date`	b. `exec date`
a. `{ foo;bar;} 2> file`	b. `(foo;bar) 2> file`
a. `{ foo;bar;} 2> file`	b. `foo 2>file; bar 2>file`

5. Write a **get** discipline function for **PS1** that formats the **SECONDS** variable to put the time of day in your prompt.

PART III

THE BUILT-IN EDITORS

---

7 INTRODUCTION

One of the major benefits of using **ksh** is that you can use an **emacs**-like or a **vi**-like interface to edit your current command line. Backspacing or starting over is tedious, time-consuming, and error-prone, not to mention that you may want to make changes or corrections several times. Thus **ksh**, unlike some other current shells, does not require that you start over or backspace to the point where you want to make a correction. You can also use the same editor interface to make changes to your previous commands, which **ksh** keeps in a history file.

emacs and **vi** are single-line editors. That is, with the exception of **vi** search/edit directives (which allow you to copy previous commands from your **ksh** history file to become the current line), you can edit **ksh** commands one line at a time.

The rest of the KornShell language is independent of these editor interfaces. Therefore, you do not have to use either of the built-in editors to use **ksh**. Some systems provide an editing mechanism that you can use whenever you are entering text. In this case, you may wish to use the editor with which you are familiar and run **ksh** without a built-in editor. You can take advantage of the history feature of **ksh** without using a built-in editor.

TERMINAL REQUIREMENTS

Environment Variable Usage

ksh uses the **COLUMNS** variable to determine the width of your screen. **ksh** does not use the **TERM**, **TERMCAP**, or **TERMINFO** variables.

Non-Screen or Paper-Only Terminals

Most people use **ksh** with screen terminals. However, you can also use **ksh** with non-screen or paper-only terminals in a very limited mode. Some points you should be aware of:

    emacs. Use *Kill Kill* (page 101) to cause each line erase to advance to the next line.

    emacs and **vi**. Use the `CONTROL` l directive (pages 105 and 114) to cause a line to be redrawn.

Space, Backspace, and Return

The following requirements apply to what your terminal should do when it receives one of these three characters. These requirements do not apply when you yourself type one of these characters. If you do not have a problem using **ksh**, you need not concern yourself with these requirements. If you do have a problem, consult the system administrator if there is one. However, there are some terminals on which these requirements may not be met, and thus on which you may not be able to use **emacs** and **vi**.

ksh works on almost all terminals. The only requirements made by **ksh** on your terminal (or your terminal emulator, if you are using one) are that if the computer sends:

- Space character. Your terminal should erase the current position and move the cursor one position to the right. This is frequently referred to as a destructive space.
- Backspace character (decimal 8). Your terminal should move the cursor one position to the left, without erasing the character at the current position. This is frequently referred to as a non-destructive backspace.
- Return character. Your terminal should move the cursor to the very first character on the line without doing a linefeed, even if the first character is a Space or a Tab. If your terminal does not meet this requirement, you can get around it by putting a control character other than Bell, for instance $\boxed{\text{CONTROL}}$ e, in your prompt.

Escape Key

If your terminal does not have an $\boxed{\text{ESCAPE}}$ key, then try using $\boxed{\text{CONTROL}}$ [.

HOW TO USE THE BUILT-IN EDITORS

This section discusses how you communicate with **ksh** and how **ksh** communicates with you, when you are using the **emacs** or **vi** built-in editors. We use the term "directives" to describe actions that are to be processed by the built-in editors.

Entering ksh Commands

You enter commands by typing them and then pressing $\boxed{\text{RETURN}}$.

If you make a mistake while typing a command, use any of the edit directives described in this chapter to position the cursor to the place where you made the mistake. Then use any of the edit directives to correct the mistake. Press $\boxed{\text{RETURN}}$ while the cursor is anywhere on the line if you want **ksh** to execute the command.

Use the directives described in this chapter to recall a command that you entered previously. These directives display a copy of the previously entered commands on your terminal for you to edit. Press RETURN when you have finished editing the command and **ksh** will execute it.

Typeahead

"Typeahead" is the term used for when you start to type a command before you get the prompt. When you do this, **ksh** will probably display the characters that you type both when you type them, and when the prompt appears, just prior to execution of the command.

Tabs

Tabs are located at every 8 columns, at columns 1, 9, 17, etc. **ksh** does this automatically. This can only be changed by using the key binding mechanism defined on page 98.

How ksh Displays Characters

See *Character Set* for information on control characters, octal codes, etc.

ksh displays letters, digits, and punctuation characters as you would expect.

CONTROL *c*. **ksh** displays this as ^, followed by a character or a symbol. This means that, for instance, if you press CONTROL g, the effect is not the same as if you type the character ^ followed by **G**, even though **ksh** displays both as ^**G**:
• CONTROL g is a control character with a special meaning.
• Typing ^**G** results in a literal ^ and a literal **G**, with no special meaning.

To tell whether a ^ on the screen is a literal ^ or a control character, move the cursor one space to the left or the right in **emacs** or **vi**. If it is a:
• Literal ^, **ksh** processes this as it does any other literal character. Thus the cursor moves just one space.
• Control character, **ksh** processes the ^ with the following character as a unit. For historical reasons, the result is that in **emacs**, it is not possible to position the cursor on the character following the ^. And in **vi**, it is not possible to position the cursor on the ^.

DELETE (octal 177). **ksh** displays this as ^?.

ksh Lines Wider Than the Screen

You can type a **ksh** line of 256 characters (more on some systems). This number is set when **ksh** is compiled, and may be different on your system. If a line comes from a file instead of being typed by you on your terminal, the line can be of unlimited size.

ksh has a one-line "window" through which you look at the current **ksh** line that you are inputting or editing. The window width is the value of the **COLUMNS** variable if you defined it (default is 80 columns). If the current line is wider than the window width minus 2 (for instance, wider than 78 columns if the width is 80 columns), **ksh** horizontally scrolls the line on your screen to the left or the right, so that you can see different segments of the line. **ksh** does this scrolling automatically when you move the cursor toward the edge of the screen. **ksh** uses the following notation in the last column displayed on the screen, on the right, to indicate that it is scrolling the line, and that there is more text to the:

> \> Right.
> \< Left.
> * Right and left.

Caution: The width of the window is affected by the width of your prompt. **ksh** may miscalculate the width of your prompt, especially if it contains escape sequences. **ksh** calculates the width of your prompt by expanding Tabs to Spaces and adding the number of characters that occur after the last Newline or Return. Therefore, if you use escape sequences in your prompt, follow them with a Newline or a Return to keep **ksh** from miscalculating the width of your prompt.

Alerting You to Disallowed Actions

ksh sends the Bell character when you try to do something that is not allowed, or a search fails, or you type ⎪ESCAPE⎪ from **vi** control mode.

Most terminals sound an audible alarm when they receive the Bell character. Others may flash the screen.

TURNING ON/OFF THE BUILT-IN EDITORS

We use the terms "turn on" and "turn off" for the **emacs** and **vi** built-in editors, rather than "invoking" and "exiting." This is because they are options, and thus they are not invoked or exited as a program would be.

You can turn on only one built-in editor at a time: **emacs**, or **vi**. The built-in editor that you want to turn on must have been compiled into **ksh** by the system administrator or whomever you obtained your system from. Your system might have **ksh** with both **emacs** and **vi**, with just one of them, or with neither of them.

Since the editors are built into **ksh**, they take virtually no time to turn on or off. You can turn on a built-in editor in any of the following three ways:

set −o vi
EDITOR=...vi
VISUAL=...vi

Note: With the last two ways, you can use any pathname (indicated here by ...) ending in **vi**. If the **EDITOR** and **VISUAL** variables are set differently, **VISUAL** overrides **EDITOR**. **set −o** overrides both.

Examples
```
VISUAL=/usr/bin/vi
VISUAL=/usr/ucb/vi
```

You can have **vi** turned on automatically by putting one of the above in your **.profile** file, or in your environment file.

You can use either of the following to turn off the **vi** edit mode.

set +o vi   Turns off **vi** and puts you in **ksh**, without a built-in editor.

set −o emacs   Turns off **vi** and turns on **emacs**.

Substitute **emacs** or **gmacs** for **vi** in the above settings, if you want to turn on or off **emacs** or **gmacs** (see page 99), respectively.

HISTORY INTERFACE

ksh stores each line you enter into a file called the history file. Each of the edit modes provides directives to navigate to or search for previous commands in the history file so that you can edit and reenter them.

Caution: If you use both **emacs** and **vi**, keep in mind this basic difference between them:

emacs   Works on **ksh** history file lines. That is, it works on just one line at a time.

vi   Works on **ksh** history file commands, which may consist of more than one line.

COMMAND AND FILE COMPLETION

If you do not remember the complete name of a command or file, enter as many characters as you can and use one of three editing directives to help find the remainder. **ksh** takes the word under the cursor, adds a * if it does not contain any pattern characters, and then expands this word to generate a list of files or commands.

Version: With versions of **ksh** newer than 11/16/88, if the word is the first word on the line (or the first word after a ;, |, or &) and does not contain a /, **ksh** will check the pattern against built-in commands, functions, and commands defined by doing a **PATH** search.

There is an editing directive to do each of the following:

• Pathname listing. Displays the list of pathnames that result from the expansion of the word under the cursor.
• Pathname completion. Characters are appended up to the point that they would match more than one pathname, or until they complete the filename . If a complete pathname results, **ksh** appends a / if the pathname is a directory; otherwise a Space.

- Pathname expansion. If any pathnames match the pattern, **ksh** replaces the pattern by the pathnames that match the pattern. Otherwise, **ksh** sends the Bell character.

KEY BINDINGS

Version: This feature is available only on versions of **ksh** newer than the 11/16/88 version.

It is possible to intercept keys as they are entered and apply new meanings or bindings. A trap named **KEYBD** is evaluated each time **ksh** processes characters entered from the keyboard, other than those typed while entering a search string or an argument to an edit directive such as **r** in **vi** control mode. The action associated with this trap can change the value of the entered key to cause the key to perform a different operation.

When the **KEYBD** trap is entered, the **.sh.edtext** variable contains the contents of the current input line and the **.sh.edcol** variable gives the current cursor position within this line. The **.sh.edmode** variable contains the ESCAPE character when the trap is entered from **vi** input mode. Otherwise, this value is Null. The **.sh.edchar** variable contains the character or escape sequence that caused the trap. A key sequence is either a single character, \X(ESCAPE) followed by a single character, or ESCAPE [followed by a single character. In **vi** control mode, the characters after the ESCAPE must be entered within half a second after the ESCAPE. The value of **.sh.edchar** at the end of the trap will be used as the input sequence.

The following uses the associative array facility of **ksh** described on page 69, and the function facility of **ksh**; to make it easy to add one key binding at a time.

Example
```
typeset -A Keytable
trap 'eval "${Keytable[${.sh.edchar}]}"' KEYBD
function keybind # key [action]
{
    typeset key=$(print -f "%q" "$2")
    case $# in
    2)      Keytable[$1]=' .sh.edchar=${.sh.edmode}'"$key"
            ;;
    1)      unset Keytable[$1]
            ;;
    *)      print -u2 "Usage: $0 key [action]"
            return 2 # usage errors return 2 by default
            ;;
    esac
}
```

8 emacs BUILT-IN EDITOR

With **emacs**, you can edit your current **ksh** line as well as lines in your **ksh** history file.

For historical reasons, **emacs** comes in two versions, one named **emacs** and the other named **gmacs**. The only difference is that when you press CONTROL **t**:
> **emacs** transposes the current character with the *previous* character and advances the cursor. *Version*: **emacs** transposes the current character with the *next* character with the 11/16/88 version of **ksh**.
> **gmacs** transposes the two previous characters.

The **emacs** built-in editor is a somewhat modified subset of the **emacs** program. It does not have all of the features of the **emacs** program. Directives sometimes differ from the **emacs** program directives, even though the directive names are the same. The **emacs** built-in editor has the following features that are not in the **emacs** program:
- Pathname listing. The ESCAPE = directive displays the list of pathnames that results from the expansion of the word under the cursor.
- Pathname completion. The ESCAPE ESCAPE directive appends characters to the word under the cursor to complete the pathname of an existing file.
- Pathname expansion. The ESCAPE * directive replaces the word under the cursor with the list of pathnames that results from expansion of the word.
- Last argument. The ESCAPE _ directive inserts the last argument of the previous command.
- Version identification. The CONTROL v directive displays the current version of **ksh**.
- Operate and get next. The CONTROL o directive causes **ksh** to operate on the current line and to fetch the next line from the history file. Use this to rerun multiline commands.

All **emacs** directives operate from any place on the line, not just at the beginning of the line. Press RETURN only when you want to execute the **ksh** command.

Whenever you type a character that is not one of the **emacs** directives, **ksh** inserts the literal character at that point.

You need to use the [ESCAPE] key with many **emacs** directives. In the usual **emacs** terminology, it is often called the "Meta" key.

In this chapter, we use the term emacs-word to indicate a string of characters consisting of only letters, digits, and underscores.

MOVING THE CURSOR

[CONTROL] **f**   [ESCAPE] *n* [CONTROL] **f**

(forward) Moves the cursor right 1 (or *n*) characters.

Example
Before   After
$ print fo<u>o</u>bar   [CONTROL] *f* $ print foo<u>b</u>ar

[CONTROL] **b**   [ESCAPE] *n* [CONTROL] **b**

(back) Moves the cursor left 1 (or *n*) characters.

Example
Before   After
$ print fo<u>o</u>bar   [CONTROL] *b* $ print f<u>o</u>obar

[ESCAPE] **f**   [ESCAPE] *n* [ESCAPE] **f**

(forward) Moves the cursor right to the first character past the end of the current emacs-word or *n* emacs-words.

Example
Before   After
$ print f<u>o</u>o bar   [ESCAPE] *f* $ print foo<u>_</u>bar

[ESCAPE] **b**   [ESCAPE] *n* [ESCAPE] **b**

(back) Moves the cursor left to the beginning of the emacs-word or *n* emacs-words.

Examples
Before   After
$ print foo ba<u>r</u>   [ESCAPE] *b* $ print foo <u>b</u>ar
$ print foo <u>b</u>ar   [ESCAPE] *b* $ print <u>f</u>oo bar

[CONTROL] **a**

Moves the cursor to the start of the line.

Example
Before   After
$ print f<u>o</u>o bar   [CONTROL] *a* $ <u>p</u>rint foo bar

| CONTROL | e

(end) Moves the cursor to the end of the line.

Example

Before

$ print f<u>o</u>o bar | CONTROL | e

After

$ print foo bar_

| CONTROL |]c | ESCAPE | *n* | CONTROL |]c

(character) Moves the cursor to the next (or *n*-th) instance of *c* on the current line; repetitions of this directive step to the next *c*(s) on the line.

Implementation-dependent: In some versions of **ksh**, *c* can be a multibyte character.

Example

Before

$ print f<u>o</u>o bar | CONTROL |]a

After

$ print foo b<u>a</u>r

DELETING

Characters that are deleted are put into a buffer that can be inserted with | CONTROL | **y**. The characters from consecutive deletes *are* appended to this buffer. ***Version***: The characters from consecutive deletes are *not* appended to this buffer with the 11/16/88 version of **ksh**.

Erase | ESCAPE | *nErase*

Deletes the preceding 1 (or *n*) characters. The default is often # or | CONTROL | **h**, depending on your system. You can set *Erase* with **stty**.

Example

Before

$ print fl<u>o</u>o bar | CONTROL | *h*

After

$ print f<u>o</u>o bar

Kill

Deletes the entire line. If you type *Kill* two times in succession, all subsequent *Kill* characters cause the cursor to move to the beginning of the next line. This feature is useful with paper-only terminals. Typing *Kill* twice in succession a second time causes **emacs** to revert to its previous behavior.

The default is often **@** or | CONTROL | **x**, depending on your system. You can set the *Kill* character with **stty**.

Example

Before

$ print f<u>o</u>o bar | CONTROL | *x*

After

$ _

| CONTROL | k |

(**kill**) Deletes from the cursor to the end of the current line.

Example

Before

$ print fo̲o bar | CONTROL | *k*

After

$ print f_

| ESCAPE | *n* | CONTROL | k |

(**kill**) Deletes:

- If column *n* is to the left of the cursor, from *n* up to, but not including, the cursor.
- If column *n* is to the right of the cursor, from the cursor up to, but not including, column *n*.

Example

Before

$ print foo ba̲r | ESCAPE | *3* | CONTROL | *k*

After

$ pri̲ar

| CONTROL | d | ESCAPE | *n* | CONTROL | d |

(**delete**) Deletes 1 (or *n*) characters. If | CONTROL | d is your *End-of-file* character, and it is the first character on the line, then it is treated as an *End-of-file*.

Example

Before

$ print fo̲o bar | CONTROL | d

After

$ print fo̲ bar

| ESCAPE | d | ESCAPE | *n* | ESCAPE | d |

(**delete**) Deletes from cursor to end of current (to right) 1 (or *n*) words.

Example

Before

$ print fo̲o bar | ESCAPE | *d*

After

$ print f_bar

ESCAPE	CONTROL	h	ESCAPE	*n*	ESCAPE	CONTROL	h
ESCAPE	CONTROL	?	ESCAPE	*n*	ESCAPE	CONTROL	?
ESCAPE	h	ESCAPE	*n*	ESCAPE	h

Deletes from the current cursor back to the beginning of the current (to left) 1 (or *n*) words. When you press | BACKSPACE |, the terminal generates | CONTROL | h. If your *Interrupt* character is the default interrupt, | CONTROL | ? (octal 177), then this directive does not work. When you press | DELETE |, the terminal generates | CONTROL | ?.

Examples

Before				After	

```
$ print foo bar    ESCAPE CONTROL h    $ print bar
$ print foo bar    ESCAPE CONTROL h    $ print foo ar
```

CONTROL **W**

(wipe out) Deletes the line, from the cursor to the mark. The first line of the following example sets a mark, as described in the next section.

Examples

Before   After

```
$ print foo bar    ESCAPE SPACE      $ print foo bar
$ print foo bar    ESCAPE f          $ print foo_bar
$ print foo_bar    CONTROL w         $ print f_bar
```

MARKING, YANKING, AND PUTTING

ESCAPE SPACE

Sets a mark at the location of the cursor. See the example above.

CONTROL **X** CONTROL **X**

(exchange) Interchanges the cursor and the mark. That is, the cursor goes to where the mark is, and the mark is set to where the cursor was. Thus you can go back to where the cursor was, by just repeating the directive.

Examples

Before   After

```
$ print foo bar    ESCAPE SPACE              $ print foo bar
$ print foo bar    ESCAPE f                  $ print foo_bar
$ print foo_bar    CONTROL x CONTROL x       $ print foo bar
```

ESCAPE **p**

(push) Selects the region from the cursor to the mark, and saves it into a buffer for subsequent use with CONTROL **y**. The previous contents of the buffer are deleted.

CONTROL **y**

Restores the last text deleted from the line, at the present location of the cursor.

Examples

Before   After

```
$ print foo bar    ESCAPE SPACE      $ print foo bar
$ print foo bar    ESCAPE f          $ print foo_bar
```

$ print foo_bar ESCAPE p	$ print foo_bar
$ print foo_bar CONTROL y	$ print foooo_bar

MISCELLANEOUS

CONTROL **t**

(transpose) This is the only difference between **emacs** and **gmacs**:
- **emacs** transposes the current character with the *previous* character and advances the cursor. *Version*: **emacs** transposes the current character with the *next* character with the 11/16/88 version of **ksh**.
- **gmacs** transposes the two previous characters.

Example

Before	emacs	After
$ pri<u>n</u>t foo bar	CONTROL t	$ prni<u>t</u> foo bar

Example

Before	gmacs	After
$ pri<u>n</u>t foo bar	CONTROL t	$ pir<u>n</u>t foo bar

CONTROL **c**   ESCAPE n CONTROL **c**

(change) Changes the current (or *n*) characters to uppercase and moves the cursor to the right 1 (or *n*) characters.

Example

Before		After
$ print f<u>o</u>o bar	CONTROL c	$ print fO<u>o</u> bar

ESCAPE **c**   ESCAPE n ESCAPE **c**

(change) Changes from the current cursor to the end of the current (or *n*th) emacs-word to uppercase, and moves the cursor to the beginning of the next (or *n*th) word.

Example

Before		After
$ print f<u>o</u>o bar	ESCAPE c	$ print fOO_bar

ESCAPE **l**   ESCAPE n ESCAPE **l**

(lowercase) Changes from the cursor to the end of the current (or *n*th) emacs-word to lowercase, and moves the cursor to the beginning of the next (or *n*th) emacs-word.

Example

Before		After
$ print F<u>O</u>O bar	ESCAPE l	$ print Foo_bar

| CONTROL | **l**

(line redraw) Moves to the next line, and displays the current line.

Use this to redraw the current line if the screen becomes garbled, or if you are using **ksh** on a non-screen terminal.

End-of-file

Acts as *End-of-file* only if it is the first character on the line. Otherwise, it acts as a normal character. The default is often | CONTROL | **d**. You can set *End-of-file* with **stty**.

If you have the **ignoreeof** option set, **ksh** displays a message telling you to type **exit** to log out. Otherwise, **ksh** terminates the current shell. If this is your login shell, you are logged out.

Caution: We recommend that you set the **ignoreeof** option in your login shell, so that you will not accidentally log yourself out by pressing *End-of-file*.

| CONTROL | **j**

| CONTROL | **m**

Executes the current line. When you press:
| LINEFEED |, the terminal generates | CONTROL | **j**.
| RETURN |, the terminal generates | CONTROL | **m**.

| ESCAPE | =

Lists pathnames that match the current emacs-word, as if an * were appended to the current emacs-word. (See **Command and File Completion** on page 97.)

Version: With versions of **ksh** newer than 11/16/88, if this directive is issued on the first word of a line then the command search rules are used to find the list of matching pathnames.

Example
Before
```
$ print foo bar      ESCAPE =
```
After
```
1) foo.c
2) fool
$ print foo bar
```

| ESCAPE | | ESCAPE |

Pathname completion. The | ESCAPE | | ESCAPE | directive appends characters to the word under the cursor to complete the pathname of an existing file. (See **Command and File Completion** on page 97.)

Version: With versions of **ksh** newer than 11/16/88, if this directive is issued on the first word of a line then the command search rules are used to find the list of matching pathnames.

Example

Before		After
$ print f_	ESCAPE ESCAPE	$ print foo

ESCAPE *

Pathname expansion. Causes an * to be appended to the current emacs-word to form a pattern, and pathname expansion to be attempted. (See **Command and File Completion** on page 97.)

Version: With versions of **ksh** newer than 11/16/88, if this directive is issued on the first word of a line then the command search rules are used to find the list of matching pathnames.

Example

Before		After
$ print foo bar	ESCAPE *	$ print foo.c fool_bar

CONTROL u

Multiplies the count of the next directive by **4**.

Example

Before		After
$ print foobar	CONTROL u CONTROL f	$ print foobar

\

Escapes the next character. Editing characters, and the user's *Erase*, *Kill*, and *Interrupt* (normally CONTROL ?) characters may be entered in a command line or in a search string if preceded by a \. The \ removes the next character's editing features, if any.

Example

Before		After
$ print foobar	\ CONTROL h	$ print f^Hoobar

CONTROL V

(version) Displays the version date of **ksh**. Press any key to resume entering commands.

Examples

Before		After
$ print foobar	CONTROL v	$ Version 12/28/93b
$ Version 12/28/93b	d	$ print foodbar

| ESCAPE | *letter*

(macro expander) Searches your alias list for an alias by the name _ *letter*.
If you have defined an alias by this name, **ksh** inserts its value on the input
queue.

letter must not be one of the letters used with | ESCAPE | above
(**f, b, d, p, l, c, h**). *Caution*: Use uppercase letters to avoid possible conflict
with new features in future releases of **ksh**.

Example
If alias _**Q** has value,
`alias _Q=' ` | ESCAPE | `b" ` | ESCAPE | `f"'`

Before   After
`$ print foo bar` | ESCAPE | *Q*   `$ print "foo" bar`

| ESCAPE | `.` | ESCAPE | *n* | ESCAPE | `.`

| ESCAPE | `_` | ESCAPE | *n* | ESCAPE | `_`

. (dot) or _ (underscore).

| ESCAPE | `_` inserts on the line, the last emacs-word of your previous **ksh**
command. | ESCAPE | `.` is identical to | ESCAPE | `_` .

| ESCAPE | *n* | ESCAPE | `.` inserts on the line, the *n*th emacs-word of your previous
ksh command.

Examples
Before
`$ print foo bar` | RETURN |

After
`foo bar`
Before   After
`$ print foo_` | ESCAPE | `_`   `$ print foobar_`

| ESCAPE | `#`

Comment. If the command does *not* begin with a #, inserts a # at the
beginning of a command in order to put the command in your **ksh** history file
as a comment. Useful for causing the current line to be inserted in your **ksh**
history file as a comment so that it won't be executed, but can be referenced for
editing in the future. If the command *does* begin with a #, then the # is
deleted. *Version*: Deletion of the # is done only with versions of **ksh** newer
than 11/16/88.

Example
Before
$ `print foo bar`   ESCAPE #
After
#print foo bar
$ _

FETCHING OLD HISTORY FILE LINE

CONTROL p   ESCAPE n CONTROL p

(previous) Fetches your previous **ksh** line (or n lines back) in your **ksh** history file. Each time you subsequently press CONTROL p, **ksh** fetches the previous **ksh** line from the line that you last fetched.

If you use both **emacs** and **vi** at different times, keep in mind that:
* **emacs** works on **ksh** history file lines. That is, **emacs** works on one line at a time.
* **vi** works on **ksh** history file commands, which may consist of more than one line.

For multiline commands, use CONTROL o rather than RETURN to cause the first line to be processed by **ksh** and to fetch the second and subsequent lines.

ESCAPE <

Fetches your least recent (oldest) **ksh** history file line.

You cannot go back more commands than are defined by the **HISTSIZE** variable.

ESCAPE >

Fetches the most recent (the one that you input last) **ksh** line that you typed.

CONTROL n   ESCAPE n CONTROL n

(next) Moves down (forward) in your **ksh** history file. Fetches the next 1 (or n) lines forward from the most recent line you fetched.

CONTROL r [*string*] RETURN

ESCAPE 0 CONTROL r [*string*] RETURN

Searches the history file for the first occurrence of a command line containing *string*. If you specify:
* *string*, and specify ESCAPE 0. Searches forward.
* *string*, and do not specify ESCAPE 0. Searches in reverse order.

- No *string*, but do specify ESCAPE **0**. Searches in the reverse direction of the previous search.
- Neither *string* nor ESCAPE **0**. Fetches the next command line containing the most recent *string*.

CONTROL **r**^*string* RETURN

ESCAPE **0** CONTROL **r**^*string* RETURN

(**reverse**) Same as above, except matches *string* only if it is at the beginning of the line.

CONTROL **o**

(**operate**) **ksh** executes the current line, and fetches the next line (relative to the current line) from the **ksh** history file. Do this repeatedly to execute multiline commands.

Examples

```
history -6
35    date
36    print foobar
37    cat foobar | wc
38    for i in *
      do  print $i
      done
39    find $HOME -name foobar -print
40    who | grep morris
```

Before		After
41$	ESCAPE >	41$ who	grep morris
41$ who	grep	CONTROL rfoo	41$ cat foobar	wc
41$ cat foobar	wc	CONTROL r	41$ print foobar
41$ print foobar	CONTROL n	41$ cat foobar	wc
41$ cat foobar	wc	CONTROL n	41$ for i in *
41$ for i in *	CONTROL o	> do print $i
> do print $i	CONTROL o	> done

9 vi BUILT-IN EDITOR

With **vi**, you can enter (in input mode) and edit (in control mode) the current command that you are typing, as well as commands in your **ksh** history file.

Press the ESCAPE key to enter control mode from input mode. If you press ESCAPE from control mode, **ksh** will send your terminal the Bell character and you will remain in control mode. On most terminals this will generate an audible sound like a bell or buzzer. Thus if you are not sure which mode you are in, you should press ESCAPE .

The **vi** built-in editor is a somewhat modified subset of the **vi** program. It does not have all of the features of the **vi** program. Directives sometimes differ from the **vi** program directives, even though the directive names are the same. The **vi** built-in editor has the following features that are not in the **vi** program:

- Comments. The # control mode directive enters the current command into the history file as a comment.
- Pathname listing. The = control mode directive displays the list of pathnames that result from the expansion of the word under the cursor.
- Pathname completion. The \ control mode directive appends characters to the word under the cursor to complete the pathname of an existing file. Characters are appended up to the point that they would match more than one pathname or until the end of the last filename. If a complete pathname results, **ksh** appends a / if the pathname is a directory; otherwise a Space.
- Pathname expansion. The * control mode directive replaces the word under the cursor with the list of pathnames that result from expansion of the word.
- Escape to **vi**. Type **v** from control mode to invoke the **vi** program from the **vi** built-in editor, on a file containing the current command. **ksh** executes the file when you leave **vi**, if the file has been modified.

We use the following special notation in this chapter:

- vi-WORD indicates a sequence of letters, digits, and/or punctuation marks delimited by Newline, Space, Tab, or the beginning of a line. Punctuation marks are counted as vi-WORDS only if they are surrounded by a Space or Tab on both sides.

- vi-word indicates a sequence of letters and/or digits delimited by Newline, Space, Tab, the beginning of a line, or a punctuation mark. A sequence of one or more punctuation marks on a line counts as one vi-WORD. For instance,) is one vi-word, whereas (") is also just one vi-WORD.

CHARACTER AND LINE INPUT

Terminology

The usual terminology for:
- Character-at-a-time input is raw (unprocessed) mode.
- Line-at-a-time input is canonical mode. It is also called "cooked" (processed) mode, which is the opposite of "raw" mode.

We use the terms character input and line input, because we feel that they are more descriptive.

Initial Status

When you get a **ksh** prompt, **ksh** puts you into line input. Then, when you press <kbd>ESCAPE</kbd>, **ksh** automatically puts you into character input for the remainder of the command, until you press <kbd>RETURN</kbd>.

To use character input at all times, type **set –o viraw**. Some systems may be configured in a way such that you are always in character input. You can type **set –o** to list all option settings, to see how the **viraw** option is set. Then, if you want to, you can type **set –o viraw**. **set –o viraw** has no effect if the **vi** mode is not turned on.

Response Time

Character input is the most reliable and full featured method, but it consumes more computer cycles. This may, under certain conditions, cause longer response times on multiuser computers, for you and/or for other users. On single user (personal) computers, character input does not cause longer response time; thus you can always use it.

Line input has fewer features, as listed below. It was created primarily for users of multiuser computers, because of the longer response time discussed above. *Caution*: Some systems have been implemented in a way that, in combination with some terminal types, may cause line input to behave at times in unpredictable ways. If you experience problems, use character input by typing **set –o viraw**, as discussed above.

Display of Characters

Character input has the following characteristics when displaying characters:
- Horizontal scrolling.

- Tabs are always expanded as they are typed. When you type a control character, for instance, CONTROL **a**, **ksh** expands it immediately, so that you can see **^A** displayed on the screen right away.
- On all systems, CONTROL **v** and CONTROL **w** work as documented in this chapter.

Line input has the following characteristics when displaying characters:
- Does not have horizontal scrolling.
- Depending on your system, when you type a control character or a Tab, you see it expanded immediately, after you press the RETURN or ESCAPE key, or you may not see it expanded at all if you press RETURN . You will see all expansions and you will enable horizontal scrolling if you press ESCAPE to enter control mode.
- On some systems, CONTROL **v** and CONTROL **w** do not work as documented in this chapter.

INPUT MODE

vi has two modes: input mode, and control mode. By default, when you enter **vi**, **ksh** puts you in input mode. *Caution*: **vi** mode thus differs from the **vi** program, which initially places you in control mode.

Press ESCAPE to exit input mode and enter control mode. In control mode, you can move the cursor wherever you want and edit what you have input, using the other **vi** directives in this chapter.

Erase

Deletes the preceding character. The default is often **#** or BACKSPACE or DELETE , depending on your system. You can set *Erase* with **stty**.

Example
Before   After
`$ print foo bar_`   BACKSPACE   `$ print foo ba_`

Kill

Deletes the entire line, and goes to the first character position after the prompt. The default is often **@** or CONTROL **x**, depending on your system. You can set *Kill* with **stty**.

Example
Before   After
`$ print foo bar_`   CONTROL *x*   `$ _`

CONTROL	**V**

Escapes the next character. That is, it enables you to insert in your **ksh** command line or in a search string, as a literal character, a non-printing or a special character such as *Erase* or *Kill* or | CONTROL | **w**.

Implementation-dependent: May not work on some systems unless **viraw** option is set.

Examples

Before			After
$ `print foobar_`		CONTROL	*v@*	$ `print foobar@_`
$ `print foobar_`		CONTROL	*v*	CONTROL	*v*	$ `print foobar^V_`

****

Similar to | CONTROL | **v**, above, except that it escapes only the next *Erase* or *Kill* character.

End-of-file

Acts as the *End-of-file* character only if it is the first character on the line. Otherwise, acts as a normal character. The default is often | CONTROL | **d**, depending on your system. You can set *End-of-file* with **stty**.

If the **ignoreeof** option is on, **ksh** displays a message telling you to type **exit** to log out. Otherwise, **ksh** terminates the current shell. If this is your login shell, you are logged out.

Caution: We recommend that you turn on the **ignoreeof** option in your login shell, so that you will not accidentally log yourself out by pressing *End-of-file*.

CONTROL	**W**

(word) Deletes the previous input vi-word. ***Implementation-dependent***: May not work on some systems unless **viraw** option is set.

Example

Before			After
$ `print foo bar_`		CONTROL	*w*	$ `print foo _`

MISCELLANEOUS CONTROL MODE DIRECTIVES

Except for | RETURN |, you must be in control mode to enter any of the directives in this and the following sections. Press | ESCAPE | to enter control mode.

RETURN

Executes the **ksh** current line, regardless of whether you are in input mode or control mode.

Synonyms
- `CONTROL` **j** is equivalent to `LINEFEED`.
- `CONTROL` **m** is equivalent to `RETURN`.

Example
Before
```
$ print foo bar     RETURN
```
After
```
foo bar
$ _
```

`CONTROL` **l**

(line redraw) Moves to the next line and displays the current line. Use this to redraw the current line if the screen becomes garbled, or if you are using **ksh** on a non-screen terminal.

Example
Before   After
```
$ print foo bar     CONTROL l         $ print foo bar
```

#

Comment. If the command does *not* begin with a **#**, inserts a **#** at the beginning of each line of the command in order to put the command in your **ksh** history file as a comment. Useful for causing the current line to be inserted in your **ksh** history file as a comment so that it won't be executed, but can be referenced for editing in the future. If the command *does* begin with a **#**, then the **#** is deleted from the beginning of each line. *Version*: Deletion of the **#** is done only with versions of **ksh** newer than 11/16/88.

Example
Before
```
$ print foo bar       #
```
After
```
#print foo bar
$ _
```

=

Lists pathnames that match the current word, as if an * were appended to it.

Version: With versions of **ksh** newer than 11/16/88, if this directive is issued on the first word of a line then the command search rules are used to find the list of matching pathnames.

Example
Before
```
$ print foo bar       =
```

After
```
1) foo.c
2) fool
$ print foo bar
```

****

Pathname completion. The \\ directive appends characters to the vi-WORD under the cursor to complete the pathname of an existing file. (See **Command and File Completion** on page 97.)

Version: With versions of **ksh** newer than 11/16/88, if this directive is issued on the first word of a line then the command search rules are used to find the list of matching pathnames.

Example
Before   After
```
$ print f_          \           $ print foo
```

*

Pathname expansion. Causes an * to be appended to the current vi-WORD, and pathname expansion to be attempted. If any pathnames match the current vi-WORD, **ksh** replaces the vi-WORD by the list of pathnames that match the matching pattern, and then enters input mode. Otherwise, **ksh** sends the Bell character.

Version: With versions of **ksh** newer than 11/16/88, if this directive is issued on the first word of a line then the command search rules are used to find the list of matching pathnames.

Example
Before   After
```
$ print foo bar     *      $ print foo.c fool_bar
```

@*letter*

Macro expander. Searches your list of aliases for an alias by the name _*letter*. If an alias of this name is defined, inserts its value on the input queue for processing.

Example
If alias _**q** has the value,
```
alias _q='1Bi" CONTROL v ESCAPE Ea" CONTROL v ESCAPE '
```
Before   After
```
$ print foo bar    @q       $ print "foo" bar
```

~   *n~*

Changes the single (or *n*) character(s) at the current cursor position to uppercase if it was lowercase, and vice-versa. Also moves the cursor 1 (or *n*) character(s) to the right.

Example

Before		After
`$ print foo bar`	~	`$ print fOo bar`

. *n.*

(dot) Repeats 1 (or *n*) times, the most recent **vi** directive that changed the contents of the current command or a previous command.

Examples

Before		After
`$ print foo bar`	~	`$ print fOo bar`
`$ print fOo bar`	*2.*	`$ print fOO Bar`

v   *n***v**

(vi) Returns the command:
`hist -e ${VISUAL:-${EDITOR:-vi}}` *n*
This command invokes the **vi** program with a file that contains the designated command. The command is the **ksh** line that you were editing with the **vi** built-in editor if you omit *n*, or command *n* in the history file. When you exit the **vi** program, **ksh** displays and executes the command if you have changed it. *Version*: With some early releases of the 11/16/88 version of **ksh**, the file was executed even if you had not changed it. Also, the 11/16/88 version of **ksh** invoked **fc** rather than **hist**.

CONTROL	**v**

(version) Displays the version date of **ksh**. Press any key to resume entering commands.

Examples

Before			After
`$ print foobar`	CONTROL	*v*	`$ Version 12/28/93b`
`$ Version 12/28/93b`	*d*		`$ print foodbar`

CONTROL MODE – MOVING THE CURSOR

l   *n***l**

SPACE	*n*	SPACE

(lowercase letter **l**, or SPACE) Moves cursor right 1 (or *n*) characters.

Example

Before		After
`$ print foo bar`	*3l*	`$ print foo bar`

w   *n***w**

(word) Moves the cursor right to the beginning of the next (or *n*th next) vi-word.

Example

Before		After
$ print f<u>o</u>o.c bar	*w*	$ print foo<u>.</u>c bar

W   *n***W**

(**W**ord) Same as above, but moves to the next (or *n*th next) vi-WORD.

Example

Before		After
$ print f<u>o</u>o.c bar	*W*	$ print foo.c <u>b</u>ar

e   *n***e**

(**e**nd) Moves the cursor right to the next (or *n*th next) end of vi-word.

Example

Before		After
$ print f<u>o</u>o.c bar	*e*	$ print fo<u>o</u>.c bar

E   *n***E**

(**E**nd) Same as above, but moves over vi-WORDS.

Example

Before		After
$ print f<u>o</u>o.c bar	*E*	$ print foo.<u>c</u> bar

h   *n***h**

Moves the cursor left 1 (or *n*) characters.

Synonyms
- *Erase*
- ☐ CONTROL **h**

Examples

Before		After
$ print fo<u>o</u>.c bar	*h*	$ print f<u>o</u>o.c bar
$ print fo<u>o</u>.c bar	*3h*	$ prin<u>t</u> foo.c bar

b   *n***b**

(**b**ack) Moves the cursor left to the preceding (or *n*th preceding) beginning of a vi-word.

Examples

Before		After
$ print foo.c ba<u>r</u>	*b*	$ print foo.c <u>b</u>ar
$ print foo.c <u>b</u>ar	*b*	$ print foo.<u>c</u> bar
$ print foo.<u>c</u> bar	*3b*	$ <u>p</u>rint foo.c bar

B   *n***B**

(**B**ack) Same as above, but backs over vi-WORDS.

Examples

Before		After
$ print foo.c ba<u>r</u>	*B*	$ print foo.c <u>b</u>ar
$ print foo.c <u>b</u>ar	*2B*	$ <u>p</u>rint foo.c bar

^

Moves the cursor left to the first character on the line that is not a Space or a Tab.

Example

Before		After
$ print f<u>o</u>o.c bar	*^*	$ <u>p</u>rint foo.c bar

0

(zero) Moves the cursor left to the first character on the line.

Example

Before		After
$ print f<u>o</u>o.c bar	*0*	$ <u> </u>print foo.c bar

$

Moves the cursor right to the last character on the line.

Example

Before		After
$ print f<u>o</u>o.c bar	*$*	$ print foo.c ba<u>r</u>

| *n|*

Moves the cursor to the *n*th character on the line. Default is 1. Moves to the last character on the line if *n* is greater than the line length.

Example

Before		After
$ print f<u>o</u>o.c bar	*10|*	$ print foo<u>.</u>c bar

CONTROL MODE – MOVING TO CHARACTER

f*c*   *n***f***c*

(find) Moves the cursor right to the next (or *n*th next) *c*.

Example

Before		After
$ print f<u>o</u>o.c bar	*fa*	$ print foo.c b<u>a</u>r

F*c*   *n***F***c*

(Find) Moves the cursor left to the preceding (or *n*th preceding) *c*.

Example

Before		After
`$ print foo.c bar`	*2Fo*	`$ print foo.c bar`

t*c*   *n***t***c*

(**to**) Moves the cursor right to the character before the next (or *n*th next) *c*.

Equivalent to **f** followed by the **h** directive.

Example

Before		After
`$ print foo.c bar`	*ta*	`$ print foo.c bar`

T*c*   *n***T***c*

(**Back To**) Moves the cursor left to the character following the preceding (or *n*th preceding) *c*.

Equivalent to **F** followed by the **l** directive.

Example

Before		After
`$ print foo.c bar`	*2To*	`$ print foo.c bar`

;   *n***;**

Repeats the most recent **f**, **F**, **t**, or **T** directive once (or *n* times). The **;** itself can, of course, be repeated. For instance, **;;;** is equivalent to **3;**.

Examples

Before		After
`$ print go to togo`	*fo*	`$ print go to togo`
`$ print go to togo`	*2;*	`$ print go to togo`

,   *n***,**

Same as above, but in the reverse direction to the original directive. Useful if you overshot the character that you wanted.

Examples

Before		After
`$ print go to togo`	*fo*	`$ print go to togo`
`$ print go to togo`	*2;*	`$ print go to togo`
`$ print go to togo`	*,*	`$ print go to togo`

%

> Moves the cursor to the balancing (,), {, }, [, or], if it exists. If the cursor is on one of the above characters, then the given line is searched to find the balancing character. If the cursor is not on one of the above characters, the remainder of the line is searched for the first occurrence of one of the above characters, and then to the balancing character. *Version*: This directive was not available on some early releases of the 11/16/88 version of **ksh**.

> ***Examples***
> | Before | | After |
> |---|---|---|
> | $ print "${foo[i]}" | % | $ print "{foo[i]}" |
> | $ print "${foo[i]}" | % | $ print "{foo[i]}" |
> | $ print "${foo[i]}" | % | $ print "{foo[i]}" |

CONTROL MODE – ADDING AND CHANGING

How to Use These Directives

Type one of the following directives. **ksh** puts you into input mode. Next type the text that you want to append or to insert. When you finish, press `ESCAPE` to go back to control mode or press `RETURN` to execute the command at once.

a

> (**append**) Appends text to the right of the current cursor position.

> ***Example***
> | Before | | After |
> |---|---|---|
> | $ print foo bar | *ad*`ESCAPE` | $ print food bar |

A

> (**Append**) Appends text to the end of the current line.

> Equivalent to **$a**.

> ***Example***
> | Before | | After |
> |---|---|---|
> | $ print foo bar | *Ad*`ESCAPE` | $ print foo bard |

i

> (**insert**) Inserts text to the left of the current cursor position.

> ***Example***
> | Before | | After |
> |---|---|---|
> | $ print foo bar | *id*`ESCAPE` | $ print fodo bar |

I

(Insert) Inserts text to the left of the first character on the line that is not a Space or a Tab. Equivalent to **^i**.

Example

Before	After
$ `print foo bar` *Id* ESCAPE	$ `dprint foo bar`

c *motion*

c *n motion*   *n* **c** *motion*

motion defines a region that consists of the text from the current cursor position to the cursor position defined by the **Moving the Cursor** or **Moving to Character** directives.

(change) Changes the characters starting at the current cursor position up to the cursor position defined by the specified directive *motion*, to the characters that you type. If the *motion* is **c**, the entire line is deleted and input mode is entered.

Notes

- **c** *n* and *n* **c** have the identical effect; use whichever form you prefer.
- If *motion* is **w** or **W**, the cursor must be at the beginning of the word if you want to change the entire word. If the cursor is within the word, only the remaining part of the word is changed.
- *Caution*: Unlike the **vi** program, the text is first deleted, and then you enter input mode.

Examples

Before		After
$ `print sand bar`	*cwfood* ESCAPE	$ `print food bar`
$ `print sand bar`	*clla* ESCAPE	$ `print salad bar`
$ `print sand bar`	*cfatee* ESCAPE	$ `print steer`
$ `print sand bar`	*c$alad* ESCAPE	$ `print salad`

C

(Change) Deletes the current character through the end of the line, and enters input mode. Equivalent to **c$**.

S

(Substitute) Deletes the entire line and enters input mode. Equivalent to **cc**.

s   *n* **s**

(substitute) Deletes characters starting at the current cursor position up to *n* characters to the right, and enters input mode.

CONTROL MODE – REPLACE

r*c*   *n***r***c*

(replace) Replaces 1 or *n* character(s) starting at the current cursor position with *c*. The cursor is positioned at the last character changed.

Example
Before   After
$ print foo<u>l</u> bar   *rd* $ print foo<u>d</u> bar

—   *n*<u> </u>

(underscore) Causes the last word (or *n*th vi-WORD from the beginning), of the previous **ksh** command to be appended, and then enters input mode.

Example
print foo.c bar
Before   After
$ grep ba<u>r</u>   *2*<u> </u> ESCAPE $ grep bar foo.<u>c</u>

R

(**R**eplace) Each character that you type replaces the character at the cursor, and moves the cursor right.

Examples
Before   After
$ print fo<u>x</u> bar   *Rod* ESCAPE $ print foo<u>d</u>bar
Before
$ print fo<u>x</u> bar   *Rod* RETURN
After
foodbar
$ <u> </u>

CONTROL MODE – X/DELETE

x   *n***x**
X   *n***X**

(x-, X-ing out) Deletes 1 (or *n*) characters.
- **x** *n***x**   Starts at the current cursor position and deletes to the right.
- **X** *n***X**   Starts immediately to the left of the current cursor position and deletes to the left.

Examples

Before			After
$ print foo<u>l</u> bar	*x*		$ print foo_bar
$ print foo<u>l</u> bar	*X*		$ print fo<u>l</u> bar
$ print f<u>o</u>ol bar	*5x*		$ print f<u>a</u>r

d*motion*

d*n* *motion*   *n***d***motion*

> *motion* defines a region that consists of the text from the current cursor position to the cursor position defined by the *Moving the Cursor* or *Moving to Character* directives.

> (delete) Deletes characters starting at the current cursor position up to, and including, the other end of the specified *motion*. **ksh** saves the characters in a buffer. You can retrieve them with the **u**ndo or **p**ut directives. **d***n* and *n***d** have the identical effect; use whichever form you prefer.

> If *motion* is **w** or **W**, the cursor must be at the beginning of the word if you want to delete the entire word. If the cursor is within the word, only the remaining part of the word is deleted.

Examples

Before		After
$ print f<u>o</u>od bar	*dw*	$ print f<u>b</u>ar
$ print f<u>o</u>od bar	*d2w*	$ print <u>f</u>
$ print f<u>o</u>od bar	*d5l*	$ print f<u>a</u>r
$ print f<u>o</u>od bar	*dta*	$ print f<u>a</u>r
$ print f<u>o</u>od bar	*d$*	$ print <u>f</u>

D

> (**D**elete) Equivalent to **d$**, immediately above.

dd

> (**d**elete) Deletes the entire command, no matter where the cursor is located on the line.

CONTROL MODE – YANK/PUT

y*motion*

y*n* *motion*   *n***y***motion*

> *motion* defines a region that consists of the text from the current cursor position to the cursor position defined by the *Moving the Cursor* or *Moving to Character* directives.

(yank) Yanks the current character through the character that *n motion* would move the cursor to, and stores the characters in a buffer for subsequent use with the **p** or **P** directive (see below). The previous contents of the buffer are deleted. The text and the cursor are not changed. **y**n and n**y** have the identical effect; use whichever form you prefer.

Y

(**Y**ank) Yanks from the current cursor position to the end of line. Equivalent to **y$**. *Caution*: This is different from the **vi** program.

yy

(yank) Yanks (copies) the entire current line into the buffer, no matter where the cursor is located on the line.

p   n**p**

(**p**ut) Puts the previously yanked or deleted text (or *n* copies of the yanked text) to the right of the cursor.

P   n**P**

(**P**ut) Puts the previously yanked or deleted text (or *n* copies of the yanked text) to the left of the cursor.

Examples

Before		After
$ print food bar	*yw*	$ print food bar
$ print food bar	*P*	$ print food_food bar
$ print food_bar	*p*	$ print food food_bar

CONTROL MODE – UNDO

u

(**u**ndo) Undoes the preceding text-modifying directive.

If you repeat the **u**, this undoes the first **u**. This is useful to compare two versions of text.

Examples

Before		After
$ print food bar	*dw*	$ print f bar
$ print f bar	*u*	$ print food bar
$ print food bar	*u*	$ print f bar

U

(**U**ndo line) Undoes all of the text modifying directives made on the current line. Use **u**, if you want to undo **U**.

Examples

Before		After
$ print f*oo*d bar	*dw*	$ print f*b*ar
$ print f*b*ar	*x*	$ print f*a*r
$ print f*a*r	*U*	$ print food bar

FETCHING PREVIOUS COMMANDS

These **vi** directives fetch commands from your **ksh** history file. Thus they act on previously entered **ksh** commands, not just on the current **ksh** command. The **HISTSIZE** variable limits how far back you can search in your **ksh** history file.

A **ksh** command can be more than one line. If it is a multiline command, then Newline characters, except the last one (i.e., the RETURN at the end of the **ksh** command), are displayed as **^J**.

k   *n***k**

−   *n*−

(minus) Moves up (back) to fetch the preceding (or *n*th preceding) **ksh** command. Each time that you enter **k**, the preceding **ksh** command back is fetched. If you specify a value for *n* that would move back more than you can access, **ksh** sends the Bell character and leaves you positioned at the command farthest up that you can access.

j   *n***j**

+   *n*+

(plus) Moves down (forward) to fetch the next (or *n*th next) **ksh** command. Each time that you enter **j**, the next **ksh** command forward is fetched. If you specify a value for *n* that would move past the most recent command, **ksh** sends the Bell character and leaves you positioned at the most recent command.

G   *n***G**

(Go back) Fetches your oldest accessible **ksh** command, or command *n* from your **ksh** history file.

/ *string* RETURN

Moves left and up (back) through your **ksh** history file to search for the most recent occurrence of *string*.

Null *string*: The previous string that you specified is used.

Caution: Differences between the **vi** built-in editor and the **vi** program:
- You cannot specify regular expressions with the **vi** built-in editor.
- **/** and **?** directives operate in the **vi** built-in editor in the opposite direction to the way that they operate in the **vi** program.

- You cannot specify a string with the format */string/+n* in the **vi** built-in editor, as you can in the **vi** program.
- There is no wraparound in the **vi** built-in editor, as there is in the **vi** program.
- *string* can contain a **/** and/or a **?** without escaping them.

/ ^*string* [RETURN]

Same as **/***string*, except matches *string* only if it is at the beginning of the line.

?*string* [RETURN]

Same as **/***string*, above, but searches in the reverse direction, right and down (that is, forward).

?^*string* [RETURN]

Same as **?***string*, except matches *string* only if it is at the beginning of the line.

n

Repeats the most recent **/** or **?** directive. That is, searches for the next match of *string*.

N

Same as above, but in the reverse direction. Useful if you overshot the string that you wanted.

Examples
```
history -6
35    date
36    print foobar
37    cat foobar | wc
38    for i in *
      do  print $i
      done
39    find $HOME -name foobar -print
40    who | grep morris
```

Before		After
41$ _	[ESCAPE] *k*	41$ who	grep morris
41$ who	grep	/foo	41$ cat foobar	wc
41$ cat foobar	wc	*n*	41$ print foobar
41$ print foobar	*j*	41$ cat foobar	wc
41$ cat foobar	wc	*38G*	41$ for i in *^Jdo print >

PART IV

PROGRAMMING
LANGUAGE

10 SYNTAX

Lexical analysis is the process of splitting input into units called tokens.
This chapter describes the lexical rules of the KornShell language. The way these
tokens are used to form commands is described in the next chapter.

SPECIAL CHARACTERS

ksh processes the following characters specially (you must use one of the quoting
mechanisms if you want them to represent themselves):

| & ; < > ( ) $ ` \ " ' Space Tab Newline

ksh processes the following pattern characters specially whenever patterns are
processed: * ? [ ]

ksh processes the following characters specially when they begin a new word:
~

ksh processes the following characters specially when processing variable
assignments: = [ ]

NEWLINES

A Newline is a token that is used both to terminate a simple command and to
separate parts of a compound command. Press the RETURN key to enter a
Newline. You can use multiple Newlines wherever a Newline is legal.

Except within a single quoted string, you can continue a command onto more than
one line by immediately preceding the Newline with an unquoted \. The \ and the
Newline are both removed.

COMMENTS

Comments begin with an unquoted # sign, and go up to the next Newline. That is,
nothing can follow a comment on the same line. A comment is legal anywhere
that a token may begin. For a multiline comment, you have to start a new
comment on each line.

Some systems use a comment of the form **#!** *pathname* in the first line of a shell script. The purpose of this is to define the name of the interpreter that will process your script if you invoke it by name, rather than specifying the script as a command argument to **ksh**.

Examples
```
# This is a comment line.
# You don't have to balance quotes in a comment.
ls -l # Displays long listing of the directory.
```

OPERATORS

Operators are tokens. They are recognized everywhere, unless you quote them. Spaces are allowed, but not needed, before and after an operator, except when an adjacent character may be concatenated to form another operator token, for example, ((. Without the Spaces this would be processed as the single operator ((.

I/O Redirection Operators: `>  >>  >&  >|  <  <<  <<-  <&  <>`

You can precede each I/O redirection operator by a single digit from 0 to 9, without any intervening Space or Tab . The digit applies to the operator.

Control Operators: `|  &  ;  ( )  ||  &&  ;;  (( ))  |&  ;&`

WORD TOKENS

A word is a token that consists of any number of characters, separated from words on the left- and right-hand side by:
- Any nonzero number of unquoted Spaces, Tabs, or Newline characters.
- Any one of the operators listed above. An operator may immediately adjoin a word without any intervening Space or Tab or Newline, but it still is an operator token and not a part of the word.

We suggest that you indent code with Tabs and/or Spaces to improve readability. See the examples in the **Shell Functions and Programs** chapter for a recommended indentation style.

ksh reads a sequence of characters grouped together with one of the quoting mechanisms described on page 141 as a word, or a part of a word.

RESERVED WORDS

Reserved words are processed specially only in the contexts described below. If you use any of these reserved words elsewhere, **ksh** processes them as regular words. The reserved words are:
{ } case do done elif else esac fi for function if in select then time until while [[ ]] !

Version: ! is a reserved word only on versions of **ksh** newer than the 11/16/88 version.

ksh recognizes reserved words only when they appear:
- As the first word on a line.
- After the operators: ; | || & && |& ( )
- As the first word after a reserved word, except after **case**, **for**, **in**, **select**, and [[.
- As the second word after **case**, **for**, and **select**. In this case, **in** is the only legal reserved word.

Example
```
for i in *    # for and in are reserved words.
do  if foo; then bar
              # do, if and then are reserved words.
fi done       # fi and done are reserved words.
```

Additionally, **ksh** does not recognize a word as a reserved word:
- When used as a pattern in a **case** command, except for **esac**.
- When used as a pattern within ( ).
- After the = within a variable assignment.
- Within a here-document.
- After [[until the end of the compound command, except for]].
- If you quote zero or more characters of the word.

Example
```
case for in      # for is not a reserved word.
do|done) [[ if -eq 0 ]]
                 # do, done and if are not reserved words.
      x=case ""do;;
                 # case and do are not reserved words.
esac <<!
while            # while is not a reserved word.
!
```

ALIAS NAMES

An alias name consists of one or more of any printable character other than one of the special characters shown on page 129. *Caution*: Since alias substitution (see page 155) is performed after reserved words are processed, an alias with the same name as a reserved word is usually ignored.

Aliases whose names are of the form _*letter* define macros for the **emacs** and **vi** built-in editors.

IDENTIFIERS

Use identifiers as the names of functions and variables. An identifier is a sequence of characters consisting of one or more of a character in the character class **alpha**, or a digit, or an _ (underscore). The first character cannot be a digit. There is no limit on how many characters an identifier may consist of. *Note*: In the POSIX locale, the character class **alpha** consists of **A-Z** and **a-z**.

Uppercase and lowercase characters are distinct. For instance, **ksh** processes **A** and **a** as different identifiers.

Examples
```
PWD   X   x   _x   Foo   A_very_long_identifier
```

VARIABLE NAMES

A *varname* is a simple variable name or a compound variable name. A simple variable name is an identifier.

A compound variable name is either:
• An identifier preceded by a . (dot).
• More than one identifier each separated by a . (dot) and optionally preceded by a . (dot).

The format for a *varname* is [.]*identifier*[.*identifier*] .... *identifier* must be in the format of an identifier. Every identifier following a . (dot) must refer to a previously-defined variable name.

*varname*s are also used as part of discipline function names, defined on page 174.

Version: Compound variable names are available only on versions of **ksh** newer than the 11/16/88 version.

Examples
```
PWD   _foo   .foo   foo.bar   .sh.name
```

SIMPLE VARIABLE ASSIGNMENTS

The format for a simple variable assignment is
varname=value
or
varname[*subscript*]=*value*

varname must be in the format described above. For associative arrays (see page 183), *subscript* can be any string. Otherwise, *subscript* is in the format of an arithmetic expression (see page 136). *value* can be any word.

No unquoted Spaces or Tabs are allowed before or after the =.

Examples
```
foo=bar   foo.bar='hello there'  .x[3]=yes  Z['hi there']=3
```

PATTERNS

ksh patterns are composed of the special pattern characters specified on page 129 and described below, and/or any other characters, called regular characters. Each regular character matches only itself. The pattern characters may appear anywhere in a word; at the beginning, middle, or end. Also, they can appear more than once in a word.

Quote any of the special characters to remove their special meaning and to cause them to behave like regular characters within a pattern.

ksh patterns are used in pathname expansion, **case** pattern matching, pattern matching within [[...]], and substring expansion.

ksh patterns differ from the regular expressions that are used in the **ed**, **grep**, and other UNIX system commands.

Pattern Characters

[...]
    (Brackets) Delimit a set of characters, any one of which will match the character position identified by the brackets. The following characters are handled specially within the brackets:
    – (minus) Indicates a range of characters. For instance, **a–z** specifies that **ksh** is to match any one character from **a** through **z**. For ranges of ASCII characters, see **Character Set**. If you specify characters in a reverse order from that shown in the **Character Set** (for instance, **z-a**), or if the characters are from two different character sets (for instance, ASCII and Kanji), then **ksh** matches only the first and last characters. The specification [**a–x–z**] is equivalent to [**a–xx–z**].
    Implementation-dependent: The ranges of characters in the same non-ASCII character set may differ on different implementations.
    – Stands for itself when it is the first character after the opening [, the character immediately after a **!** following the opening [, or the last character before the closing].
[:*class*:]
    Indicates a class of characters as defined by the ANSI C standard. For instance, with the ASCII character set [[:**alpha:**]] specifies that **ksh** is to match any one character from **a** through **z** or **A** through **Z**. **ksh** recognizes the following character classes (see **Character Set**):
    [:alnum:] [:alpha:] [:blank:] [:cntrl:] [:digit:] [:graph:] [:lower:] [:print:] [:punct:] [:space:] [:upper:] [:xdigit:]
    Version: This feature is available only on versions of **ksh** newer than the 11/16/88 version.

[=*c*=]
>	Indicates the set of collation elements that have the same primary weight as
>	*c*. **Version**: This feature is available only on versions of **ksh** newer than the
>	11/16/88 version.

[.*symbol*.]
>	Indicates the collating element defined by *symbol*; for instance, [**.ch.**] in
>	Spanish. **Version**: This feature is available only on versions of **ksh** newer
>	than the 11/16/88 version.

!	Immediately after the opening [, reverses the match. That is, it matches any
>	character(s) except those specified. For example, [**!a–z**] matches anything
>	that is not a lowercase letter.

]	Stands for itself when it is the first character after the opening [, or the
>	character immediately after a ! following the opening [.

\	Removes the special meaning of –,], !, and \.

Examples

```
chap[259]
# Matches chap2, chap5, chap9.
para[!1-3]
# Matches para4, para5, parax, etc.
chap[12][01]
# Matches chap10, chap11, chap20, chap21.
para[1-3]
# Matches para1, para2, para3.
para[[:digit:]t]
# Matches para0, para1, ..., para9, and parat.
```

?	Matches any single character. In multibyte character sets (e.g., Kanji),
	matches a complete multibyte character, not just a single byte.

Example

```
para?
# Matches all 5-character strings, beginning with para
# and ending with any single character.
```

*	Matches zero or more occurrences of any and all characters.

Examples

```
para*
# Matches all character strings that begin with para.
x*y
# Matches all strings beginning in x and ending in y.
```

A *pattern-list* is one or more patterns separated by | or **&**. A | between two
patterns indicates that either pattern needs to be matched. An **&** between patterns
indicates that both patterns need to be matched. The **&** takes precedence over |.

A *sub-pattern* is a pattern-list enclosed in parentheses and preceded by one of the characters as shown below. A pattern-list can contain one or more sub–patterns and each sub-pattern can contain one or more sub-patterns. A pattern can consist of one of the following sub-pattern expressions:

?(*pattern-list***)**

Matches zero or one occurrence of *pattern-list*.
Example
```
para?([345]|99)1
# Matches the string para1, para31, para41,
# para51, or para991.
```

*(*pattern-list***)**

Matches zero or more occurrences of *pattern-list*.
Example
```
para*([0-9])
# Matches the string para, and para followed by
# any number of digits.
```

+(*pattern-list***)**

Matches one or more occurrences of *pattern-list*.
Example
```
para+([0-9])
# Matches para followed by one or more digits.
```

@(*pattern-list***)**

Matches exactly one occurrence of *pattern-list*.
Example
```
para@(chute|graph)
# Matches the string parachute or paragraph.
```

!(*pattern-list***)**

Matches all strings except those matched by *pattern-list*.
Examples
```
para!(*.[0-9])
# Matches any string beginning with para, and not
# ending in a . followed by a digit.
@(*.c&!(para*))
# Matches any string ending in .c, and not beginning
# with para.
```

The sub-patterns can be referred to by number as determined by the order of open parentheses in the pattern starting from 1. Within a pattern, you can refer to the string that matched an earlier completed sub-pattern with *digit*, where *digit* is the number of the sub-pattern. This is called a backreference. At most 9 possible backreferences are possible. A backreference must match the same string as the sub-pattern to which it refers. *Version*: Backreferences are available only on versions of **ksh** newer than the 11/16/88 version.

Examples
```
@(?)*\1
#Matches any string that begins and ends in the same letter.
+(?)\1
#Matches doubled strings such as foofoo and barbar.
```

ARITHMETIC EXPRESSIONS

Use an arithmetic expression:
- As an indexed array subscript.
- For each argument in **let**.
- Inside double parentheses ((...)).
- Inside double parentheses preceded by a dollar sign. $((...)) is replaced by the value of the enclosed arithmetic expression.
- As the shift count in **shift**.
- As operands to the arithmetic comparison operators of **test**, [, or [[...]].
- As resource limits in **ulimit**.
- As the right-hand side of a variable assignment to an integer or floating point variable.
- As operands to arithmetic formats with **print** or **printf**.

Example
```
print -f '%d\n' 3+4
```

ksh performs all calculations using the double precision floating point arithmetic type on your system. **ksh** does not check for overflow. *Version*: Floating point arithmetic is available only on versions of **ksh** newer than the 11/16/88 version. Previous versions use integer arithmetic.

An integer constant has the form [*base#*] *number* where:

base   A decimal integer between 2 and 64 that defines the arithmetic base. The default is base 10.

number   Any non-negative number. Use the unary minus operator described below for negative numbers. A number in a base greater than 10 uses uppercase or lowercase letters of the alphabet to represent a digit whose value is 10 or greater. For example, **16#b** or **16#B** represents 11 in base 16. For bases greater than 36, uppercase and lowercase letters are distinct. **@** and **_** are the two highest digits. For example, **40#b** represents 11 whereas **40#B** represents 37. Anything after a decimal point is truncated.

Version: Bases greater than 36 are available only on versions of **ksh** newer than the 11/16/88 version.

A floating point constant has the form [±] *number* [*.number*] [*exponent*] where:
number   Any non-negative decimal number.
exponent   **E** or **e** optionally followed by + or – and a non-negative decimal number.
The decimal point character is comma in some locales.
Version: Floating point constants are available only on versions of **ksh** newer than the 11/16/88 version.

A variable is denoted by a *varname*. If a variable in an arithmetic expression has the integer attribute (see attributes on page 178), then **ksh** uses the value of the variable. Otherwise, **ksh** assumes that the value of the variable is an arithmetic expression, and tries to evaluate it. A variable whose value is Null evaluates to **0**. For example, if variable **x** has value **y+1**, variable **y** has value **z+2**, and **z** has value **3**, then the expression **2∗x** evaluates to **12**. **ksh** can evaluate variables 9 levels deep.

An arithmetic function is denoted by *function*(*expression*), where *function* is one of the following:

abs	Absolute value
acos	Arc cosine of angle in radians
asin	Arc sine
atan	Arc tangent
cos	Cosine
cosh	Hyperbolic cosine
exp	Exponential with base *e* where $e \approx 2.718$
int	Greatest integer less than or equal to value of *expression*
log	Logarithm
sin	Sine
sinh	Hyperbolic sine
sqrt	Square root
tan	Tangent
tanh	Hyperbolic tangent

Arguments to any of the above functions that require angles are in radians.
Version: The above mathematical functions are available only on versions of **ksh** newer than the 11/16/88 version.

Expressions:
- Value: The value of an expression with a comparison operator or a logical operator is **1** if non-zero (true), or **0** (false) otherwise.
- Precedence: Items are listed below in order of precedence, with the highest ones first. Items of the same precedence are listed under the same bullet.
- Associativity: **ksh** evaluates all items of the same precedence left-to-right, except for = and *op=* and other assignment operators, which it evaluates right-to-left.

An *expression* is a constant, a variable, or is constructed with the following operator(s) (listed here from highest to lowest precedence):
- (*expression*) Overrides precedence rules.
- *varname*++ / ++*varname* Postfix / prefix increment.
  varname −− / −−*varname* Postfix / prefix decrement.
  +*expression* Unary plus.
  −*expression* Unary minus.
  !*expression* Logical negation. The value is **0** for any *expression* whose value is not **0**.
  ~*expression* Bitwise negation.
- *expression* ∗ *expression* Multiplication.
  expression / *expression* Division.
  expression % *expression* Remainder of 1st expression after dividing by the 2nd expression.
- *expression* + *expression* Addition.
  expression − *expression* Subtraction.
- *expression* << *expression* Left shift first expression by the number of bits given by the second expression.
  expression >> *expression* Right shift first expression by the number of bits given by the second expression.
- *expression* <= *expression* Less than or equal to.
  expression >= *expression* Greater than or equal to.
  expression < *expression* Less than.
  expression > *expression* Greater than.
- *expression* == *expression* Equal to.
  expression != *expression* Not equal to.
- *expression* & *expression* Bitwise and. Value contains a **1** in each bit where there is a **1** in both expressions, and a **0** in every other bit position. Both expressions are always evaluated.
- *expression* ^ *expression* Bitwise exclusive or. Value contains a **1** in each bit where there is a **1** in exactly one of the expressions, and a **0** in every other bit position.
- *expression* | *expression* Bitwise or. Value contains a **1** in each bit where there is a **1** in either expression, and a **0** in every other bit position. Both expressions are always evaluated.

- *expression* **&&** *expression* Logical and. If the first expression is zero, then the second expression is not evaluated.
- *expression* | | *expression* Logical or. If the first expression is non-zero, then the second expression is not evaluated.
- *expression* **?** *expression* **:** *expression* Conditional operator. If the first expression is non-zero, then the second expression is evaluated. Otherwise, the third expression is evaluated.
- *varname* = *expression* Assignment.
  varname op= *expression* Compound assignment. This is equivalent to *varname* = *varname op expression. op* must be ∗ / % + − << >> & ^ or |.
- *expression* **,** *expression* Comma operator. Both expressions are evaluated. The resulting value is the value of the second expression. ***Caution***: The comma is used as the decimal point character in some locales. Therefore, for maximum portability you should leave a space before the comma when it is preceded by a number.

Version: The unary +, ++, − −, ?:, and , operators are available only on versions of **ksh** newer than the 11/16/88 version.

CONDITIONAL EXPRESSION PRIMITIVES

Conditional expression primitives are unary and binary expressions that evaluate to True or False. They are used within expressions with the **test** and [simple commands, and within the [[...]] compound command. Spaces or Tabs are required to separate operators from operands.

A primitive can be any of the following unary file expressions:

	True if:
−**e** *file*	*file* exists. ***Version***: −**e** *file* is available only on versions of **ksh** newer than the 11/16/88f version.
−**a** *file*	*file* exists. ***Caution***: The −**a** option is obsolete and may be replaced in the future. You should use −**e** rather than −**a**.
−**r** *file*	*file* exists and is readable.
−**w** *file*	*file* exists and is writable. True indicates only that the write bit is on. *file* will not be writable on a readonly file system even if this test indicates True.
−**x** *file*	*file* exists and is executable. True indicates only that the execute bit is on. If *file* is a directory, True indicates that *file* can be searched.
−**f** *file*	*file* exists and is a regular file.
−**d** *file*	*file* exists and is a directory.
−**c** *file*	*file* exists and is a character special file.
−**b** *file*	*file* exists and is a block special file.
−**p** *file*	*file* exists and is a named pipe (fifo).
−**u** *file*	*file* exists and its set-user-id bit is set.
−**g** *file*	*file* exists and its set-group-id bit is set.

–k *file*	*file* exists and its sticky bit is set.
–s *file*	*file* exists and it has a size greater than zero.
–L *file*	*file* exists and is a symbolic link.
–h *file*	*file* exists and is a symbolic link.
–O *file*	*file* exists and its owner is the effective user id.
–G *file*	*file* exists and its group is the effective group id.
–S *file*	*file* exists and it is a special file of type socket.

ksh checks file descriptor *n* when pathname of *file* is of the form **/dev/fd/***n*.

A primitive can be any of the following unary expressions:

	True if:
–t *fildes*	The file whose file descriptor number is *fildes* is open and is associated with a terminal device.
–o *option*	The *option* is on.
–z *string*	Length of *string* is zero.
–n *string*	Length of *string* is non-zero.

A primitive can be a string by itself. In this case the primary is True if the string is not Null. *Version*: With the 11/16/88 version of **ksh**, this primary was only available in **test** and **[**.

With **test** and **[**, a primitive can be any of the following binary string expressions:

	True if:
string1 = *string2*	*string1* is equal to *string2*.
string1 != *string2*	*string1* is not equal to *string2*.

With **[[...]]**, a primitive can be any of the following binary string expressions:

	True if:
string == *pattern*	*string* matches pattern *pattern*. Quote *pattern* to treat it as a string.
string = *pattern*	*string* matches pattern *pattern*. **Caution**: = is obsolete and may be replaced in the future. Use == rather than =.
string != *pattern*	*string* does not match pattern *pattern*.
string1 < *string2*	*string1* comes before *string2* in the collation order defined by the current locale.
string1 > *string 2*	*string1* comes after *string2* based on the collation order in the current locale.

A primitive can be any of the following binary file expressions:

	True if:
file1 **–nt** *file2*	file *file1* is newer than file *file2* or if *file2* does not exist.
file1 **–ot** *file2*	file *file1* is older than file *file2* or if *file2* does not exist.
file1 **–ef** *file2*	*file1* is another name for file *file2*. This will be true if *file1* is a hard link or a symbolic link to *file2*.

Example:
```
[[ /dev/fd/2 -ef /dev/null ]]
# True if standard error is redirected to /dev/null.
```

A primitive can be any of the following expressions that compare two arithmetic expressions:

	True if the value of:
exp1 **–eq** *exp2*	*exp1* and *exp2* are equal.
exp1 **–ne** *exp2*	*exp1* and *exp2* are not equal.
exp1 **–gt** *exp2*	*exp1* is greater than the value of *exp2*.
exp1 **–ge** *exp2*	*exp1* is greater than or equal to the value of *exp2*.
exp1 **–lt** *exp2*	*exp1* is less than the value of *exp2*.
exp1 **–le** *exp2*	*exp1* is less than or equal to the value of *exp2*.

QUOTING

Quoting is the means for negating the normal processing of many items. You can apply any of the quoting mechanisms to:
- Use any of the special characters with their literal meaning.
- Prevent reserved words from being recognized as reserved words. Quote zero or more characters of the reserved word, for example **"for"**, **\for**, **""for**, or **for""**.
- Prevent alias names from being recognized as aliases. Quote zero or more characters of the alias name.
- Prevent parameter expansion and command substitution within here-document processing. Quote zero or more characters of the delimiter word of a here-document.

\ *Escape Character*

(backslash) When \ is:
- Within a comment, it has its literal meaning.
- Not quoted, the \ is removed and the single next character, other than Newline, is treated with its literal meaning. A Newline following the \ is also removed.
- Within literal quotes, it has its literal meaning.
- Within ANSI C strings (see page 142), it formats according to the escape conventions listed under **print** on page 226.
- Within grouping (double) quotes, it has its literal meaning except when followed by $, `, \, or ".
- Within old command substitution, it has its literal meaning except when followed by $, `, or \.

Example
```
print -r \#  \\\\ $'don\'t'
# \\ don't
```

\Newline *Line Continuation*

(backslash, followed by Newline) Joins two lines together. This is a special case of the \, in that the \ removes the usual meaning of the Newline character.

Does not have this effect if the \ is within single quotes, or if it follows a # (comment) symbol.

Examples
```
print this is a line \
continuation
this is a line continuation
# The following works but is not recommended.
wh\
ile ((x<3)); do ((x++));command; do\
ne
```

'...' *Literal (Single) Quotes*

(pair of single quotes) Removes special meaning of all enclosed characters. A single quote cannot appear within single quotes because a single quote denotes the end of the string. That is, even \' is not legal within single quotes. Use \' or "'" outside of single quotes to refer to the literal ' character.

Example
```
print -r '!*+\'"'"'    # Concatenates ' to a literal
                       # string.
!*+\'
```

$'...' *ANSI C Strings*

(pair of single quotes preceded by a dollar sign) Removes special meaning of all enclosed characters except for escape sequences, which are introduced by the escape character (\) and are followed by special meaning characters, described under **print** on page 226.

Version: ANSI C strings are available only on versions of **ksh** newer than the 11/16/88 version.

Example
```
print $'hello\n\tworld'
# \t is a tab character
# \n is a newline character
hello
        world
```

"..." *Grouping (Double) Quotes*

(pair of double quotes) Removes special meaning of all enclosed characters, except $, `, ", and \.

Inside double quotes, backslash followed by one of the above four characters causes the \ to be removed and that character to be interpreted with its literal meaning. When not preceded by a backslash, the four characters are interpreted as:

$ Parameter expansion.

$(...)   New command substitution. All of the tokens between (and) form the command.

`   Old command substitution.

$((...))   Arithmetic expansion.

"   End of this string.

\   As stated above, if followed by one of these four characters, \ escapes the meaning of the next characters. Otherwise, it is interpreted as a literal \.

Examples

```
print -r   "$PWD   \"   \$PWD   \\$PWD   \\\$PWD"
/usr/dgk   "  $PWD  \/usr/dgk   \$PWD
```

$"..." *Message Grouping (Double) Quotes*

(pair of double quotes preceded by a dollar sign) Same as double quotes except that the string will be looked up in a locale-specific message dictionary and replaced if found. The $ is always deleted.

Version: This feature is available only on versions of **ksh** newer than the 11/16/88 version.

Example

```
LANG=french
print -r   $"hello world"
bonjour monde
```

`...` *Old Command Substitution*

(pair of backquotes, also known as grave accents) *Bourne shell*: This is the syntax from the Bourne shell, and is accepted by **ksh** but is obsolete. However, its quoting rules are complex, so **ksh** offers a simpler syntax that does the same thing (see *New Command Substitution*, below).

ksh constructs the command to be executed from the characters that are left after **ksh** makes the following deletions. A \ that is followed by a $, ` , or \, is removed. The following example illustrates the complexity of quoting with ``.

Example

```
print -r "`print -r \$PWD "\$PWD" ')a\`\$\\'`"
/home/dgk /home/dgk )a`$\
```

You can include backquotes, `...`, within grouping (double) quotes. If you do that, and you also want to include one or more double quotes within the backquotes, then you must precede each included double quote by a backslash. **ksh** removes the backslash when it constructs the command.

$(...) *New Command Substitution*

All of the tokens (not characters, as for the old command substitution, above), between the (and the matching), form the command. Thus you do not have to change a command to put it within $(...) as you often do with `` `...` ``.

Nesting is legal. That is, you can include $(...) within grouping (double) quotes.

You can use unbalanced parentheses within the command, providing that you quote them. *Version*: With the 11/16/88 version of **ksh**, you must put a (in front of each pattern list of any **case** commands contained within $(...), to keep the parentheses balanced.

Example
```
print -r "$(print -r \$PWD "\$PWD" ')a\`\$\\')"
$PWD $PWD )a\`\$\\
```

${...} *Parameter Expansion*

Parameter expansion is described starting on page 183. The characters between the braces are processed as part of the same token.

Example
```
foo=${foo:-<This is the default>}
```

((...)) *Arithmetic Evaluation*

Arithmetic expressions. The characters between the parentheses are processed as if they are contained within double quotes, since this is equivalent to **let** "...".

Example
```
while (( (X*=2) < 100 )); do print $X; done
```

$((...)) *Arithmetic Expansion*

Arithmetic expressions. $((...)) is replaced by the value of the arithmetic expression within the double parentheses.

Example
```
print -- $((celsius * 9./5 + 32))
# use -- in case result is negative
```

varname[...]= *Array Variable Assignment*

Subscript for array variable assignment. The characters within the brackets follow the rules for grouping (double) quotes.

Example
```
X[2*(i+1)]=6
x[hello world]=hi
```

I/O REDIRECTION

To redirect the input and/or output of a command, use the notation in this section anywhere in a simple command, or following a compound command.

Example
```
while read -r line
do    print -r "$line"
done <fromfile >tofile
```

You can also use this notation with **exec** to open and close files in the current environment.

Example
```
exec 3< $infile 4>&-
```

For systems that support socket connections, pathnames of the form **/dev/tcp**/*hostid*/*portid* and **/dev/udp**/*hostid*/*portid* are treated specially as **tcp** and **udp** socket connections, respectively. *hostid* is the id of the current host, and *portid* is the port number. **Version**: This feature is not available on all versions of the 11/16/88 version of **ksh**.

See the table on page 157 for how *word*s are expanded. In particular, note that pathname expansion occurs only if a unique pathname would result.

Any of the operators below may be preceded by a single digit, with no intervening Space or Tab allowed. In this case the digit specifies the file descriptor number, instead of the default 0 or 1.

The order in which you specify redirection is significant. **ksh** evaluates each redirection from left-to-right in terms of the file descriptor association at the time of evaluation.

Example
```
cat 1>fname 2>&1
# First associates file descriptor 1 with file fname.  It
# then associates file descriptor 2 with the file associated
# with file descriptor 1 (that is, fname).  If the order of
# redirections were reversed, file descriptor 2 would be
# associated with the terminal (assuming that file
# descriptor 1 had been specified), and then file descriptor
# 1 would be associated with file fname.
```

Note: In the following formats, one or more Spaces or Tabs are optional between the operator and *word*, and no Space or Tab is allowed between the digit and the I/O operator.

< *word*   *n*< *word*   **Reading**

> Opens the file with the name that results from the expansion of *word*, for reading as standard input (or file descriptor *n*). When used with a command, redirects the input (or file descriptor *n*) of the command, from the file expanded from *word*.

Example
```
mail abc < F2
# Sends message in file F2 to user whose login
# is abc.
```

`<< word      n<< word`   **Here-Document**

Creates a here-document file, and opens it as the standard input (or file descriptor *n*).

Any input on the same line after the delimiter *word*, is read normally. You can even have another command on the same line. Common practice is to put *word* at the end of the command it refers to. The here-document begins just after the next Newline even when the Newline is part of a compound command. It continues up to a line that matches *word* character for character (there must be just the one *word* on the line for a match), or to the end of the file. If you specify more than one here-document on a command line, then **ksh** reads them in the order given.

ksh does not do any parameter expansion, command substitution, or pathname expansion on *word*. If you quote zero or more characters of *word* with a \, single quote, or double quote, then **ksh** does not do any expansions on the characters of the here-document. Otherwise, **ksh** reads and processes the here-document just as it does a double quoted string, except that **ksh** does not process double quotes specially.

Examples
```
cat <<!* | tr '[a-z]' '[A-Z]'
this is a here-document
$HOME is my home directory
!*
THIS IS A HERE-DOCUMENT
/USR/DGK IS MY HOME DIRECTORY
cat << ""EOF
this is a here-document
$HOME is my home directory
EOF
this is a here-document
$HOME is my home directory
```

`<<- word      n<<- word`   **Here-Document**

Same as above, except that **ksh** strips leading Tabs from the here-document and the line containing the matching delimiter word.

Example
```
cat <<-\!@
    this is a here-document
    $HOME is my home directory
    !@
this is a here-document
$HOME is my home directory
```

<& word   *n<& word*   ***Duplicating/Moving/Closing Input***

word must expand to:
- A digit, in which case **ksh** makes standard input (or file descriptor *n*) a *duplicate* of the file descriptor whose number is given by the digit.
- A digit − , in which case **ksh** *moves* the file descriptor whose number is given by the digit to standard input (or file descriptor *n*). ***Version***: digit − is available only on versions of **ksh** newer than the 11/16/88 version.
- − (minus), in which case **ksh** closes standard input (or file descriptor *n*).
- **p**, in which case **ksh** connects the output of the co-process (see page 167) to standard input (or file descriptor *n*). This makes it possible to create another co-process and/or to pass the output from the co-process to another command.

Examples
```
exec 3<&4     # Opens file descriptor 3 as a copy of 4.
exec 3<&4-    # Moves file descriptor 4 to 3.
exec 4<&-     # Closes file descriptor 4.
```

<> word   *n<> word*   ***Reading/Writing***

Opens the file with the name that results from the expansion of *word*, for reading and writing as standard input (or file descriptor *n*). When used with a command, redirects the input (or file descriptor *n*) of the command, from the file expanded from *word*.

Example
```
exec 3<> /dev/tty
# Opens /dev/tty on file descriptor 3 for reading
# and writing.
```

> word   *n> word*   ***Writing***
>| word   *n>| word*   ***Writing***

ksh opens the file that results from the expansion of *word*, for writing as standard output (or as file descriptor *n*). When used with a command, **ksh** redirects the output (or file descriptor *n*) of the command, to the file expanded from *word*.

If the file does not exist, **ksh** creates it if possible. If the file exists and the **noclobber** option is:

- Set, **ksh** displays an error message. The syntax >| *word* (or *n*>| *word*) causes **ksh** to truncate the file to zero length even if you set the **noclobber** option.
- Not set, **ksh** truncates the file to zero length.

Examples
```
exec 3> foobar    # Opens file foobar for writing.
cat F1 F2 > F3    # Concatenates files F1 and F2, and
                  # places result in F3.
cat F1 F2 >| F3   # Same as above except also works if
                  # F3 exists and noclobber is on.
```

>> word   *n>> word*   **Appending**

ksh opens the file that results from the expansion of *word* for appending as standard output (or as file descriptor *n*). When used with a command, **ksh** redirects standard output (or file descriptor *n*) of the command, and appends it to the end of the file expanded from *word*.

If the file does not exist, **ksh** creates it if possible.

Example
```
cat F1 >> F2
# Appends file F1 to F2.
# Creates F2 if it doesn't already exist.
```

>& word   *n>& word*   **Duplicating/Moving/Closing Output**

word must evaluate to:

- A digit, in which case **ksh** makes standard output (or file descriptor *n*) a *duplicate* of the file descriptor whose number is given by the digit.
- A digit – , in which case **ksh** *moves* the file descriptor whose number is given by the digit to standard output (or file descriptor *n*). *Version*: digit – is available only on versions of **ksh** newer than the 11/16/88 version.
- – (minus), in which case **ksh** closes standard output (or file descriptor *n*).
- **p**, in which case **ksh** connects the input of the co-process (see page 167) to standard output (or file descriptor *n*). This makes it possible to direct the output from any command to the co-process.

Example
```
foobar |& # Creates cooperating process foobar.
exec 3>&p # Moves write end of cooperating process
          # to file descriptor 3.
date >&3  # Directs the output of date to the
          # cooperating process.
exec 3>&- # Closes connection to cooperating process.
```

EXERCISES

1. Identify each of the following:
   - a. `#foo`
   - b. `> foo`
   - c. `?*`
   - d. `esac`
   - e. `foo=bar`
   - f. `_abc`
   - g. `'ab$x'`
   - h. `3b2`
   - i. `(`
   - j. `{`
   - k. `~`
   - l. `&&`
   - m. `select`
   - n. `"abc$x"`
   - o. `` `date` ``
   - p. `$(date)`
   - q. `:foo`
   - r. `foo[i]=bar+1`
   - s. `foo.bar=bam`
   - t. `.foo=(hello world)`
   - u. `[[.space.]x]`

2. What do each of the following patterns match?
   - a. `?`
   - b. `foo??`
   - c. `foo*`
   - d. `foo.*`
   - e. `foo*bar`
   - f. `foo.[cho]`
   - g. `foo*.[!cho]`
   - h. `foo[!a-z][!a-z]`
   - i. `*foo\**`
   - j. `foo[-*]`
   - k. `*/`
   - l. `???[z-a]`
   - m. `[a-z]*([a-z0-9])`
   - n. `*([0-9])?(.)+([0-9])`
   - o. `[0-9]!(*([0-9]))`
   - p. `@(foo|bar|bam)?(.c|.o)`
   - q. `!(*.o|core)`
   - r. `[[:alnum:]_]*([[:alpha:]_])`
   - s. `*@(?)\1*`

3. In each of the following character strings, identify which characters are special and which characters retain their literal meaning.
   - a. `abc\d\$e`
   - b. `'abc\d\$e'`
   - c. `"abc\d\$e"`
   - d. `""'abc\d\$e'`
   - e. `"`abc\d\$e`"`
   - f. `'`abc\d\$e`'`
   - g. `$'#$\'\0123'`
   - h. `.foo[hi there]=1`
   - i. `$"a\b$x"`

4. What do each of the following I/O redirections do?
   - a. `> foobar`
   - b. `>> foobar`
   - c. `3< foobar`
   - d. `4>& -`
   - e. `5<> foobar`
   - f. `3<< foobar`
   - g. `5<<- 'foobar'`
   - h. `4<& p`
   - i. `5<& 0`
   - j. `2>| foobar`
   - k. `4<& 5-`

5. What do each of the following conditional primitives do?

a.	`-e foobar`	b.	`-w foobar`
c.	`$x`	d.	`-e /dev/fd/2`
e.	`-O foobar`	f.	`$x == ?`
g.	`$x == "?"`	h.	`/bin -ef /usr/bin`
i.	`$x -nt $y`	j.	`-x =`
k.	`-t`	l.	`! !`

11 COMMAND PROCESSING

This chapter presents the logical order that **ksh** follows to read and process a command. This is not necessarily the actual order within the code of any given **ksh** implementation.

Commands are processed in two stages. In the first stage, **ksh** reads each command and splits it into tokens. **ksh** determines whether the command is a simple command or a compound command to determine how much to read.

In the second stage, **ksh** expands and executes a command each time that it is used. A compound command such as a **while-do-done** loop is expanded and executed each time that the loop is iterated. A function is expanded and executed each time that it is referenced.

This chapter describes how **ksh** reads its input, and how **ksh** expands and executes simple commands. Refer to *Compound Commands* to see how **ksh** processes them.

See the *Quick Reference* for a more concise description of the grammar for the KornShell language.

READING COMMANDS

ksh first reads commands and then executes them. This section describes how much **ksh** reads at a time, and how **ksh** splits the input into commands.

Splitting Input into Commands

It is important for you to understand how aliases and **set –k** interact with **ksh** in the reading of commands. **set –k** is an obsolete feature that causes all arguments of the form *name=value* to be treated as assignments no matter where they appear on the command line. You can avoid problems caused by the order in which commands are read and processed by **ksh**, if you:
- Use **alias** and **unalias** with no other commands on the same line.
- Do not use **alias** and **unalias** in compound commands.
- Do not use **set –k** at all. *Bourne shell*: **set –k** is a feature of **ksh** only for compatibility with the Bourne shell.

ksh reads at least one line at a time. Therefore new aliases and **set –k** do not affect subsequent commands on the same line, but affect only subsequent lines. This means that if you have two or more simple or compound commands on a single line, **ksh** reads all of the commands on the line before executing them.

Example
```
alias foo=bar; foo
# In this case, foo will not become bar.  If foo were on
# a line following the alias, then foo would become bar.
```

ksh reads entire commands at a time. Therefore, if you use aliases or **set –k** within a compound command, they do not affect the commands within the compound command. They affect only the reading of commands that are read after the execution of the compound command. *Note*: A function definition (see page 174) is a compound command. Therefore, alias definitions within them do not affect how the function is read. In addition, a function may be referenced and thus executed many lines after the code for the function definition command, or never at all. Thus an **alias** or **unalias** command in a **function** command may take affect only many lines after the function definition, or never at all.

Example
```
for  i in 0 1
do   if   ((i==0))
     then alias print=date
     fi
     print +%H:%M:%S
done
print +%H:%M:%S
+%H:%M:%S
+%H:%M:%S
11:02:28
```

ksh reads a complete dot script and splits it into tokens before it executes any of the commands in the file. The dot script is the file specified as the first argument to the **.** (dot) command. Therefore, if you use aliases or **set –k** in a dot script, they do not affect the commands in the dot script. They affect only the reading of subsequent commands.

ksh reads the smallest number of complete lines that constitute a complete command when it reads its input from your terminal, a shell script other than a dot script, profile files, or your environment file.

When you type an incomplete **ksh** command from a terminal, and then press RETURN , **ksh** displays its secondary prompt, **PS2** (default is >), to indicate that it expects you to continue entering more of the command.

Example
```
for i in One two three
> do print $i
> done
```

```
One
two
three
```

Splitting Input into Tokens

The process of splitting your **ksh** input commands into tokens is called lexical analysis and was described in the previous chapter. A token is one of the following:
- I/O redirection operator.
- Control operator.
- Newline.
- Reserved word.
- Simple assignments.
- Word.
- Here-document.

When you type an incomplete token from a terminal, and then press RETURN , **ksh** displays its secondary prompt, **PS2** (default is >), to indicate that it expects you to continue entering more of the token.

Example
```
print "One two three
> four five six
> seven"
One two three
four five six
seven
```

ksh performs alias substitutions (see page 155) as it splits input into tokens.

ksh converts each message string into a double quoted string by looking up the message in a locale-specific message catalog. If **ksh** cannot find the message catalog, or the message is not in the catalog, the message string is not translated.

Determining the Type of a Command

If the first token of the command is one of the following reserved words, then **ksh** reads it as a compound command: **{ case for function if until select time while [[!**. *Note*: **ksh** processes these as reserved words only if there are no quotes of any type, or any backslash, in or around them, and they are the first token in the command.

If the first token of the command is one of the following operators:
- (**ksh** reads it as a compound command, until the matching closing).
- ((**ksh** reads it as an arithmetic expression until the matching closing)).
  ksh processes this as though it were a double quoted argument to **let**.

If the first token of the command is one of the following, then **ksh** displays a syntax error and, when not interactive, exits:

- Reserved words:
  do done elif else esac fi in then }]]
- Operators: **| || & && ; ;; |& ;&**

ksh reads any other token at the beginning of a command, including I/O redirection operators, as the first token of a simple command.

Variable Assignments

Compound assignment is a mechanism for assigning values to one or more variables. A compound assignment can appear wherever a simple assignment token can appear. A compound assignment is in one of the following forms:

varname=(*value* ...) to assign values to indexed array *varname* (page 183).

varname=([*expression*]=*value* ...) to assign values to associative array
  varname (see page 183).

varname=(*assignment* ...) to assign values to a set of variables whose names are of the form *varname.name*. Each *assignment* can be one of:

- A simple assignment.
- A compound assignment.
- The **typeset** command defined on page 213. Use a Newline or **;** to separate each **typeset** command.

In this case, the value of *varname* after an assignment is in the format of a compound variable assignment consisting of all variables whose names begin with *varname.*.

No Spaces or Tabs are allowed before the =. The (must appear on the same line as the =. Newlines are permitted between values or assignments and before the).

Version: Compound assignments are available only on versions of **ksh** newer than the 11/16/88 version.

Examples
```
files=(*)
age= ( [Adam]=18 [Jeff]=21 [Flip]=23 )
point=( x=3.5 y=4.2 )
record= ( name=joe ;  typeset -i age=31 )
```

Reading Simple Commands

ksh reads all of the tokens until the following as a simple command:
; | & || && |& Newline

ksh organizes the tokens in simple commands into three classes:

- I/O redirections (the I/O redirection operator, plus the word following the operator; e.g., **>x**). **ksh** reads and processes I/O redirections left-to-right. You can mix I/O redirections and command words in any order, although it is not considered good practice to do so. However, this "mixing" ability makes it possible to specify I/O redirections as part of an alias definition, which is sometimes useful.

- Variable assignments. If the **keyword** option (**set –k**) is on, **ksh** recognizes any word in the syntax of a variable assignment (page 132) as a variable assignment. If the **keyword** option is off, **ksh** recognizes any word of the syntax of a variable assignment as a variable assignment word, only until it encounters a token which is not of this format and is not an I/O redirection word. If **ksh** encounters the variable assignment syntax later on, it reads and processes the word as a command word.
- Command words. The remaining words are called command words. **ksh** constructs the command name and the command arguments by expanding command words. **ksh** checks the first command word when it reads it, to see if there is an alias of that name to expand (see next section). If the command name is **alias**, **readonly**, **typeset**, or **export**, **ksh** processes each argument of the format of a variable assignment specially, regardless of whether **keyword** is on or off. These arguments are read and expanded with the same rules as variable assignments, except that they are expanded and evaluated when command arguments are processed.

Alias Substitution

ksh checks the command name word of each simple command to see if it is a legal alias name. If it is not quoted in any way, and it is a legal alias name, and there is a non-tracked alias of that name defined, then **ksh** checks to see if it is currently processing an alias with the same name. If it is, **ksh** does not replace the alias name. This prevents infinite recursion. If it is not currently processing an alias with the same name, **ksh** replaces the alias name by the value of the alias.

ksh performs alias substitution as part of the process of splitting a command into tokens. When **ksh** performs alias substitution, the token containing the alias is replaced by the tokens defined by the value of the alias.

You create and display aliases with **alias**, and remove aliases with **unalias**. *Version*: The 11/16/88 version had a **–x** option to **alias** to allow alias definitions to be inherited by scripts invoked by name. The **–x** option of **alias** does not have any affect with newer versions of **ksh**.

If the value of an alias ends with a Space or a Tab, **ksh** checks the next command word for alias substitution. For example, the preset alias **nohup**, defined below, ends in Space. Thus the word after **nohup** will be processed for alias substitution.

Examples
```
alias foo='print '
alias bar='hello world'
foo bar
hello world
```

```
alias od=done
for i in foo bar
do    print $i
od
foo
bar
```

Alias definitions are not inherited by scripts run by **ksh** or across invocations of **ksh**.

Preset Aliases

Preset aliases are aliases that are predefined by **ksh**. You can unset or change them if you wish to do so. However, we recommend that you do not change them, as this may later confuse you and/or others who expect the alias to work as predefined by **ksh**.

> **autoload='typeset –fu'**
> **command='command '**
> **fc=hist**
> **float='typeset –E'**
> **functions='typeset –f'**
> **hash='alias –t – –'**
> **history='hist –l'**
> **integer='typeset –i'**
> **nameref='typeset –n'**
> **nohup='nohup '**
> **r='hist –s'**
> **redirect='command exec'**
> **stop='kill –s STOP'**
> **times='{ {time;}2>&1;}'**
> **type='whence –v'**

Message Substitution

ksh checks each double quoted string that is preceded by an unquoted $ for message substitution. The $ is deleted. If not in the POSIX locale, **ksh** looks for the string in a locale-specific message catalog and replaces it with a string contained in the message catalog. In the POSIX locale, or if it is not found in the locale-specific message catalog, the double quoted string is not changed.

EXPANDING A SIMPLE COMMAND

Prior to execution, **ksh** processes the word tokens of each simple command to generate the command name and/or command arguments as described in this section.

ksh performs tilde expansion, command substitution, parameter expansion, and arithmetic expansion on a word from left to right first. This is followed by field splitting, and then by pathname expansion. Quote removal is always done last.

As stated above, simple commands are composed of three types of tokens: variable assignment words, command words, and I/O redirections. Command words are expanded first from left to right. The following table summarizes what processing **ksh** does to each type.

	Variable Assignment	*Command Word*	*I/O Redirection*
Reading commands			
Alias substitution	No	Note 1	No
Message substitution	Yes	Yes	Yes
Executing commands			
Tilde expansion	Note 2	Yes	Yes
Command substitution	Yes	Yes	Yes, Note 3
Parameter expansion	Yes	Yes	Yes, Note 3
Arithmetic expansion	Yes	Yes	Yes, Note 3
Field splitting	No	Note 4	No
Pathname expansion	No	Yes, Note 5	Note 6
Quote removal	Yes	Yes	Yes

Yes	This is done.
No	This is not done.
Note 1	Always applies to first word. If the **alias** value ends with a Space or a Tab, then alias substitution also applies to the next word and so on.
Note 2	Done after the = and after each **:**.
Note 3	Except after << and <<– operators.
Note 4	Done only on portions of word resulting from command substitution and parameter expansion.
Note 5	Done, unless **set –f** (**set –o noglob**) is on.
Note 6	Done for interactive shells only if expansion yields a unique pathname with versions of **ksh** newer than 11/16/88.

Tilde Expansion

ksh checks each word to see if it begins with an unquoted ~. If it does, then **ksh** checks the word up to a / to see if it matches:

~ by itself. It is replaced by the value of the **HOME** variable.

~ followed by +. It is replaced by the value of the **PWD** variable.

~ followed by – (minus). It is replaced by the value of the **OLDPWD** variable.

~ followed by user login name. It is replaced by the home (login) directory of the matched user.

~ followed by anything else. The original word is left unchanged.

Also, **ksh** checks the value of each variable assignment to see if a ~ appears after the = or after a : in the assigned value. If it does, **ksh** attempts tilde expansion.

Version: Tilde expansion was performed while reading the command with the 11/16/88 version. Tilde expansion is performed on the word following the parameter expansion modifier (see page 185), when the parameter expansion is not inside double quotes in versions of **ksh** newer than the 11/16/88 version.

Command Substitution

ksh checks each word to see if it contains a command enclosed in $(...) (new command substitution), or in a pair of backquotes `...` (old command substitution). If it does, then **ksh** does the following:

- If you use the old command substitution form, **ksh** processes the string between the backquotes using the quoting rules on page 143 to construct the actual command.
- If you use the new command substitution form, **ksh** executes the command represented by the ellipsis (...).
- $(...) or `...` is replaced by the output of the command represented by the ..., with the trailing Newlines (if any) removed. **ksh** does not process this output for parameter expansion, arithmetic expansion, or command substitution.
  Example
  ```
  x=$(date)   # x is assigned the output from date.
  ```
- If the command substitution appears within grouping (double) quotes, then **ksh** does not process the output from the command for field splitting or for pathname expansion.

$(<*file*) is equivalent to $(**cat** *file*), but executes faster because **ksh** does not create a separate process.

Command substitution is carried out in a subshell environment. No side effects occur in the current **ksh** environment as a result of executing the command substitution. For instance, $(**cd**) does not change the working directory in the current environment.

Arithmetic Expansion

Each $((...)) is replaced by the value of the arithmetic expression within the double parentheses.

Example
```
x=$((RANDOM%5))
# x is assigned a random number from 0 to 4.
```

Parameter Expansion

ksh checks all words that contain an unquoted $ to see if the $ specifies parameter expansion. If it does, then **ksh** replaces the parameter portion of the word.

If the parameter is not set and you specified the **nounset** option (**set –u**), **ksh** displays an error message on standard error. If the error occurs within a script, the program terminates with a False return value.

Example
```
set -u
unset foobar
rm $foobar
ksh: foobar: parameter not set
```

If you include a parameter expansion within grouping (double) quotes, then **ksh** does not process the result of the parameter expansion for field splitting and pathname expansion.

Field Splitting

ksh scans the results of command substitution, arithmetic expansion, and parameter expansion of command words for the field delimiter characters found in the value of the **IFS** variable, provided that the expansion isn't inside double quotes. If the value of **IFS** is Null, then **ksh** does not perform field splitting. Otherwise, **ksh** splits the results of command substitution and parameter expansion into distinct fields as described on page 201.

Example
```
IFS=: foobar="foo:bar"
set foo:bar $foobar "$foobar"
for i
do  print "$i"
done
foo:bar
foo
bar
foo:bar
```

Pathname Expansion

Following field splitting, **ksh** checks each field for unquoted characters *, ?, [, and (, unless you use the **noglob** option (**set –f**). Any (or) character that results from an expansion is quoted so that patterns using (...) must be present as part of the command input. For example, **print !(*.o)** will match filenames that do not end in **.o**, whereas **x='(*.o) '; print $x** will not.

If any of these characters do not appear, the field is left unchanged. Otherwise, **ksh** processes the field as a pattern. **ksh** replaces the pattern with all pathnames that match, sorted alphabetically, with the following additional rules:
- * and ? in a pattern do not match /. The pathname must explicitly match each / in the pattern.

- The pathname must explicitly match . (dot) when . is the first character of the pathname, and when the . immediately follows a / . If the **FIGNORE** variable is set, then filenames matching the pattern defined by the value of the **FIGNORE** variable are excluded from the match rather than filenames that contain a leading . (dot). *Version*: **FIGNORE** is only available on versions of **ksh** newer than the 11/16/88 version.

If there are no matches, **ksh** leaves the word unchanged.

Quote Removal

The special characters \, ", and ' are removed by **ksh** unless they are themselves quoted. **ksh** does not remove quotes that result from expansions.

Null arguments that are:
- Explicit (within single or double quotes, for instance "$*name*" where *name* has no value), are retained.
- Implicit (for instance, $*name* where *name* has a Null value or no value), are removed.

Examples
```
x='"'  y=""
print "'hello'" ${x}there${x}
'hello' "there"
set "$y" $y
print $#
1
```

EXECUTING A SIMPLE COMMAND

This section describes how **ksh** searches for and executes a simple command. A simple command can be a variable assignment command, I/O redirections, a special built-in command, a function, a regular built-in command, or a program.

No Command Name or Arguments

ksh does each of the I/O redirections in a subshell environment. Therefore, the only redirection operators that are useful in this context are > and >|, which you can use to create files.

ksh performs variable assignments from left to right in the current environment.

The return value of a variable assignment is True in all cases except when:
- The last variable assignment involves a command substitution that fails.
- Redirection fails within a script or a function.
- Attempt to assign to a variable that has the readonly attribute.
- Attempt to assign an invalid arithmetic expression to an integer or floating point variable.

Special Built-in Commands

ksh executes special built-in commands (designated by daggers in the *Built-in Commands* chapter) in the current environment. Many of these commands have side effects. They are listed below:

. (dot) : (colon) alias break continue eval exec exit export newgrp readonly return set shift trap typeset unalias unset

Except for **exec**, I/O redirection applies only to the built-in command itself. It does not affect the current environment. However, I/O redirection applied to **exec** with no arguments affects open files in the current environment.

ksh processes these built-ins specially in the ways noted below:
* **ksh** evaluates variable assignment lists specified with the command before I/O redirection. These assignments remain in effect when the command completes.
* Errors in these built-ins cause the script that contains them to terminate.

Return value: Noted under each command in the *Built-in Commands* chapter.

Version: The **times** and **wait** built-in commands are no longer special built-ins in versions of **ksh** newer than the 11/16/88 version. The **set**, **unset**, and **unalias** built-in commands have been made special built-in commands in versions of **ksh** newer than the 11/16/88 version.

Functions

If the command is not a special built-in, **ksh** checks to see if it is a defined function. If a function has not been defined, but has been marked as an undefined function with **typeset –fu**, **ksh** will search **FPATH** to find the function definition and execute it before it does a **PATH** search.

I/O redirections specified with the function reference apply only to the function itself. They do not affect the current environment. I/O redirections specified within the function with **exec** do affect the current environment.

The following are shared by the function and the invoking script, so that they can produce side effects:
* Variable values and attributes, unless you use **typeset** within the function body of a non-POSIX function to declare a local variable.
* Working directory.
* Aliases, function definitions, and attributes.
* Special parameter **$**. *Caution*: Take care that functions do not create a temporary file with the same name as a temporary file created by the invoking script.
* Open files.

If you declare a function with the **function** *name* syntax, then **ksh** executes the function in a separate function environment. The following are not shared between this kind of function and the invoking script, and thus cannot cause side effects:
- Positional parameters.
- Special parameter #.
- Variables in a variable assignment list when the function is invoked.
- Variables declared using **typeset** within the function.
- Options.
- Traps. However, signals ignored by the invoking script will also be ignored by the function.

ksh executes a trap on **EXIT** set within this kind of function right after the function completes, but in the environment of the invoking script.

If you declare a function with the *name* ( ) format, then **ksh** executes the function in the current environment like a dot script. The following are not shared between this kind of function and the invoking script, and thus cannot cause side effects:
- Positional parameters.
- Special parameter #.

Version: **ksh** executes a *name*( ) function in the current environment like a dot script only on versions of **ksh** newer than the 11/16/88 version.

The return value of a function is the return value of the last command executed within the function.

Regular Built-in Utilities

ksh executes the following regular built-in utilities in the current environment:
bg builtin cd command disown echo false fg getconf getopts hist jobs kill print printf read test true umask wait whence. *Version*: **builtin, command, disown, getconf, hist**, and **printf** are available only on versions of **ksh** newer than the 11/16/88 version.

They are executed regardless of the contents of the **PATH** variable.

The **builtin** command can be used to add or delete regular built-ins.

Many of these commands have side effects on the current environment. These side effects are listed in the *Built-in Commands* chapter.

PATH Search

If the given command contains a / character, then **ksh** executes the command with the specified pathname. Otherwise, **ksh** checks each of the directories located in the path search parameter **PATH**. The search occurs in the order that the directories are listed in the **PATH** variable. If **ksh** does not locate the given command in any of the directories in the **PATH** parameter, then **ksh** displays an error message and the return value is 127.

If **ksh** locates the given command in a directory in the **PATH** parameter, then **ksh** checks for that directory located in the function path search parameter **FPATH**. If the directory is located in **FPATH**, then **ksh** reads this file in the current environment and then executes the function. *Caution*: A directory that is both in **PATH** and **FPATH** should contain no executable files other than function definitions.

Otherwise, if **ksh** determines that the given command has been implemented as a built-in, then **ksh** executes the built-in in the current environment.

Otherwise, **ksh** executes the given command as a program in a separate environment. Therefore the programs cannot have side effects on the current environment.

ksh remembers the pathnames of any commands executed and will not search for them again unless the **PATH** variable has been assigned to again.

If the program terminates with a return value False (non-zero) and if a trap on **ERR** is specified, **ksh** executes the action associated with it. If the **errexit** option (**set –e**) is set, **ksh** exits with a return value of the command that terminated with the False value. Otherwise, **ksh** executes the next command.

If the program terminates with a return value True, **ksh** processes the next command.

Version: In versions of **ksh** up to and including 11/16/88, builtins are always executed first. Also, pathnames of commands are *not* remembered unless the **trackall** option is set (which it is by default).

EXERCISES

1. Which of the following are simple commands?

a.	`foo bar`		b.	`for bar`
c.	`> bar`		d.	`for=bar`
e.	`foo`		f.	`for>bar`
g.	`foo|bar`		h.	`for ~bar`
i.	`#foo bar`		j.	`fi bar`

2. Split each of the following commands into parameter assignments, command arguments, and I/O redirections.

   a. `foo bar > file`
   b. `foo=$bar bar=abc print $foo $bar > file`
   c. `foo=$bar bar=abc print > file $foo $bar`
   d. `foo=$bar bar=abc print > $foo file $bar`
   e. `$foo foo=bar > file`
   f. `> file foo bar`
   g. `> file foo < bar $bar`

12 COMPOUND COMMANDS

This chapter defines the format and meaning of **ksh** compound commands. A compound command is a pipeline or a list, or else the compound command begins with a reserved word or the control operator (.

I/O redirection after any compound command, except a pipeline, the **time** command, or a list, applies to the complete command. I/O redirection following a pipeline, the **time** command, or a list applies to only the last command. Use the grouping command beginning with the reserved word { around any command if you need to specify I/O redirection for the complete sequence of commands. I/O redirection does not affect the environment in which **ksh** executes the command.

You cannot specify variable assignments with a compound command.

See the **Quick Reference** chapter for a more concise description of the grammar for the KornShell language.

PIPELINE COMMAND

command [| [*newline...*] *command*] ...

A pipeline is a sequence of one or more simple or compound commands, each separated by |. As the above format and definition specify, a pipeline can consist of a single simple or compound command with no pipeline operator |. In practice we would not refer to this as a pipeline (since there is no pipeline operator |). We define it this way so that we do not have to single out this case for commands that allow pipelines within them.

Standard output of each command except the last one, is connected to the standard input of the next command.

ksh runs each command except possibly the last as a separate process. If the **monitor** option is off, **ksh** waits for the last command to terminate. Otherwise, **ksh** runs each pipeline as a separate job. For instance, **date | wc** would be run as a job. **ksh** waits for all processes in a pipeline to complete.

Return value: Return value of last specified *command*.

Example
```
grep foo bar | sort | uniq
food menu
```

TIME COMMAND

time [*pipeline*]

> If *pipeline* is specified, **ksh** executes *pipeline*, and displays on standard error the elapsed time, user time, and system time. Otherwise, **ksh** displays the cumulative time for the shell and its children. *Version*: With the 11/16/88 version of **ksh**, **time** required *pipeline*, and the **times** built-in command was used to display the cumulative time for the shell and its children.

> Redirections following *pipeline* apply to the last command in *pipeline* rather than to **time**. To save the output from **time** in a file, enclose the **time** command in one of the grouping commands (see page 173) and redirect the standard error for the grouping command to the file.

> *Return value*: Return value of *pipeline*.

> *Examples*
> ```
> time grep foo bar | sort | uniq
> food menu
>
> real    0m2.03s
> user    0m0.85s
> sys     0m0.49s
>
> time
> user    0m0.85s
> sys     0m0.49s
> ```

NEGATION COMMAND

! *pipeline*

> **ksh** executes *pipeline*. The return value of **!** is:
> - True (zero) if the return value of *pipeline* is False (non-zero).
> - False (non-zero) if the return value of *pipeline* is True (zero).

> *Example*
> ```
> if    ! grep -c ^$user: /etc/passwd
> then  print There is no account for $user
> fi
> ```

> *Version*: **!** is available only on versions of **ksh** newer than the 11/16/88 version.

LIST COMMANDS

list

A *list* can be a *pipeline*, or any combination of the following formats. That is, wherever *list* appears in a format below, you can substitute *pipeline* or a complete format recursively, to whatever depth you wish.

The list operators have lower precedence than the pipeline operator |. If you specify two or more operators in the same *list*, **ksh** evaluates them left to right, and uses the following precedence:
- Highest: **&&** **||**
- Lowest: **;** **&** **|&**

list [**&&** [*newline...*] *pipeline*]... ***And List***

ksh runs the first *pipeline*. If its return value is:
- True: **ksh** runs the second *pipeline*, and so on to the following *pipeline*(s), as long as the return values of the preceding *pipeline*(s) are True.
- False (non-zero): **ksh** does not run the remaining *pipeline*(s).

Return value: Return value of the last *pipeline* run by **ksh**.

Example
```
cd foobar && print -r $PWD
```

list [**||** [*newline...*] *pipeline*]... ***Or List***

ksh runs the first *pipeline*. If its return value is:
- True: **ksh** does not run the remaining *pipeline*(s).
- False (non-zero): **ksh** runs the second *pipeline*, and so on to the following *pipeline*(s), as long as the return values of the preceding *pipeline*(s) are False.

Return value: Return value of the last *pipeline* run by **ksh**.

Example
```
read -r line || error_exit 'Unexpected end-of file'
```

list [**;** *pipeline*]... ***Sequential List***

ksh runs each of the *pipeline*(s) in sequence.

Return value: Return value of the last *pipeline* run by **ksh**.

Example
```
who|wc ; date
```

list **&** [*pipeline* **&**]... ***Background Processes***

ksh runs each of the *pipeline*(s) without waiting for any of them to complete. If the **monitor** option is on, **ksh** runs each *pipeline* as a separate job.

Return value: True.

Example
```
nohup find / -name foobar -print &
```

list **|&** ***Co-Processes***

ksh runs *list* as a separate job with its standard input and standard output connected to **ksh**.

To write onto the standard input of this process, use **print –p**. To read the standard output from this process, use **read –p**.

Return value: True.

Example
```
ed - foobar |&
```

[*newline...*] *list* [*newline...*] ***Compound List***

When a list appears within any of the compound commands listed below, it can optionally be preceded and followed by one or more Newlines. We designate this by *compound-list*.

You can use one or more Newlines instead of **;** to specify a sequential list within a compound list.

CONDITIONAL COMMANDS

[[*test-expression* [*newline...*] **]]**
Note: You must type the brackets shown in boldface.

test-expression must be one of the conditional expression primitives defined on page 139, or some combination of these conditional primitives formed by combining one or more of them with one of the following. The following are listed in order of precedence, from highest to lowest:
- **(** *test-expression* **)**. Evaluates to value of *test-expression*. The ( ) are used to override normal precedence rules.
- **!** *test-expression*. Logical negation of *test-expression*.
- *test-expression* **&&** *test-expression*. Evaluates to True if both *test-expression*s are True. The second *test-expression* is expanded and evaluated only if the first *test-expression* is True.
- *test-expression* **||** *test-expression*. Evaluates to True if either of the *test-expression*s is True. The second *test-expression* is expanded and evaluated only if the first *test-expression* is False.

ksh expands the operand(s) for each conditional expression primitive for command substitution, parameter expansion, arithmetic expansion, and quote removal as required to evaluate the command. **ksh** tests the primitive expression to determine whether it is True or False.

Return value: Value of *test-expression*.

Example
```
[[ foo > bar  &&  $PWD -ef . ]]  &&  print foobar
foobar
```

if   *compound-list*
then   *compound-list*
[**elif**   *compound-list*
then   *compound-list*]
...
[**else**   *compound-list*]
fi

ksh runs the **if** *compound-list*. If the return value is:
- True: **ksh** runs the **then** *compound-list*.
- False: **ksh** runs each **elif** *compound-list*(s) (if any) in turn, until one has a return value of True. If there are no **elif** *compound-list*(s), or if none have a return value of True, ksh runs the **else** *compound-list*, if any.

Return value:
- Return value of the last **then** or **else** *compound-list* that was executed.
- True if no **then** *compound-list* or **else** *compound-list* was executed.

Example
```
if    ((score < 65))
then  grade=F
elif  ((score < 80))
then  grade=C
elif  ((score < 90))
then  grade=B
else  grade=A
fi
```

case *word* **in**

[[**(**] *pattern* [**|** *pattern*]...**)** *compound-list* **;;**]
[[**(**] *pattern* [**|** *pattern*]...**)** *compound-list* **;&**]
...
esac

ksh runs the first command *compound-list* for which *word* matches *pattern*.

ksh expands *word* for command substitution, parameter expansion, arithmetic expansion, and quote removal.

ksh expands each ¦-separated list of *pattern*s, in turn, for command substitution, parameter expansion, and quote removal. The order of evaluation for patterns within the same list is not defined. If the expanded value of *word* matches the pattern resulting from the expanded value of *pattern*, the corresponding *compound-list* is executed.

Once **ksh** matches a *pattern*, it does not execute any more *compound-list*s unless *compound-list* is followed by **;&**. In this case, **ksh** will fall through to the next *compound-list*.

The parenthesis before each list of *pattern*(s) is optional. ***Version***: The parenthesis is required when a **case** command appears within a **$(...)** command substitution with the 11/16/88 version of **ksh**.

Return value:
- If *word* matches any *pattern*, the return value of the last *compound-list* that **ksh** executed.
- If *word* does not match any *pattern*, True.

Example
```
case $x in
-d*)    dflag=1;&          # fall through
-e*)    eflag=1;;
"")     print -r -u2 -- "x must have a value";;
*)      if   [[ ! -r $x ]]
        then print -ru2 -- "$x: no read permission"
        fi;;
esac
```

ITERATION COMMANDS

select   *varname* [**in** *word...*]
do   *compound-list*
done

ksh does command substitution, parameter expansion, arithmetic expansion, field splitting, pathname expansion, and quote removal for each *word* to generate a list of items, before it processes the **do** *compound-list* command. If you do not specify **in** *word*, **ksh** uses the positional parameters starting at **1** as the list of items as if you had specified **in "$@"**.

ksh displays the items in one or more columns on standard error, each preceded by a number, and then displays the **PS3** prompt. The number of columns is determined by the value of the **LINES** variable and the value of the **COLUMNS** variable.

ksh then reads a selection line from standard input. If the line is the number of one of the displayed items, **ksh** sets the value of the variable *varname* to the item corresponding to this number. If the line is empty, **ksh** again displays the list of items and the **PS3** prompt; **ksh** does not run *compound-list*. Otherwise, **ksh** sets the variable *varname* to Null.

ksh saves the contents of the selection line read from standard input in the variable **REPLY**.

ksh runs *compound-list* for each selection until **ksh** encounters a **break**, **return**, or **exit** command in *compound-list*. The **select** command also terminates when it encounters an *End-of-file*.

If the value of the **TMOUT** variable is greater than zero, **select** will time out after the number of seconds given by **TMOUT**. *Version*: Available only on versions of **ksh** newer than the 11/16/88 version.

Example
```
PS3='Please enter a number '
select i in fo*
do    case $i in
      food|fool|foot)
              print good choice
              break;;
      for|foxy)
              print poor choice;;
      *)      print -u2 'Invalid number';;
      esac
done
1) food
2) fool
3) foot
4) for
5) foxy
Please enter a number
```

Return value:
- True if no *compound-list* was executed.
- False if **select** times out.
- Return value of last *compound-list* executed.

for   *varname* [**in** *word*...]
do   *compound-list*
done

> **ksh** does command substitution, parameter expansion, arithmetic expansion, field splitting, pathname expansion, and quote removal for each *word* to generate a list of items, before it processes the **do** *compound-list* command. If you do not specify **in** *word*, **ksh** uses the positional parameters starting at **1** as the list of items as if you had specified **in** "**$@**".
>
> **ksh** sets *varname* to each item in turn, and runs *compound-list*. Execution ends when there are no more items. If *varname* has the reference attribute set, then a new reference will be created for each *word*.
>
> ***Example***
> ```
> for i in fo*
> do  print "$i"
> done
> food
> fool
> foot
> for
> foxy
> ```
>
> ***Return value***:
> • Return value of last *compound-list* executed.
> • True if no *compound-list* was executed.

for   (([*init_expression*] ; [*loop_condition*] ; [*loop_expression*]))
do   *compound-list*
done

> The arithmetic **for** command is very similar to the C programming language **for** statement. *init_expression, loop_condition, and loop_expression* are arithmetic expressions. **ksh** evaluates *init_expression* before executing the **for** loop. Use the comma operator within *init_expression* to specify multiple initializations. **ksh** evaluates *loop_condition* before each iteration.
> If *loop_condition* is non-zero, then *compound-list* is executed again.
> *loop_expression* specifies an expression that is executed after each iteration.
>
> If *loop_condition* is omitted, it defaults to 1.
>
> ***Version***: The arithmetic **for** is available only on versions of **ksh** newer than the 11/16/88 version.

Example
```
for     ((i = 0; i < 5; i++))
do      print -- ${array[i]} # Prints the first five
                             # elements of the array.
done
```
Return value:
- Return value of last *compound-list* executed.
- True if no *compound-list* was executed.

while   *compound-list*

do   *compound-list*

done

The **while** command repeatedly runs the **while** *compound-list*. Each time, if the return value of *compound-list* is:
- True: Runs **do** *compound-list*.
- False (non-zero): Loop terminates.

A **break** command within the **do** *compound-list* causes the **while** command to terminate with a return value of True. A **continue** command causes the **do** *compound-list* to terminate and the **while** *compound-list* to be run again.

Return value:
- Return value of last **do** *compound-list* executed.
- True if no **do** *compound-list* was executed.

Example
```
# Reads lines and prints them until an end-of-file.
while read -r line
do      print -r - - "$line"
done
```

until   *compound-list*

do   *compound-list*

done

The **until** command repeatedly runs the **until** *compound-list*. Each time, if the return value of *compound-list* is:
- False (non-zero): Runs **do** *compound-list*.
- True: Loop terminates.

A **break** command within the **do** *compound-list* causes the **until** command to terminate with a return value of True. A **continue** command causes the **do** *compound-list* to terminate and the **until** *compound-list* to be run again.

Return value:
- Return value of last **do** *compound-list* executed.
- True if no **do** *compound-list* was executed.

Example
```
until cc -c foo.c
do    vi foo.c
done
```

COMMAND GROUPING

(*compound-list*) Subshell Grouping

ksh runs *compound-list* in a subshell environment. Therefore, there will not be side effects in the current environment.

Caution: If you need to nest this command, you must insert Spaces, Tabs, or Newlines between the two open parentheses to avoid arithmetic evaluation.

Return value: Return value of *compound-list*.

Example
```
( find . -print | wc ) >foobar 2>&1 &
```

Brace Grouping

```
{
      compound-list
}
```

ksh runs *compound-list* in the current environment.

Caution: { and } are reserved words here. See page 131 for rules governing reserved words.

Return value: Return value of *compound-list*.

Example
```
{ time foobar ;} 2> savetimes
```

ARITHMETIC COMMAND

((*word...*))

ksh does command substitution, parameter expansion, arithmetic expansion, and quote removal for each *word* to generate an arithmetic expression that is evaluated as described on page 136.

Return value: True if arithmetic expression evaluates to nonzero; otherwise False.

FUNCTION DEFINITION

function [*varname.*]*identifier*
{
      compound-list
}

[*varname.*]*identifier* ( )
{
      compound-list
}

Either of these declarations defines a function which is referenced by *varname.identifier* or *identifier*. The body of the function is the compound-list of commands between { and }. If you declare a function with the **function** *name* format, then **ksh** executes the function in a separate function environment described on page 263. If you declare a function with the *name* ( ) format, then **ksh** executes the function in the current environment. This form is called a POSIX function and is included for compatibility with the POSIX standard. See page 161 for a description of function execution.

Function names of the form *varname.identifier* are called *discipline* functions. Three special *discipline* functions are permitted to be defined for all variables: **get**, **set**, and **unset**. They are used to define a function to be executed when a variable is expanded, assigned, and unset (respectively). Additional discipline functions can be defined for variables defined by builtins added to **ksh** by an application library or a user.

Version: **ksh** executes an *identifier* ( ) function in the current environment only on versions of **ksh** newer than the 11/16/88 version. With the 11/16/88 version of **ksh**, the name of a function was limited to an *identifier*.

Caution: { and } are reserved words here. See page 131 for rules governing reserved words.

Return value: True.

Examples
```
function affirmative # question
{
    typeset -l reply
    while true
    do    read -r "reply?$1? " || return 1
          case $reply in
          y|yes)  return 0;;
          n|no)   return 1;;
          *)      print 'Please answer y or n';;
```

```
            esac
        done
}

# The following references this function.
while affirmative 'Do you want to continue?'
do     foobar
done

# The following displays a message when an assignment
# is made to foo.
function foo.set
{
    print "variable foo[${.sh.subscript}] is ${.sh.value}"
}
foo[3+4]=bar
variable foo[7] is bar
```

EXERCISES

1. Write a compound command to do each of the following:
    a. Run a given command once an hour.
    b. Execute a given command only if the variable named **x_flag** is set.
    c. Display the files in your directory in the same format as a **select** list.
    d. Time how long a **while** loop takes to execute.
    e. Time how long it takes to run a command 100 times with the time output directed to a file.
    f. Display the arguments of a command that do not begin with **–**.

2. In what ways do the following two commands differ?
    a. ```
        for i in *
        do cmd >> output
        done
        ```
    b.  ```
        for i in *
        do cmd
        done > output
        ```

---

13 PARAMETERS

---

ksh entities that store values are called parameters. Some parameters have names predefined by **ksh**, and values that are set by **ksh**. Other parameters also have names predefined by **ksh**, but values that are set by you. And other parameters (called user variables) have names that you choose and values that you set and use.

Named parameters, that is, parameters denoted by a *varname*, have attributes that you can set. You can use attributes to format data, and for other purposes.

There are several modifiers that you can use to alter the value of a parameter when it is referenced. An important example is substring operations.

All of these operations are discussed in this chapter.

PARAMETER CLASSES

Named Parameters (Variables)

Named parameters are called variables and are denoted by a varname. You:
- Assign the values of variables with a variable assignment list.
- Assign/unassign attributes with **typeset**.
- Unassign the values and attributes of variables with **unset**.

Caution: By convention, **ksh** (and other commands) uses variable names containing three or more uppercase characters (for instance, **CDPATH**) for its own use. Therefore, we suggest that you do not use all uppercase identifier names of three or more characters for user variables. If you do, you run the risk of a future release of **ksh** using that same name for its own use. In addition, variable names beginning with **.sh.** are reserved for use by **ksh**.

Many variables are inherited through the environment of the parent process.

Variables can also be arrays (see page 183).

Positional Parameters

Positional parameters are parameters that are denoted by one or more digits. They are initially assigned values when you invoke **ksh,** or any shell script or function, as follows:

- Parameter **0** is the name of the shell, script, or function.
- Parameter **1**, **2**, ... are the values of each of the arguments to the shell, script, or function as it was invoked.

You can reassign or unset all of the positional parameters from **1** up with **set**. You cannot reset the value of an individual positional parameter.

You can shift positional parameters (except **0**) to the left only (for instance, you can move **3**, **4**, **5**, ... to **1**, **2**, **3**, ...), with **shift 2**.

Special Parameters

Special parameters are parameters denoted by the characters
* @ # ? – $!
ksh automatically sets the values for each of these parameters.

See page 190 for a description of each of these special parameters.

ATTRIBUTES

You can assign each variable one or more of the following attributes. When you change an attribute of a variable, the value that the variable expands to may change to conform to the new attribute. Use **typeset** to turn attributes on/off, or to list the attributes.

Note: You do not have to specify the integer or floating point attribute to use variables within arithmetic expressions. However, performance may be better if you do specify these attributes.

–u Uppercase

Whenever **ksh** expands the variable, **ksh** changes lowercase characters to uppercase.

ksh turns off the lowercase attribute.

Example
```
typeset -u x=abc
print  $x
ABC
```

–l Lowercase

Whenever **ksh** expands the variable, **ksh** changes uppercase characters to lowercase.

ksh turns off the uppercase attribute.

Example
```
typeset -l x=ABC
print  $x
abc
```

–E or –En *Floating Point – Scientific Notation*

If, after the –E, you:
- Do not specify *n*, the default is 10.
- Do specify *n*, **ksh** expands the value to that number of significant digits.

Whenever you assign a value to the variable, the value is evaluated as an arithmetic floating point expression. When you print the value of the variable, it will be displayed in the **printf %g** format (see page 227).

You can use the preset alias **float** to declare floating point variables.

Version: The –E attribute is available only on versions of **ksh** newer than the 11/16/88 version.

–F or –Fn *Floating Point – Fixed Precision*

If, after the –F, you:
- Do not specify *n*, the default is 10.
- Do specify *n*, **ksh** expands the value to that number of digits after the decimal point.

Whenever you assign a value to the variable, the value is evaluated as an arithmetic floating point expression. When you print the value of the variable, it will be displayed in the **printf %f** format (see page 227).

Version: The –F attribute is available only on versions of **ksh** newer than the 11/16/88 version.

–i or –ibase *Integer*

If, after the –i, you:
- Do not specify *base*, the default is 10 (decimal).
- Do specify *base*, **ksh** expands the value in that arithmetic base. You cannot specify a base above 64. *Version*: In the 11/16/88 version of **ksh** the maximum base was 36.

Whenever you assign a value to the variable, the value is evaluated as an arithmetic integer expression.

If the base is other than 10, **ksh** prepends the base number followed by a # sign, to the value of the variable when it is expanded.

You can use the preset alias **integer** to declare integer variables.

Example
```
integer x=6
typeset -i8 y=x+x
print $y
8#14
```

–A *Associative Array*

Defines an associative array, as opposed to an indexed array. The subscript for an associative array element is an arbitrary string.

Version: The –A attribute is available only on versions of **ksh** newer than the 11/16/88 version.

Example
```
typeset -A color
color[apple]=red color[banana]=yellow color[grape]=purple
for i in ${!color[@]}   # list of array subscripts
do     print $i ${color[$i]}
done
apple red
grape purple
banana yellow
```

–L or –L*width* *Left-justified*

width is any number. If you don't specify *width*, then **ksh** uses the number of characters of the first assignment to the variable.

Whenever **ksh** expands the variable, it left justifies the characters to fit *width*, and puts trailing Spaces at the right, if needed, to fill *width*.

If you assign a value to the variable that is too big to fit *width*, **ksh** truncates excess characters on the right.

ksh turns off the right-justified attribute.

Implementation-dependent: In multibyte versions of **ksh**, *width* refers to the number of columns (rather than to the number of characters). During expansion, if there isn't enough room in *width* for the last complete character, **ksh** does not include that character in the expansion, and uses Spaces to fill up *width*.

Example
```
typeset -L3 x=abcd y
y=3
print "$y-$x"
3  -abc
```

–LZ or –LZ*width* *Strip Leading Zeros*

This is similar to the left-justified attribute (above), except that whenever **ksh** expands the variable, it strips leading zeros at the left.

ksh turns off the right-justified attribute.

Example
```
typeset -LZ3 x=abcd y z=00abcd
y=03
print "$y-$x z=$z"
3  -abc z=abc
```

–R or –R*width* *Right-justified*

width is any number. If you don't specify *width*, then **ksh** uses the number of characters of the first assignment to the variable.

Whenever **ksh** expands the variable, it right justifies the characters to fit *width*, and puts leading Spaces at the left, if needed, to fill *width*.

If you assign a value to the variable that is too big to fit the *width*, **ksh** truncates excess characters on the left.

ksh turns off the left-justified attribute.

Implementation-dependent: In multibyte versions of **ksh**, *width* refers to the number of columns rather than to the number of characters. During expansion, if there isn't enough room in *width* for the first complete character, **ksh** does not include that character in the expansion and uses Spaces to fill up *width*.

Example
```
typeset -R3 x=abcd y
y=3
print "$y-$x"
  3-bcd
```

–Z or –Z*width* *Zero-filled*

–RZ or –RZ*width* *Zero-filled*

This is similar to the right-justified attribute. However, whenever **ksh** expands the variable it prepends leading zeros at the left. **ksh** does this only if needed, and only if the first character (other than Space or Tab) is a digit. If the first character is not a digit, then **ksh** fills with leading Spaces.

ksh turns off the left-justified attribute.

Example
```
typeset -Z3 x=abcd y
y=3
print "$y-$x"
003-bcd
```

−r *Read-only*

Once you set this attribute, you will get an error message if you attempt to change the value of this variable, turn off its readonly attribute, or unset it. However, **ksh** can still change the value if it is a variable that **ksh** automatically changes, such as **PWD**.

You can use **readonly** or **typeset** **−r** to set this attribute. Within a function, **typeset** creates a local variable while **readonly** does not.

Example
```
readonly foo=bar
foo=nobar
ksh: foo: is read only
unset foo
ksh: foo: is read only
```

−n *Name Reference*

Causes the value of a variable to be treated as a reference to another variable so that variables can be indirectly named. Reference variables are often used inside functions whose arguments are the names of shell variables. The attribute is particularly useful when the shell variable is an array.

The names of reference variables cannot contain a . (dot). Whenever a shell variable is referenced, the portion of the variable up to the first . is checked to see whether it matches the name of a reference variable. If it does, then the name of the variable actually used consists of the concatenation of the name of the variable defined by the reference, plus the remaining portion of the original variable name.

Version: The **−n** attribute is available only on versions of **ksh** newer than the 11/16/88 version.

Example
```
typeset -n z=foo.bar      # z is a name reference for
                          # foo.bar
z.bam="hello world"       # foo.bar.bam is changed
                          # accordingly
print ${foo.bar.bam}
hello world
```

–x *Exported*

This attribute causes the name and value of the variable to be passed to the environment of each child process. **ksh** automatically sets this attribute for all variables inherited from the parent environment. Therefore, if you change the value of any variable that is inherited from the environment, then **ksh** automatically exports the new value to the environment of each child process. *Bourne shell*: This is different from the Bourne shell, where you must explicitly export the variable to export the new value to the environment of any child process.

ksh also passes the attributes of exported variables to the environment of each child process.

The names for exported variables cannot contain a . (dot).

Use **export** or **typeset –x** to set this attribute. Within a function, **typeset** creates a local variable while **export** does not.

Example
```
export foo=bar PATH
```

–H *Host Operating System Pathname Mapping*

Applicable only to non-UNIX systems. **ksh** ignores this if you specify it on UNIX systems.

Whenever **ksh** expands the variable, **ksh** changes the format of the value from a UNIX system pathname to a host operating system pathname.

Example
In this example, it is assumed that each filename in a pathname is delimited by a \ rather than a / on the host operating system.
```
typeset -H file=/system/win32
print "$file"
c:\system\win32
```

–t *Tagged*

ksh does not use this attribute. It is intended for you to use as you wish.

Example
```
typeset -t PWD foo=bar
typeset +t    # Display names of all variables with
              # the tagged attribute.
PWD
foo
```

ARRAYS

You can use any variable as a one-dimensional array, with the format *varname*[*subscript*]. Use the syntax on page 132 to assign values to individual array elements. There are two types of arrays in **ksh**: indexed arrays and associative arrays.

For indexed arrays, the *subscript* must be an arithmetic expression that evaluates to a number in the range **0-4095**. *Implementation-dependent*: Some implementations of **ksh** may have a larger limit for integer subscripts. *Version*: The range of subscripts was limited to **0-1023** for some versions of the 11/16/88 version of **ksh**. See program on page 279 to see how to test whether a given subscript is valid.

For associative arrays, the subscript can be an arbitrary string. Associative arrays must be declared with **typeset –A**. You do not have to declare indexed arrays. However, if you know the size of the indexed array, and/or you want to specify an attribute for the array, use **typeset** to declare the size and or attributes, for instance, **typeset –u x[100]**. When you reference any variable with a valid subscript, an array will be created if you did not declare it. Each attribute applies to all elements of the array.

The form of any array element reference is **${**name[*subscript*]**}** for both indexed and associative arrays.

To reference all of the elements of an indexed or associative array, use *subscript* * or **@**. The subscripts * and **@** differ only when the expansion is contained within double quotes. In this case they differ in the same way that the expansion of special parameters * and **@** differ (see page 190).

To reference all of the subscripts of an array, use the prefix operator **!** in the parameter expansion. For example, **${!foo[@]}** expands to the list of array subscripts for variable **foo**.

Caution: Current implementations of **ksh** do not allow you to export array variables to separate invocations of **ksh**.

Version: Associative arrays and referencing all subscripts with **${!foo[@]}**, are available only in versions of **ksh** newer than the 11/16/88 version.

PARAMETER EXPANSION – INTRODUCTION

$** triggers parameter expansion. Read **$ as "value of."

When we say that a parameter is not set, we mean that the parameter has never been given a value or that the parameter has been unset; for example, using **unset** or **shift**.

ksh expands parameters even inside grouping (double) quotes. *Note*: If you put double quotes around the parameter expansion of a command word, or a word in the list of words for the **for** compound command or the **select** compound command, **ksh** does *not* do field splitting or pathname expansion on the result of the expansion.

ksh expands parameters inside here-documents if you do not quote the delimiter word.

PARAMETER EXPANSION – BASIC

${*parameter*}

> **ksh** expands this format to the value of the *parameter*.
>
> If the **nounset** option is on and *parameter* is not set, then **ksh** displays an error message. If this occurs within a script, **ksh** terminates execution of this script with a False return value. If **nounset** is off, then **ksh** treats unset parameters as if their value was Null.
>
> *Note*: If *parameter* value is Null, and if you:
> * Put grouping (double) quotes around *parameter*, then when **ksh** does quote removal, it retains the expansion of *parameter*, and counts it as a Null argument. *Exception*: When there are no positional parameters (or array elements), "**$@**" (or "${*varname*[**@**]}") does not count as a Null argument.
> * Do not put double quotes around ${*parameter*}, then when **ksh** does quote removal, it throws away the expansion of *parameter* and does not count it as an argument.
>
> { } Braces are optional, except for a:
> * *parameter* followed by a letter, digit, or underscore that is not to be interpreted as part of its name.
> * Variable that is subscripted.
> * Positional parameter of more than one digit.
> * Variable names with . (dot).
>
> If *parameter* is one or more digits, then it is a positional parameter.
>
> *Example*
> ```
> print $PWD ${11} $$
> /usr/dgk arg11 1234
> ```
>
> **ksh** evaluates the subscript before it expands an array variable. You should be alert to this, in case the subscript evaluation causes side effects.
>
> *Example*
> In the expansion **${x[y=1]}**, **ksh** first evaluates the assignment **y=1**, and then it expands **x[1]**.

PARAMETER EXPANSION – MODIFIERS

${*parameter*:–*word*} *Using default values*
Note: The **:** is optional.

If *parameter* is:
- Unset, **ksh** expands the above format to the expanded value of *word*.
- Null, and you specified **:**, same as above.
- Otherwise, **ksh** expands the above format to the value of *parameter*.
  ksh does not perform any expansion on *word*.

Example
In this example, **ksh** executes **date** only if **d** is Null or is unset.
```
print ${d:-$(date)}
```
In this example, **ksh** performs a tilde expansion if **d** is Null or is unset.
```
print ${d:-~}
/usr/dgk
```

${*parameter*:=*word*} *Assigning default values*
Note: The **:** is optional.

If *parameter* is:
- Unset, **ksh** assigns the expanded value of *word* to *parameter*, and then expands the above format to the value of *parameter*.
- Null, and you specified **:**, same as above.
- Otherwise, **ksh** expands the above format to the value of *parameter*.
  ksh does not perform any expansion on *word*.

Only variables may be assigned to in this way.

Example
```
unset X
typeset -u X
print ${X=abc}
ABC
```

${*parameter*:?*word*} *Displaying error if Null or unset*
Note: The **:** is optional.

If *parameter* is:
- Unset, **ksh** expands and displays *word* on standard error, and causes your shell script, if any, to terminate with return value False (1). If you omit *word*, then **ksh** displays a message on standard error.
- Null, and you specified **:**, same as above.
- Otherwise, **ksh** expands the above format to the value of *parameter*.
  ksh does not perform any expansion on *word*.

Example
```
print ${foo?}
ksh: foo: parameter null or not set
```

${*parameter*:+*word*} *Using alternate value*
Note: The : is optional.

If *parameter* is:
- Unset, **ksh** expands the above format to Null. **ksh** does not expand *word*.
- Null, and you specified :, same as above.
- Otherwise, **ksh** expands the above format to the expanded value of *word*.

Example
```
set a b c
print ${3+foobar}
foobar
```

PARAMETER EXPANSION – SUBSTRINGS

Note: *pattern* represents any pattern.

${*parameter*#*pattern*} *Remove small left pattern*

The value of this expansion is the value of the *parameter*, with the smallest portion matched on the left by *pattern* deleted. If *pattern* begins with a # it must be quoted.

Example
```
cd $HOME/src/cmd
print ${PWD#$HOME/}
src/cmd
```

${*parameter*##*pattern*} *Remove large left pattern*

The value of this expansion is the value of the *parameter*, with the largest portion matched on the left by *pattern* deleted.

Example
```
x=/one/two/three
print ${x##*/}
three
```

${*parameter*%*pattern*} *Remove small right pattern*

The value of this expansion is the value of the *parameter*, with the smallest portion matched on the right by *pattern* deleted. If *pattern* begins with a % it must be quoted.

Example
```
x=file.c
print ${x%.c}.o
file.o
```

${*parameter*%%*pattern*} *Remove large right pattern*

The value of this expansion is the value of the *parameter*, with the largest portion matched on the right by *pattern* deleted.

Example
```
x=foo/fun/bar
print ${x%%/*}
foo
```

${*parameter*:*offset*:*length*} *Substring starting at offset*
${*parameter*:*offset*}

See page 188 for the description when *parameter* is **@** or *****. The value of this expansion is a substring of the *parameter* starting at the character position defined by the arithmetic expression *offset,* and terminating after *length* characters, where *length* is an arithmetic expression. If :*length* is not specified or if the value of *length* will cause the expansion to exceed the length of *parameter*, then the substring terminating at the last character of *parameter* is produced. The first character of *parameter* is defined by an offset of 0.

Examples
```
x=foo/fun/bar
print ${x:4:3}
fun
print ${x:3}
/fun/bar
```

Version: The ${*parameter*:*offset*:*length*} and ${*parameter*:*offset*} parameter expansions are available only on versions of **ksh** newer than the 11/16/88 version.

${*parameter*/*pattern*/*string*} *Substitute string for pattern*
${*parameter*/#*pattern*/*string*}
${*parameter*/%*pattern*/*string*}
${*parameter*//*pattern*/*string*}

The value of this expansion is the value of *name* with one or more occurrences of the longest match of *pattern* replaced by *string*. Any / contained within *pattern* must be quoted. Each occurrence of *digit* in *string* that is not the result of an expansion, is replaced by the corresponding backreference in *pattern*. For:
• /*pattern*/ The first occurrence of pattern in name is replaced.

- */#pattern/* If *pattern* occurs at the beginning of name, then it is replaced by string.
- */%pattern/* If pattern occurs at the end of name, then it is replaced by string.
- *//pattern/* Each occurrence of *pattern* is replaced by *string*.

Leaving off */string* deletes the matched text.

Examples
```
x=foo/fun/bar
print ${x/fun/bam}
foo/bam/bar
print ${x//f?/go}
goo/gon/bar
print ${x/%n*r/mble}
foo/fumble
print ${x/*+(o)*/\1}
oo
```

Version: These parameter expansions are available only on versions of **ksh** newer than the 11/16/88 version.

PARAMETER EXPANSION – OTHER

${#*parameter*} *String length*

If *parameter* is * or **@**, **ksh** substitutes the number of positional parameters. Otherwise, **ksh** substitutes the length of the value of *parameter*.

Example
```
HOME=/usr/dgk
print ${#HOME}
8
```

${#*varname*[*]} *Number of elements of an array*
${#*varname*[@]}

ksh expands the above format to the number of elements in the array *varname* that are set.

Example
```
unset x
x[1]=5 x[3]=8 x[6]=abc x[12]=
print ${#x[*]}
4
```

${!*varname*} *Name of variable*

ksh expands the above format to the name of the variable that *varname* is set to. In most cases, *varname* will simply be expanded to *varname*. However, if *varname* is a reference variable, this format will expand to the variable name that *varname* is referring to.

Example
```
nameref foo=bar
print ${!foo}
bar
```

Version: The ${!*varname*} parameter expansion is available only on versions of **ksh** newer than the 11/16/88 version.

${!*prefix*@} *Names of variables beginning with prefix*
${!*prefix**}

ksh expands the above format to the list of variable names that begin with *prefix* and are set.

Example
```
print ${!HIST@}
HISTEDIT HISTCMD HISTFILE HISTSIZE
```

Version: The ${!*prefix*@} and ${!*prefix**} parameter expansions are available only on versions of **ksh** newer than the 11/16/88 version.

${!*varname*[@]} *Names of subscripts of an array*
${!*varname*[*]}

ksh expands the above format to the list of subscripts of the array *varname* that are set. For a variable that is not an array, the value is 0 if the variable is set. Otherwise, it is null.

When used in double quotes, **ksh** expands the ${!*varname*[*]} format to one argument, and the ${!*varname*[@]} format to separate arguments for each array subscript.

Example
```
x[1]=5 x[3]=8 x[6]=abc x[12]=
print ${!x[@]}
1 3 6 12
typeset -A class
class[Monday]=algebra class[Thursday]=history
print ${!class[@]}
Monday Thursday
```

Version: These parameter expansions are available only on versions of **ksh** newer than the 11/16/88 version.

${@:*offset*:*length*} ***Expand positional parameter, sub-array***
${*:*offset*:*length*}
${@:*offset*}
${*:*offset*}
${*varname*[@]:*offset*:*length*}
${*varname*[*]:*offset*:*length*}
${*varname*[@]:*offset*}
${*varname*[*]:*offset*}

The value of this expansion is a sub-array of *varname*, or a subset of the positional parameters (see **Positional Parameters**, just below), starting at the position defined by the arithmetic expression *offset* and terminating after *length* parameters, where *length* is an arithmetic expression. If :*length* is not specified or if the value of *length* will cause the expansion to exceed the number of array elements or positional parameters, the remaining elements are used.

Examples
```
set foo/fun/bar hello.world /dev/null
print ${@:2}
hello.world /dev/null
print ${*:2:4}
hello.world /dev/null
print ${@:0:2}
ksh foo/fun/bar
x=( foo/fun/bar hello.world /dev/null)
print ${x[@]:1:2}
hello.world /dev/null
```

Version: These parameter expansions are available only on versions of **ksh** newer than the 11/16/88 version.

SPECIAL PARAMETERS SET BY ksh

Note: You cannot initialize or assign values to these parameters.

@ Positional Parameters

ksh expands the positional parameters, starting with **$1**, separating them with Space characters.

If you include this parameter expansion in grouping (double) quotes, then **ksh** includes the value of each positional parameter as a separate double quoted string. This contrasts with the way that * is handled, where **ksh** includes the entire value in one double quoted string (the usual way that parameters are expanded). Therefore, **"$@"** is equivalent to **"$1"** **"$2"** up to **"$***n***"** where *n* is the value of **$#**. When there are no positional parameters, **ksh** expands **"$@"** to an unquoted Null string.

Example
```
set "hello there" world
for i in $@
do print "$i"
done
hello
there
world
for i in "$@"
do print "$i"
done
hello there
world
```

* *Positional Parameters*

ksh expands the positional parameters, starting with **$1**, separating them with the first character of the value of the **IFS** variable.

If you include this parameter expansion in grouping (double) quotes, then **ksh** includes, in double quotes, the values of all of the positional parameters, separated by *d*, where *d* is the first character of the **IFS** variable. Therefore, **"$*"** is equivalent to **"$1*d*$2*d*..."**.

Example
```
set "hello there" world
IFS=,$IFS
for i in $*
do print "$i"
done
hello
there
world
for i in "$*"
do print "$i"
done
hello there,world
```

Number of Positional Parameters

This is initially the number of arguments to **ksh**. Its value can be changed by the **set**, **shift**, and **.** (dot) commands, and by calling a function.

Example
```
set a b c
print $#
3
```

– *Option Flags*

(minus) These are the options supplied to **ksh** at invocation or via **set**. **ksh** also automatically sets some options. Each option corresponds to a letter in the value of this parameter.

Example
```
case $- in
*i*) print interactive ;;
*)   print not interactive ;;
esac
interactive
```

? *Return Value*

The value is that returned by the last executed command, function, or program. If value is:
- Zero, indicates successful completion.
- Non-zero, indicates error or unusual condition. A command terminated by a signal has a return value of 256 plus the signal number.
  Version: The 11/16/88 version of **ksh** used 128 instead of 256.

Example
```
let 0
print $?
1
```

$ *Process Id of This Shell*

The process id is a unique integer guaranteed to be different in every process active at the same time. It is normally obtained from the operating system. This parameter expands to the process id.

Suppose you are writing a shell script that may be used by two or more users at the same time, and that the script creates a temporary file for its use. You can use this parameter as part of the pathname, to cause each use of the script to generate a distinct name for the temporary file.

The value of $ does not change when **ksh** creates a subshell, even on systems that create a separate process for a subshell.

Example
```
exec 3> /tmp/foo$$
print /tmp/foo$$
( print /tmp/foo$$ )
/tmp/foo1234
/tmp/foo1234
```

! *Background Process Id*

The process id number of the last background command or co-process spawned.

Example
```
sleep 30 &
print $!
784
```

VARIABLES SET BY ksh

If you assign values to most of these variables, you will remove their usual meanings. For instance, if you change **PWD**, it will not change your working directory. In addition, if you then say **print $PWD**, **ksh** will not print your working directory. However, the next time **ksh** executes **cd**, it will set **PWD** to the pathname of your working directory.

_ *Temporary Variable*

(underscore) This variable has several functions. It contains:
- Last argument of the previous simple command run in the current environment.
- Name of matching **MAIL** file when checking for mail.
- Value of the pathname of each program that **ksh** invokes. This value is passed in the environment. The value of _ in a script is initialized to the pathname of the script.

Caution: If you unset _, **ksh** removes its special meaning even if you subsequently set it.

Example
```
print hello world
hello world
print $_
world
```

HISTCMD *History Command Number*

The value of **HISTCMD** is the number of the current command in the history file.

Version: The **HISTCMD** variable is available only on versions of **ksh** newer than the 11/16/88 version.

LINENO *Current Line Number*

ksh sets **LINENO** to the current line number within a script or function before it executes each command.

When you assign a value to **LINENO**, it only affects the line number for commands that **ksh** has not yet read.

Caution: If you unset **LINENO, ksh** removes its special meaning even if you subsequently set it.

Example
```
function foobar
{
    print $0 line $LINENO
}
foobar
foobar line 2
```

OLDPWD *Last Working Directory*

Previous working directory set by **cd**.

Example
```
print $PWD $OLDPWD
/usr/dgk /usr/src
cd -
/usr/src
print $OLDPWD
/usr/dgk
```

OPTARG *Option Argument*

ksh sets the value of the **OPTARG** variable when **getopts** encounters an option that requires an argument.

Caution: If you unset **OPTARG, ksh** removes its special meaning even if you subsequently set it.

OPTIND *Option Index*

getopts sets the value of the **OPTIND** variable to the index of the argument to search for the next option.

OPTIND is initialized to **1** whenever **ksh**, a script, or a function is invoked. You can assign **1** to **OPTIND** to reinitialize **getopts** to process another argument list.

Caution: If you unset **OPTIND, ksh** removes its special meaning even if you subsequently set it.

Example
```
OPTIND=1
while getopts u:xy:z foo -y bar -zx -unew foobar
do    print OPTIND=$OPTIND OPTARG=$OPTARG foo=$foo
done
OPTIND=3 OPTARG=bar foo=y
OPTIND=3 OPTARG= foo=z
OPTIND=4 OPTARG= foo=x
OPTIND=5 OPTARG=new foo=u
```

PPID *Parent Process Id*

Process id of the process that invoked this shell. *Caution*: If you unset **PPID**, **ksh** removes its special meaning even if you subsequently set it.

The value of **PPID** does not change when **ksh** creates a subshell, even on systems that create a separate process for a subshell.

Example
```
print $PPID $(print $PPID)
777 777
```

PWD *Working Directory*

Working directory set by **cd**.

Example
```
cd /usr/src
print $PWD
/usr/src
```

RANDOM *Random Number Generator*

RANDOM has the integer attribute. **ksh** assigns **RANDOM** a uniformly distributed random integer from **0** to **32767** each time it is referenced.

You can initialize the sequence of random numbers by assigning a numeric value to **RANDOM**.

Caution: If you unset **RANDOM**, **ksh** removes its special meaning even if you subsequently set it.

Example
```
RANDOM=$$   # Initialize the random number generator.
print $RANDOM $RANDOM
7269 32261
```

REPLY *Reply Variable*

When you use the **select** compound command, the characters that you type are stored in this variable.

When you use the **read** built-in command, and you do not specify any arguments, the characters that are read are stored in this variable.

Example
```
read; print "$REPLY"
hello    world
hello  world
```

SECONDS *Elapsed Time in Seconds*

By default, **SECONDS** has the floating point attribute displayed to three places after the decimal point. Its value is the number of seconds since you invoked **ksh**. If you assign a value to **SECONDS**, then the value of **SECONDS** is the value that you assigned, plus the number of seconds since the assignment. See *Customizing Your Prompt*.

Caution: If you unset **SECONDS**, **ksh** removes its special meaning even if you subsequently set it.

Version: The **SECONDS** variable was an integer number of seconds with the 11/16/88 version of **ksh**.

Example
```
SECONDS=35
print $SECONDS; sleep 10; print $SECONDS
35.069
45.103
```

.sh.edchar *Character that Caused KEYBD Trap*

.sh.edchar contains the value of the keyboard character (or sequence of characters if the first character is Escape) that was entered when processing a **KEYBD** trap. If the value is changed as part of the trap action, then the new value replaces the key (or key sequence) that caused the trap.

.sh.edcol *Cursor Position Before KEYBD Trap*

.sh.edcol is set to the current character position of the cursor within the input buffer when entering a **KEYBD** trap.

.sh.edmode *Escape Character for vi*

.sh.edmode is set to the ESCAPE character when in the **vi** input mode when entering a **KEYBD** trap.

.sh.edtext *Contents of Input Buffer Before KEYBD Trap*

.sh.edtext is set to the current contents of the input buffer when entering a **KEYBD** trap.

.sh.name *Name of Variable in Discipline Function*

.sh.name is set inside a discipline function to the name of the variable associated with the discipline function.

.sh.subscript *Subscript in Discipline Function*

.sh.subscript is set inside a discipline function to the name of the subscript of the variable associated with the discipline function.

.sh.value *Value of Variable in Discipline Function*

.sh.value is set inside a **set** discipline function to the value that is intended to be assigned to the variable associated with the **set** discipline function.
The value of **.sh.value** when the discipline function completes will be the value of the assignment.

If **.sh.value** is given a value inside a **get** discipline function, it will become the value of the variable that is being expanded.

Example
```
unset foo
function foo.set
{
 print "old: ${.sh.name}[ ${.sh.subscript}]=${.sh.value}"
 .sh.value=good
}
foo[3]=bad
old: foo[3]=bad
print "new: foo[3]=${foo[3]}"
new: foo[3]=good
```

Example
```
function bar.get
{       .sh.value=$(date)
}
print "$bar"
Sat Aug 28, 1993 15:32 EST
```

Example
```
foo=( float x=1.0 y=0 sum=1.0 )
function foo.x.set
{       (( foo.sum = foo.y + .sh.value ))
}
function foo.y.set
{       (( foo.sum = foo.x + .sh.value ))
}
foo.x=3.5  foo.y=5
print "${foo.sum}"
8.5
```

.sh.version *Running Version of Shell*

.sh.version is set to the version string for the shell currently running.

Example
```
print "${.sh.version}"
Version 12/28/93b
```

Version: Variables beginning with **.sh.** are available only with versions of **ksh** newer than 11/16/88.

VARIABLES USED BY ksh

This section describes variables you can set to affect the behavior of **ksh**. Many people assign values to these variables in their profiles, so that they do not have to do it each time they log in.

System administrators often assign values to some of these variables in the **/etc/profile** file. You can use **cat** to display the contents of **/etc/profile**. However, normally only system administrators can make changes to this file.

Defaults: You can assign values to these variables. If you do not, **ksh** does one of the following:
- Assigns an explicit default value. In this case, you could print the value of the variable.
- Uses an implicit default value. In this case, you could not print the value of the variable.
- Has no default. In this case, **ksh** does neither of the above, and does not use that variable at all. For instance, if you do not assign a value to **CDPATH**, then if you specified **cd**, it would not do a search.

CDPATH *Search Path for* cd *Built-in*

: (colon)-separated list of directories used by the **cd** command as described below. The working directory is specified by a **.** (dot) or a Null directory name, which can appear before the first **:**, after the last **:**, or between **:** delimiters.

If the directory that you specify for **cd** does not begin with **/**, **./**, or **../**, then **ksh** searches each of the directories in the **CDPATH** in order for the specified directory, and tries to **cd** to that directory.

No Default

Example
```
CDPATH=$HOME:/usr/src
cd cmd
/usr/src/cmd
```

COLUMNS *Number of Columns on Terminal*

If you set **COLUMNS**, **ksh** uses the value to define the width of the edit window for the **ksh** edit modes, and for printing **select** lists.

Besides **ksh**, several other programs also use this variable.

Implicit Default: 80

EDITOR *Pathname for Your Editor*

If you set the value of **EDITOR** to a pathname that ends in **emacs**, **gmacs**, or **vi**, and if the **VISUAL** variable is not set, then **ksh** turns on the corresponding option.

Implicit Default: /bin/ed

ENV *User Environment File*

Each time that you invoke **ksh** interactively, it expands this variable and does parameter expansion, command substitution, and arithmetic expansion to generate the pathname of the shell script, if any, that will be executed when **ksh** is invoked. Typical uses are for **alias** and **function** definitions, and for setting options with **set**. *Version*: ENV was also expanded and executed for non-interactive shells with the 11/16/88 version of **ksh**.

When the **privileged** option is set, **ksh** does not expand this variable and does not execute the resulting script.

No Default

Example
```
ENV=$HOME/envfile
```

FCEDIT *Editor for* hist *Built-in*

You assign a value to **FCEDIT** if you want to change the editor that **hist** will use, when you do not specify an editor on the **hist** command line.

Implicit Default: /bin/ed

Caution: The **FCEDIT** variable is obsolescent. The **HISTEDIT** variable is preferred.

FIGNORE *Ignore Filenames that Match Pattern*

ksh ignores each name which matched the pattern defined by the value of **FIGNORE**, when reading a directory during file expansion.

No Default

Version: The **FIGNORE** variable is available only on versions of **ksh** newer than the 11/16/88 version.

Example
```
print /usr/*/include/*      # Displays a listing for files
                            # in all include directories.
/usr/local/include/sys  /usr/gcc/include/sys
FIGNORE=gcc                 # Pattern to match C source
                            # files.
print /usr/*/include/*
/usr/local/include/sys
```

FPATH *Search Path for Auto-load Functions*

: (colon)-separated list of directories that **ksh** searches in order for a function definition file. The format of the **FPATH** variable is the same as the **PATH** variable.

No Default

Example
```
FPATH=$HOME/fundir # Look for function definitions here.
autoload foobar    # Specify that foobar is a function.
foobar             # Load $HOME/fundir/foobar to define
                   # function, and then execute it.
```

HISTEDIT *Editor for* hist *Built-in*

You assign a value to **HISTEDIT** if you want to change the editor that **hist** will use, when you do not specify an editor on the **hist** command line.

Implicit Default: **/bin/ed**

Version: The **HISTEDIT** variable is available only on versions of **ksh** newer than the 11/16/88 version. On earlier versions, the variable is called **FCEDIT** and the **hist** command is named **fc.**

HISTFILE *History Pathname*

If **HISTFILE** is set when **ksh** first accesses the history file, then **ksh** uses this value as the name of the history file. **ksh** first accesses the history file when it encounters the first function definition which does not have the **nolog** option set, or after it completes processing the environment file, whichever occurs first.

If the history file does not exist and **ksh** cannot create it, or if it does exist and **ksh** does not have permission to append to it, then **ksh** uses a temporary file as the history file.

Implicit Default: **$HOME/.sh_history**

Example

This example shows how to create a separate history file for each "window" on systems that have windows (sometimes termed "layers"), and that also have a program named **tty** that returns a separate pathname for each window.

```
ttyname=$(tty)
HISTFILE=$HOME/${ttyname##*/}.hist
```

HISTSIZE *Number of History Commands*

If **HISTSIZE** is set when **ksh** first accesses the history file, then the maximum number of previously entered commands that you can access via **ksh** will be equal to this number.

Caution: Setting this number to an outrageously large value, such as 10000, may result in a slow startup for a new invocation of **ksh**.

Implicit Default: 128

HOME *Your Home Directory*

The value of the **HOME** variable is the default argument used by **cd**.

Default: The value of **HOME** is automatically set when you log in, as assigned by your system administrator.

IFS *Internal Field Separator*

ksh uses each of the characters in the value of the **IFS** variable to split into fields:
- The result from command substitution or parameter expansion of command words.
- The result from command substitution or parameter expansion of words after **in** with **for** and **select**.
- The characters that **ksh** reads with **read**.

ksh uses the first character of the value of **IFS** to separate arguments when **ksh** expands the * parameter, and when **ksh** expands ${*varname*[*]}.

Any sequence of characters belonging to the **space** class that are contained in **IFS** delimit a field, except for any character that appears in **IFS** more than once consecutively. Otherwise, each occurrence of an **IFS** character and adjacent **space** characters contained in **IFS**, delimit a field. If a **space** character is repeated consecutively in **IFS**, the character behaves like a non-**space** character so that each occurrence delimits a field. If **IFS** is set to Null, **ksh** does not perform field splitting. *Version*: Repeating a **space** character to cause each instance to act as a delimiter is available only on versions of **ksh** newer than the 11/16/88 version.

The value of **IFS** is reset to the default value after executing the environment file and before the execution of a script begins. Therefore, you cannot influence the behavior of a script by exporting **IFS**.

Default: Space-Tab-Newline characters, in that order.

Examples
```
x=$'foo\t\tbar'
IFS=$'\t'
set -- $x
print second arg=$2
second arg=bar
IFS=$'\t\t'
set -- $x
print second arg=$2
second arg=
IFS=:
read name passwd  uid gid rest
root::0:0:superuser:
print "User $name has userid $uid and groupid $gid"
User root has userid 0 and groupid 0
```

LANG *Language Locale*

Determines the locale category for any category not specifically selected via a variable starting with **LC_**.

Implicit Default: POSIX

LC_ALL *Locale Settings*

Overrides the value of the **LANG** variable and any other variable starting with **LC_**.

No Default

LC_COLLATE *Locale Collation*

Determines the locale category for sorting and for character classes.

No Default

LC_CTYPE *Locale Character Classes*

Determines the locale category for character handling functions such as classification of characters.

No Default

LC_NUMERIC *Locale Numeric Formatting*

Determines the locale category for the decimal point character.

No Default

LINES *Number of Lines on Terminal*

If you set **LINES**, **ksh** uses the value for printing **select** lists (**select** compound command). **select** lists will display vertically until about two-thirds of **LINES** lines are filled.

Besides **ksh**, several programs also use this variable.

Implicit Default: 24

MAIL *Name of Your Mail File*

If **MAIL** is set to the name of a file that has grown, and **MAILPATH** is not set, then **ksh** informs you when there is a change in the modification time of the file whose name is the same as that of the value of **MAIL**. **ksh** does this periodically as determined by **MAILCHECK** (see below).

Default: Set by system administrator.

MAILCHECK *Frequency of Mail Check*

MAILCHECK has the integer attribute. You can set the value of **MAILCHECK** to specify how often (in seconds) **ksh** will check for changes in the modification time of any of the files specified by the value of **MAIL** (see just above) or **MAILPATH** (see just below). When the time has elapsed, **ksh** will check before issuing the next prompt.

If **MAILCHECK** is not set or is zero, then **ksh** checks the file before each prompt.

Caution: If you unset **MAILCHECK**, **ksh** removes its special meaning even if you subsequently set it.

Default: 600 seconds.

MAILPATH *List of Mail Files*

: (colon)-separated list of pathnames. You can follow each pathname with a **?** and a message for **ksh** to display. Default message is **You have mail in $_**.

Before **ksh** displays a message, **ksh** sets the variable _ (underscore) to the name of the file that changed and performs parameter expansion on the message.

No Default

Example
```
MAILPATH=~uucp/dgk:/usr/spool/mail/dgk
```

PATH   *Search Path for Commands*

: (colon)-separated list of directories. The working directory is specified by a . (dot) or a Null directory name, which can appear before the first :, after the last :, or between : delimiters.

Use the **PATH** variable to specify where **ksh** should search for the command that you want it to execute. Searches apply only to programs that do not contain a / in their names. **ksh** searches for the program in each of the directories in the **PATH** in the order specified, until it finds the program to execute.

Whenever you assign a value to the **PATH** variable, **ksh** unsets the values of all tracked aliases.

You may not change **PATH** if the **restricted** option is on.

Implementation-Dependent Default: /**bin**:/**usr**/**bin**:

The path in the following example causes **ksh** first to look in your own bin directory, then in /**bin**, then in /**usr**/**bin**, and finally in the working directory.

Example
```
PATH=$HOME/bin:/bin:/usr/bin:
```

PS1 *Primary Prompt String*

If the **interactive** option is on, **ksh** does parameter expansion, command substitution, and arithmetic substitution on the value of **PS1** and displays it via standard error when **ksh** is ready to read a command.

ksh replaces the character ! in **PS1** by the command number. If you want to include an ! in your prompt, use !!.

For more information and examples, such as how to customize your prompt, see *Customizing Your Prompt*.

Default: $Space (#Space for the superuser)

PS2 *Secondary Prompt String*

ksh displays **PS2** via standard error after you have pressed ⌷RETURN⌷ and thus started a new line, without your having entered a complete command.

Default: >Space

Example
```
$ print Tod\
> ay is Tuesday
Today is Tuesday
```

PS3 *Select Command Prompt*

ksh does parameter expansion, command substitution, and arithmetic substitution on the value of **PS3** and displays it via standard error to prompt you to select one of the choices that you specified with the **select** compound command.

Default: #?

Example
```
PS3='Please enter a number: '
select i in foo bar1 bar2 bar3
do   command
done
1) foo
2) bar1
3) bar2
4) bar3
Please enter a number:
```

PS4 *Debug Prompt String*

ksh does parameter expansion, command substitution, and arithmetic substitution on the value of **PS4**, and displays it via standard error when **ksh** is ready to display a command during execution trace.

Default: +

Example
```
PS4='[$LINENO]+ '
set -x
print $HOME
[3]+ print /usr/dgk
/usr/dgk
```

SHELL *Pathname of the Shell*

If the last component of the value of **SHELL** is **rsh**, **rksh**, or **krsh** when **ksh** is invoked, then **ksh** sets the **restricted** option. Several UNIX system commands use the **SHELL** variable to invoke a new shell.

Default: May be set to the pathname for **ksh** during login.

TERM *Terminal Type*

Specifies what terminal you are using. It is not used by **ksh**. However, it is used in some examples in this book and several other programs use this variable.

No Default

TMOUT *Timeout Variable*

TMOUT has the integer attribute.

If you set **TMOUT** to a value greater than zero, **ksh** terminates if you do not enter a command within the prescribed number of seconds after **ksh** issues the **PS1** prompt (plus an additional 60-second grace period).

Implementation-dependent: **ksh** may have been compiled on your system with a maximum bound for this value that you cannot exceed.

Caution: If you unset **TMOUT**, **ksh** removes its special meaning even if you subsequently set it. However, the value of **TMOUT** at the time that it is unset continues to be the timeout value for terminating **ksh**.

Version: The **TMOUT** variable is used as a timeout for **select** in versions of **ksh** newer than 11/16/88.

Default: Zero, which means unlimited. Or set by system administrator.

Example
```
# In this example, it is assumed that 5 minutes have
# elapsed after the $ prompt.
TMOUT=300
$
shell timeout in 60 seconds
```

VISUAL *Visual Editor*

If you set the value of **VISUAL** to a pathname that ends in **emacs**, **gmacs**, or **vi**, then **ksh** turns on the corresponding option no matter what the value of **EDITOR** is.

No Default

EXERCISES

1. Assuming that variable **y** has value 3, what is the value of variable **x** after each of the following assignments?

   a. `x=4`
   b. `typeset -i x=y`
   c. `typeset -i2 x=3`
   d. `typeset -x x=y`
   e. `typeset -E x=y/2`
   f. `typeset -u x=y`
   g. `typeset -R3 x=$y`
   h. `typeset -Z3 x=$y`
   i. `typeset -L3 x=y`
   j. `typeset -n x=y`
   k. `typeset -F3 x=y/3`
   l. `typeset -r x=y`

2. For each of the following assume that variable **x** has the value `/foo/bar/bar/foo`. What is the result of each of the following?

   a. `$x`
   b. `${x}`
   c. `${#x}`
   d. `${!x}`
   e. `${x-foo}`
   f. `${x+foo}`
   g. `${x%*foo}`
   h. `${x%%*foo}`
   i. `${x#*/}`
   j. `${x%%*/}`
   k. `${x/foo/FOO}`
   l. `${x//foo/FOO}`
   m. `${x:4}`
   n. `${x:5:3}`
   o. `${x[0]}`
   p. `${x[1]}`

3. For each of the following assume that variable **x** has the value with **x=(foo bar 'foo bar' foo)**. Also assume that **IFS=/**. What is the result of each of the following?

   a. `$x`
   b. `${x[@]}`
   c. `${#x}`
   d. `${#x[@]}`
   e. `${x[@]}`
   f. `${x[*]}`
   g. `"${x[*]}"`
   h. `"${x[@]}"`
   i. `${x[2]}`
   j. `"${x[@]:2}"`
   k. `"${x[*]:1:2}"`
   l. `${!x[1+1]}`
   m. `${x[@]%?}`
   n. `"${x[@]/oo/u}"`

---

14 BUILT-IN COMMANDS

INTRODUCTION

Built-in Commands

Built-in commands (we refer to them as "built-ins") are processed by **ksh** itself. On most systems **ksh** causes a separate process to be created for programs but not for built-ins. Most built-ins behave the same as do programs. However, some built-ins differ in the way that I/O redirection and variable assignment lists work. These differences are defined on page 209. These special built-ins are denoted by a dagger (†) next to the formats for the command.

Reasons for having built-ins:
- You can change the current environment with them, either directly or via side effects.
- **ksh** executes them much faster than other commands doing the same thing.
- They always behave as documented in this chapter. The behavior of programs may differ on different systems.

Return Values

The normal return value is specified under each built-in. The return value is False (1) for all built-ins for which you have specified an:
- Invalid option.
- Incorrect number of arguments.
- Incorrect argument (for instance, an argument that should be numeric, but that is not numeric).
- Invalid I/O redirection.
- Invalid variable assignment, such as an invalid identifier or a non-numeric assignment to an integer variable.
- Invalid alias name.
- Expansion for a parameter that has not been set and the **nounset** option is on.

Output

Unless otherwise specified, **ksh** writes output for a built-in on standard output, file descriptor 1. Thus you can use built-ins in pipelines.

ksh writes error messages on standard error.

Example
```
set | wc  # set is a built-in command.
29   43   310
```

Caution About Side Effects:
- **ksh** executes each element of a pipeline, except the last, in a subshell environment. Therefore, any side effects of built-ins, except in the last element of a pipeline, do not affect the current environment as built-ins normally do.
- You must enclose the command in parentheses if you need to guarantee that the built-in will execute in a subshell environment, as illustrated in the second example, below.
- *Example*
```
word=murrayhill
print foobar | read word
print $word
foobar
```
- *Example*
```
word=murrayhill
print foobar | (read word)
print $word
murrayhill
```

Notation

Each built-in command described below uses the command syntax notation defined on page 11. Whenever a command is specified as allowing options of the form *–letters*, you can specify each of the options separately, each preceded by a –. You can specify – – to cause the next argument to be processed as an argument rather than an option. The – – is required whenever the first non-option argument to a command begins with a –. Whenever a command is specified as allowing options of the form ±*letters*, then the + is processed in the same way as the –.

† A dagger designates special built-ins that are treated differently as follows:
  - **ksh** processes variable assignment lists specified with the command before I/O redirection. These assignments remain in effect when the command completes.
  - Errors in these built-ins cause the script that contains them to terminate.

DECLARATIONS

ksh expands command arguments to declaration commands that are in the format of a variable assignment in a special way. **ksh** performs tilde expansion after the equal sign, and does not perform field splitting or pathname expansion on these arguments.

- *Example*
```
bar='one two'
export foo=~morris/$bar
```

```
print -r -- "$foo"
/usr/morris/one two
```

† **alias** [**–pt**] [*name* [*=value*]...]

> *Version*: The 11/16/88 version of **ksh** supported a **–x** option that exported alias definitions to scripts run by **ksh**. The **–x** option no longer has any effect and is not listed here.

> Use **alias** to define and display aliases.

> Do not specify any *name* arguments if you want to display aliases. **ksh** displays the list of aliases, one per line, on standard output, in the form *name=value*. The **–p** option causes the word **alias** to precede each one so that it is displayed in a re-enterable format. If you specify **–t**, then **ksh** displays only tracked aliases. *Version*: The **–p** option is available only on versions of **ksh** newer than the 11/16/88 version.

> Use **–t** to set and list tracked aliases. The value of a tracked alias is the full pathname corresponding to the program of the given *name*. Tracked aliases become undefined when the value of the **PATH** variable is reset.

> If *name* is specified, it must be a valid alias name, or **alias** displays an error message. In a valid alias name, the first character is a printing character other than one of the special characters listed on page 129, and the other characters are alphanumeric.

> **ksh** defines an alias for each *name* whose *value* you specify. Previous definitions for each *name* are removed.

> If you specify *name* only, then:
> - Without **–t**, **ksh** displays the name and value of the alias *name*.
> - With **–t**, **ksh** sets the tracked attribute, and sets the value of the alias *name* to the pathname obtained by doing a path search.

> *value* can contain any valid shell text. During alias substitution, if the last character of *value* is a Space or a Tab, **ksh** also checks the word following the alias to see if it should do alias substitution. Use a trailing Space or a Tab when the next argument is supposed to be a command name.

> Enclose *value* in single quotes if you want *value* expanded only when **ksh** executes a reference to the alias. Otherwise, **ksh** also expands *value* when it processes **alias**.

> ***Examples***
> ```
> x=1
> alias foo='print $x' bar="print $x"
> ```

---

† See page 209

```
x=2
foo
2
bar
1
alias -t date
alias -t
date=/bin/date
```

Return value:
- If all *name*(s) are aliases or if you specify attributes: True.
- Otherwise: False. Value is the number of *name*(s) that are not aliases.

Examples
```
alias ls='ls -C'
alias nohup='nohup  '
```

† **export** [**–p**] [*name* [=*value*]] ...

name(s) are marked for automatic export to the environment of subsequently executed commands.

export is the same as **typeset –x**, except that if you use **export** within a function, **ksh** does not create a local variable.

If you don't supply any arguments to **export**, **ksh** displays a list of variables with the export attribute, and their values. Each *name* starts on a separate line.

If you specify **–p**, **ksh** displays the list of variables in re-enterable format. *Version*: The **–p** option is available only on versions of **ksh** newer than the 11/16/88 version.

Return value: True.

Examples
```
export PWD HOME   # Exports PWD and HOME variables.
export PATH=/local/bin:$PATH
                  # Sets and exports PATH variable.
export            # Lists all exported variables.
```

† **readonly** [**–p**] [*name* [=*value*]] ...

name(s) are given the readonly attribute.
- You cannot change *name* by subsequent variable assignment in this **ksh** environment.
- **ksh** itself can still assign a new value to a readonly variable. For instance, if **PWD** is set to **readonly**, you cannot assign it a new value. But **ksh** will assign it a new value whenever you change your working directory (see **cd**).

---

† See page 209

- You cannot unset readonly variables.

readonly is the same as **typeset –r**, except that if you use **readonly** within a function, **ksh** does not create a local variable.

If you do not specify any *name*(s), **ksh** displays a list of your variables that have the readonly attribute, and their values.

If you specify **–p**, **ksh** displays the list of variables in re-enterable format. *Version*: The **–p** option is available only on versions of **ksh** newer than the 11/16/88 version.

Return value: True.

Example
```
readonly HOME PWD
```

† **typeset ±f** [**tu**] [*name...*]

Version: The 11/16/88 version of **ksh** supported a **–x** option that exported function definitions to scripts run by **ksh**. The **–x** option no longer has any effect and is not listed here.

Use this form of **typeset** to display function names and values, and to set and unset function attributes.

Use the flags:
t To specify the **xtrace** option for the function(s) specified via *name*.
u To specify that *name* refers to a function that has not yet been defined.

To set attributes, specify **–f** and one or more of the above flags and the *name*s to which they apply.

To unset attributes, specify **+f** and one or more of the above flags and the *name*s to which they apply.

Use **typeset** to display function names and definitions on standard output. Use **–f** to display both function names and definitions. Use **+f** to display function names only. Because **ksh** stores function definitions in your history file, even if you specify **–f**, **ksh** will not display a function definition if you do not have a history file, or if the **nolog** option was on when the function was read. To display:
- Specific functions, specify *name* and none of the above flags.
- All functions with a given attribute, specify a flag and no *name*.
- All functions, specify neither *name* nor flags.

---

† See page 209

Return value:
- If all *name*(s) are functions or you specify **–u**: True.
- Otherwise: False. Value is the number of *name*(s) that are not functions.

Examples
```
typeset -f   # Displays all function names, and their
             # values if known.
typeset -fu foobar
             # Specifies foobar to be an undefined
             # function.
```

† **typeset** [±**AHlnprtux**] [±**ELFRZi**[*n*]] [*name*[=*value*]]...

Use this command on variables to:
- Set attributes. Specify a **–** and the *name*(s).
- Unset attributes. Specify a **+** and the *name*(s).
- Set *value*(s). Specify *name*(s) and *value*(s). You can also specify:
  - **–** To set attribute(s) after setting *value*(s)
  - **+** To unset attribute(s) after setting *value*(s).
- Display on standard output, variables and/or their attributes. Do not specify any *name*(s), and specify:
  - **–** To display names and values of all variables that have the attribute(s) that you specify.
  - **+** To display only the names.

  Nothing (neither **–** nor **+**) to display names and attributes of all variables.

The **–p** option displays variable names, attributes, and values in re-enterable format.

If you specify **typeset** inside a function defined with the **function** reserved word syntax, **ksh** creates a new instance of each variable *name* if *name* is an identifier. That is, **ksh** creates local variable(s), and restores the value(s) and attribute(s) of these variables when the function completes.

You can specify the following attributes:
- **–u** Uppercase.
- **–l** Lowercase.
- **–i** Integer. *n* specifies arithmetic base.
- **–n** Name reference.
- **–A** Associative array.
- **–E** Exponential number. *n* specifies significant figures.
- **–F** Floating point number. *n* specifies decimal places.
- **–L** Left-justifies. *n* specifies field width.
- **–LZ** Left-justifies and strips leading zeros. *n* specifies field width.
- **–R** Right-justifies. *n* specifies field width.

---

† See page 209

–RZ Right-justifies. *n* specifies field width and fills with leading zeros.

–Z Zero-filled. *n* specifies field width. Equivalent to **–RZ**.

–r Readonly.

–x Export.

–H UNIX system-to-host operating system pathname mapping.

–t User-defined tag.

Note: Some of these attributes, such as **–u** and **–E**, are mutually exclusive and cannot be used together.

Version: The **–A**, **–E**, **–F**, **–n**, and **–p** options are available only on versions of **ksh** newer than the 11/16/88 version.

Return value: True.

Examples

```
typeset -p       # Displays names and attributes of all
                 # variables.
typeset          # Same as typeset -p.
typeset -xi      # Displays names and values of all
                 # variables with both the export and
                 # integer attributes.
typeset +xi      # As above, but displays names only.
typeset a b c    # Defines variables a, b, and c without
                 # any special attributes. If executed
                 # inside a function, this creates local
                 # variables.
typeset -i8 x    # x will be an integer variable and will
                 # print in octal (base 8).
typeset -u x     # Whenever x is given a value, all
                 # lowercase characters are converted to
                 # uppercase.
typeset -r x=abc # First gives x the value abc, and then
                 # makes it readonly.
typeset -L4 z    # Whenever z is given a value, it is
                 # truncated to four places and filled
                 # with trailing spaces as needed.
typeset -LZ4 z   # Same as above, except that leading
                 # zeros are stripped.
typeset -R4 z    # Whenever z is given a value, it is
                 # truncated on the left to four
                 # characters.  It is filled in with
                 # leading spaces if the value is fewer
                 # than four characters.
typeset -RZ4 z   # Same as above, except leading zeros
                 # are prepended instead of spaces.
typeset -H file  # On non-UNIX systems, this takes a
                 # UNIX system pathname and converts it
                 # to the host system name.  On UNIX
```

```
                        # systems the -H has no effect.
    typeset -E x        # x will be a floating point variable.
    typeset -F2 x       # x will be a floating point variable
                        # which will print with two places
                        # after the decimal point.
    typeset -Ai a       # a will be an associative array whose
                        # values will be integers.
    typeset -n x=y      # x will be a name reference for y.
    z=1
    function foo
    {
        typeset z=3     # z will be a local to the function.
        typeset .y=$z   # .y is not an identifier, thus global.
    }
    foo
    print z=$z y=${.y}
    z=1 y=3
```

[†] **unalias** [**–a**] *name*...

unalias removes the *name*(s) from the alias list.

If you specify **–a**, then all of the aliases are cleared from memory.

Version: The **–a** option is available only on versions of **ksh** newer than the 11/16/88 version.

Return value :
• If all *name*(s) are aliases: True.
• Otherwise: False. Value is the number of *name*(s) that are not aliases.

Example
```
unalias ls nohup # Remove ls and nohup alias definitions.
```

[†] **unset** [**–fnv**] *name*...

If you specify **–v** or you do not specify **–f** or **–n** , then *name* refers to a variable. In this case, for each of the *name*(s):
• **ksh** unsets value(s) and attribute(s).
• An unsubscripted array name refers to all elements of the array.
• You cannot unset readonly variables.

If you specify **–n** and *name* is a name reference to another variable, *name* will be unset rather than the variable it refers to. Otherwise, **–n** is equivalent to **–v**.

If you specify **–f**, then *name* refers to a function. In this case, **ksh** unsets the function definition(s) and removes *name*. The **–f** option overrides the other options.

[†] See page 209

Caution: If you specify **unset** with the following predefined variabl⸱ ⸱, **ksh** removes their special meaning even if you subsequently set them: _ (Temporary) **LINENO MAILCHECK OPTARG OPTIND RANDOM SECONDS TMOUT**

Version: The **–n** and **–v** options are available only on versions of **ksh** newer than the 11/16/88 version.

Return value :
- If all *name*(s) are functions or variables: True.
- Otherwise: False. Value is the number of *name*(s) that are not functions or variables.

Examples
```
unset VISUAL        # Unsets VISUAL variable.
unset -f foo bar    # Unsets functions foo and bar.
```

POSITIONAL PARAMETERS AND OPTIONS

† **set** [±**Cabefhkmnopstuvx–**] [±**o** *option*]... [±**A** *name*] [*arg*...]
Note: You can repeat the [±**o** *option*] argument.

You can specify options on your **ksh** invocation line (see page 260), as well as with **set**.

Use **set** to:
- Set options. Specify – (minus) and option letter, or **–o** *option*.
- Unset options. Specify + and option letter, or **+o** *option*.
- Set positional parameters. Specify *arg*(s).
- Assign values to an array variable. Specify ±**A** *name* and *arg*(s).
- Sort positional parameters or *arg*. Specify **–s**.
- Unset positional parameters. Specify – – and do not specify *arg*.

Do not specify *arg* for the following:
- Display option setting(s) on standard output. Specify **–o** and do not specify *option*. *Note*: The special parameter – (minus) contains the letter of each option that has a letter and that is set.
- Display names and values of all variables. Specify **set** by itself, with nothing else.

Option names are shown below, together with option letters in parentheses.
allexport (a)
> While **allexport** is set, **ksh** sets the export attribute for each variable whose name does not contain a **.** (dot) to which you assign a value.

---

† See page 209

(b)   See **notify**, below.

bgnice   **ksh** runs all background jobs at a lower priority.

(C)   See **noclobber**, below.

emacs   Puts you in the **emacs** built-in editor.

errexit (e)

If a command has False return value, **ksh** executes the **ERR** trap if set, and immediately exits. **ksh** disables **errexit** while reading profiles and environment files.

(f)   See **noglob**, below.

gmacs   Puts you in the **gmacs** built-in editor.

(h)   See **trackall**, below.

ignoreeof

When the **interactive** option is also set, **ksh** does not exit on *End-of-file* (default CONTROL d). Type **exit** to terminate **ksh**.

keyword (k)

When **ksh** reads a command, **ksh** places each word that has the syntax of a variable assignment in the variable assignment list. Ordinarily, variable assignments must precede the command name word, and words that look like variable assignments but appear after the command name word are treated as command argument words. *Caution* (*Bourne shell*): **keyword** is provided for compatibility with the Bourne shell and is obsolete. We recommend that you not use it. It is not essential. It may be omitted from future versions of **ksh**.

markdirs

ksh appends a trailing **/** to all directory names resulting from pathname expansion.

monitor (m)

ksh runs background jobs in a separate process group, and displays a line upon completion. **ksh** reports the return value of background jobs in a completion message. **ksh** automatically turns on **monitor** for interactive shells on systems with job control.

noclobber (C)

ksh will not overwrite an existing file with the **>** redirection operator. You must specify **>|** to overwrite an existing file.

noexec (n)

ksh reads commands but does not execute them. You can use this option to have **ksh** check your shell script for syntax errors. **ksh** ignores **noexec** for interactive shells.

noglob(f)

ksh disables pathname expansion.

nolog   **ksh** does not store function definitions in the history file.

notify (b)

> **ksh** displays a completion message on standard error immediately after each background job completes. *Version*: This option is available only on versions of **ksh** newer than the 11/16/88 version.

nounset (u)

> **ksh** displays an error message when it tries to expand a variable that is unset.

privileged (p)

> Turning **privileged** off sets the effective user id to the real user id, and the effective group id to the real group id. Turning **privileged** on restores the effective user id and effective group id to their values when **ksh** was invoked (see page 260). The **privileged** option is on whenever the effective user id is not equal to the real user id, or the effective group id is not equal to the real group id. When **privileged** is on, **ksh**:
>
> - Disables processing of the **$HOME/.profile** file.
> - Uses the file **/etc/suid_profile** instead of the file you specify with the **ENV** variable. The system administrator can use this file to change **PATH** or insert commands.

(t)
> **ksh** reads and executes one command, and then exits. This option is obsolete.

trackall (h)

> **ksh** causes each command whose name has the syntax of an alias name to become a tracked alias when it is first encountered.
> **ksh** automatically turns on **trackall** for non-interactive shells.

(u)
> See **nounset**, above.

verbose (v)

> **ksh** displays its input on standard error as it is read.

vi
> Puts you in **vi** built-in editor.

viraw
> Specifies **vi** character-at-a-time input.

xtrace (x)

> After expanding each simple command, **ksh** expands **PS4** and displays it on standard error followed by the command and its expanded arguments. The **set +x** command that turns off this option is not displayed.

–s sorts positional parameters. This option has a different meaning when used on the **ksh** invocation line (see page 261).

Use ±A *name* to assign values *arg* to array *name* starting sequentially from zero. When –s is also specified, *arg* is sorted before the assignment. Use –A to cause **ksh** to unset *name* prior to the assignment.

Options are terminated by an argument not beginning with a + or −,
a −, or a − −. **ksh** interprets any argument(s) that follow the − or − −, even if
the argument(s) begin with a −, as an *arg*, not as an option. Thus you must
use − or − − to set positional parameter **1** to a value beginning with a −. Use:

− Turns off −**x** and −**v** options. *Caution (Bourne shell)*: This is
obsolescent. It is included only for compatibility with the Bourne shell.
Use +**xv** to turn off the −**x** and −**v** options instead.

− − Does not change any of the options. If you do not specify any arguments
following the − −, then **ksh** unsets the positional parameters.

Return value: True.

Examples
```
set                 # Lists all variables and their values.
set -o              # Lists all option settings.
set c a b           # Sets $1 $2 and $3.
set -s              # Sorts $1 $2 and $3.
set -o vi -o viraw
                    # Turns on vi and viraw options.
set -xv             # Turns on verbose and xtrace options.
set --              # Unsets all positional parameters.
set -- "$x"         # Sets $1 to value of x, even if x
                    # begins with -.
set -- $x           # Splits x using the IFS variable,
                    # then does pathname expansion on each
                    # item.  Then sets positional parameters
                    # to the items that result, even if x
                    # begins with -.
set -A foo c a b    # Assigns foo[0]=c foo[1]=a foo[2]=b.
set +A foo d x      # Assigns foo[0]=d foo[1]=x, leaves
                    # foo[2] alone.
```

[†] **shift** [*n*]

ksh shifts positional parameter(s) to the left by *n*. **ksh** discards the first *n*
positional parameter(s).

n is an arithmetic expression that must evaluate to zero, or a positive number
less than or equal to the value of special parameter #. Default is 1.

Return value: True.

Example
```
set a b c d e
shift 2
print $*
c d e
```

[†] See page 209

CONTROL FLOW

[†] *.* *name* [*arg...*]   ***Dot Command***

If *name* refers to a function defined with the **function** *name* syntax, **ksh** executes this function in the current environment. Otherwise, **ksh** reads the complete *file* (called a dot script) and executes commands from it in the current environment. *Note*: **ksh** reads the complete dot script before executing commands in it. Thus, if you set or unset aliases or use **set –k** within a dot script, they will not affect the commands within that dot script.

ksh uses the search path specified by the **PATH** variable for a file to find the file. If you specify *args*, they replace the positional parameters during the execution of *name*. Otherwise, the positional parameters are unchanged.

Version: *name* could not be a function with the 11/16/88 version of **ksh**. Also, if *args* were specified, the positional parameters were not restored when the dot script completed.

Return value: Return value of last command in *name*.

Example
```
cat foobar
foo=hello bar=world
print $foo $bar
. foobar
hello world
```

[†] **break** [*n*]

break exits from the smallest enclosing **for**, **while**, **until**, or **select** loop, or from the *n*th enclosing loop if you specify *n*. Execution continues with the command immediately following the loop(s).

n is an integer equal to or greater than 1.

Return value: True.

Example
```
for i in *
do    for j in foo bar bam
      do    if    [[ $j == $i ]]
            then    break 2  # Break out of both for loops.
            fi
      done
done
```

[†] See page 209

command [−pvV] *command* [*arg*...]

Executes *command* with the specified arguments, with functions eliminated from the search order. Also, if *command* is a special built-in command (designated with a dagger), then *command* is treated as a regular built-in. (See page 209 for the description of how a special built-in command is normally treated.)

If you specify −**p**, then **ksh** performs the command search using the default value for **PATH**.

command −**v** is equivalent to **whence**.   **command** −**V** is equivalent to **whence** −**v**.

Return value:
- If you specified −**v** or −**V**, same as return value for **whence**.
- Otherwise, return value of *command*.

Version: **command** is available only on versions of **ksh** newer than the 11/16/88 version. Naming a function with the name of a built-in command was not possible in the older version. You had to use aliases for this purpose.

Examples
```
function cd
{
        # call the builtin cd rather than the cd function
        command cd "$1"  && title $PWD
}
# command prevent scripts from exiting on exec error
command exec 3< "$1"  || exec 3< "$foo/$1"
IFS=: command set -- $*   # value of IFS is restored
```

† continue [*n*]

Goes to top of smallest enclosing **for**, **while**, **until**, or **select** loop, or to top of *n*th enclosing loop if specified, and causes it to repeat execution.

n is an integer equal to or greater than 1.

Return value: True.

Example
```
for i in *
do    if    [[ -d $i ]]
      then  continue  # Continue with next for value.
      fi
      print -r -- "$i is not a directory"
done
```

---

† See page 209

† **eval** [*arg...*]

> **eval** constructs a command by concatenating *arg*(s) together, separating each with a Space. **ksh** then reads and executes this command in the current environment. Note that command words are expanded twice; once to construct *arg* and again when **ksh** executes the constructed command.

> *Return value*: Value of the command determined by *arg*(s).

> *Examples*
> ```
> foo=10 x=foo
> y='$'$x
> print $y
> $foo
> eval y='$'$x
> print $y
> 10
> if    eval [[ -d \${$#} ]]
> then  print $0: Last argument must be a directory.
>       exit 1
> fi
> ```

† **exec** [**-c**] [**-a** *name*] [*command* [*arg...*]]   (See page 225)

† **exit** [*n*]

> Causes **ksh** to exit. If this is the login shell, **ksh** logs you out. Otherwise, **ksh** returns to the program that invoked **ksh**. If set, a trap on **EXIT** is executed before **ksh** terminates.

> *End-of-file* also causes **ksh** to exit, unless the **ignoreeof** option is on.

> *Return value*
> - *n*, if you specify it.
> - Otherwise, value of preceding command. When invoked inside a trap, the "preceding command" means the command that invoked the trap.

> *Examples*
> ```
> exit 0       # Exits True.
> exit 1       # Exits False.
> ```

---

† See page 209

[†] **return** [*n*]

> Causes a **ksh** function or dot script to return to the invoking shell script.
> **return** outside a function or dot script is equivalent to **exit**.
>
> If set, a trap on **EXIT** defined in a non-POSIX function is executed in the
> environment of the calling program after the function returns.
>
> ### Return value
> - *n*, if you specify it.
> - Otherwise, value of preceding command.
>
> ### Example
> ```
> function foo # filename
> {
>     if    [[ ! -d $1 ]]
>     then  print "$PWD/$1: No such directory"
>           return 1
>     fi
>     cd "$1"
>     foo "$1"
>     cd ..
> }
> ```

[†] **trap** [*action condition...*]

[†] **trap –p** [*condition...*]

> Use **trap** to:
> - Specify the action for **ksh** to take when the *condition*(s) arise. If *action* is:
>   - Null, then when any specified *condition* arises, **ksh** ignores it.
>   - –, then **ksh** resets *condition*(s) to their original value(s).
>   - *n*, then **ksh** performs the action described for –, and *n* becomes the first
>   *condition*. Thus, **trap** *n* is equivalent to **trap** – *n*.
>   - A command, then **ksh** executes the command each time that any of the
>   *condition*(s) arise.
> - Display a list of *action*(s) and *condition*(s) in the format of the **trap**
>   command for all of your trap settings. To do this, specify **trap** with or
>   without **–p,** and no *action* and no *condition*(s).
> - Display the *action*(s) corresponding to each *condition* in re-enterable form.
>   To do this, specify **–p** and the list of *condition*(s). ***Version***: The **–p** option is
>   available only on versions of **ksh** newer than the 11/16/88 version.
>
> **ksh** expands *action* once when it executes **trap**, and again whenever one or
> more of the *condition*(s) arise.

[†] See page 209

A *condition* is one of:
- Name or number of a signal.
  Implementation-dependent: The specific signal numbers and names (uppercase or lowercase) differ on different systems. Use **kill –l** to list signal names and numbers on your system. For portability, we recommend that you specify names rather than numbers, because names are more likely to be the same on different systems.
- **ERR**. **ksh** executes *action* whenever a command has a non-zero return value. This trap is not inherited by functions.
- **0** or **EXIT**. If **trap** is executed inside the body of a non-POSIX function, *action* is executed after the function completes, in the environment that called the function. If outside the body of a function, *action* is executed upon exit from **ksh** or from the current subshell,
- **DEBUG**. **ksh** executes *action* after each simple command. This trap is not inherited by functions.
- **CHLD**. **ksh** executes *action* when a background job stops or exits.
- **KEYBD**. **ksh** executes *action* after each key entered from the terminal. See example on page 98. ***Version***: The **KEYBD** trap is available only on versions of **ksh** newer than the 11/16/88 version.

If more than one condition arises at about the same time, **ksh** executes:
- First, **DEBUG**, if specified.
- Second, **ERR**, if applicable.
- Then, any other applicable trap command(s) in order of signal number.
- Last, **EXIT**.

When **ksh** is invoked, it ignores traps that were ignored by its parent process. Even if you specify an action for a signal that the parent ignored, the signal will never reach **ksh**.

Return value: True, unless an invalid signal name or number is supplied. This will not cause the script that invokes the trap to terminate.

Examples
```
trap '$HOME/.logout' EXIT
        # Sets a trap so that logout in your HOME
        # directory will execute when shell terminates.
trap '$HOME/.logout' 0
        # Same.
trap -p # Displays all traps and actions.
trap -- '$HOME/.logout' EXIT
trap -p EXIT # Displays EXIT trap.
'$HOME/.logout'
trap - INT QUIT TERM EXIT
        # Unsets traps on INT QUIT TERM EXIT.
```

INPUT/OUTPUT

echo [*arg...*]

Echoes each *arg* on standard output, separating each by a Space.

Implementation-dependent: The behavior of **echo** depends on your system:
- On UNIX System V compatible systems, **echo** is equivalent to **print –**.
- On other systems that have a command named **/bin/echo**, and for which **/bin/echo –n** means not to print a trailing Newline, **echo** depends on the **PATH** variable. If a path search for **echo** would yield **/bin/echo**, **echo** is equivalent to **print –R**. Otherwise, **echo** is equivalent to **print –**.
- On all other systems, **echo** is equivalent to **print –**.

Return value: True.

Example
```
echo - foobar
- foobar
```

† **exec** [**–c**] [**–a** *name*] [*command* [*arg...*]]

Use **exec** to:
- Replace **ksh** with *command*, without creating a new process. You must specify *command* . If you specify *arg*(s), they are arguments to *command*. I/O redirection affects the current process environment. If you specify **–c**, **ksh** clears the environment of all variables before execution except variable assignments that are part of the current **exec** command. If you specify **–a**, **ksh** passes *name* as the zero'th argument of *command*. *Version*: The **–a** and **–c** options are available only on versions of **ksh** newer than the 11/16/88 version.
- Open, close, and/or copy file descriptors as specified by I/O redirection. Do not specify any options, *command*, or *arg*. **ksh** sets to close-on-exec file descriptor numbers greater than **2** that are opened in this way, so that they will be closed when **ksh** invokes another program.

Return value:
- If you specify *command*, **exec** does not return to **ksh**.
- Otherwise, True.

Examples
```
exec 3< readfile  # Opens readfile as file descriptor 3
                  # for reading.
exec 4> writefile # Opens writefile as unit 4 for
                  # writing.
```

---

† See page 209

```
exec 5<&0              # Makes unit 5 a copy of unit 0.
exec 3<&-              # Closes file unit 3.
exec prog              # Overlays ksh with prog.
SHELL=/bin/sh PATH=$PATH exec -c -a -sh sh
                       # Clears the environment, creates new
                       # environment containing PATH and
                       # SHELL, and overlays ksh with sh.
                       # The zero'th argument, -sh, causes
                       # it to be a login shell.
```

print [**–Rnprs**] [**–f** *format*] [**–u** [*n*]] [**–**] [*arg...*]

Use **print** to display output on standard output, or wherever you specify. **print** displays each *arg*, separating each by a Space, and normally adding a Newline after all the *arg*(s).

Unless you specify **–r** or **–R** , **print** formats using the following escape conventions:

\a   Bell character.
\b   Backspace.
\c   Print line without adding Newline. The remaining *arg*s are ignored.
\f   Formfeed.
\n   Newline.
\r   Return.
\t   Tab.
\v   Vertical Tab.
\\   Backslash.
\E   Escape. *Version*: The \E escape sequence is available only on versions of **ksh** newer than the 11/16/88 version.
\0*x*   The 8-bit character whose ASCII code is the 1-, 2-, or 3-digit octal number *x*.

Caution: \ is a quote character. **ksh** removes it when it expands the command, unless the \ is quoted.

You can specify the following with **print**:

–   **ksh** processes anything following the **–** as an *arg*, even if it begins with a **–**. *Caution*: **–** is obsolete; use **– –**.
–R   **ksh** does not use the \ conventions listed above. **ksh** processes anything following the **–R**, other than **–n**, as an *arg*, even if it begins with a **–**.
–f *format*
        Arguments are processed as described with the **printf** command. A Newline is not appended. *Version*: The **–f** option is available only on versions of **ksh** newer than the 11/16/88 version.
–n   **ksh** does not add a trailing Newline to the output.
–p   **ksh** redirects *arg*(s) onto the co-process.
–r   **ksh** does not use the \ conventions listed above.

-s   **ksh** redirects *arg*(s) to the history file.

-u   **ksh** redirects *arg*(s) to file descriptor *n*, or to default 1. *n* must be 1, 2, or a file descriptor that you opened with **exec**. The -u option has the same effect as redirecting the standard output of **print** but does not cause the file to be opened and closed, or the file descriptor to be duplicated, each time.

Return value: True.

Examples
```
print -r 'hi\\\\there'
hi\\\\there
print 'hi\\\\there'
hi\\there
print -r hi\\\\there
hi\\there
print hi\\\\there
hi\there
```

printf *format* [*arg...*]

Use **printf** to format and display output on standard output. **printf** displays all characters in *format* except for escape sequences, which begin with the \ character, and conversion control strings, which begin with the % character. The syntax of *format* is an extension of that in the C programming language **printf** ( ) function.

printf formats using the escape sequences listed under **print** above.

printf formats according to the following conversion control string syntax:
%[flags][field_width][precision][base]conversion

conversion specifies how the corresponding *arg* is to be displayed. You must specify exactly one of the following conversion characters:

b   String with the **print** escape conventions followed.

c   Unsigned character.

d   Signed decimal.   "[−]*n*"

e,E   Scientific notation.   "[−]*n.n*e±*n*" or "[−]*n.n*E±*n*"

f   Floating point. "[−]*n.n*"

g,G Scientific notation with significant digits.

n   The number of bytes printed at this point is stored in a variable whose name is given by *arg*.

o   Unsigned octal.

P   Regular expression is printed as a shell pattern.

q   String within special characters quoted.

s   String.

u   Unsigned decimal.

x   Unsigned hexadecimal with digits 0123456789abcdef.

X   Unsigned hexadecimal with digits 0123456789ABCDEF.

%   % character.

Flag sequences are zero or more of the following characters:

–   Left-justify *arg* within field.

+   Prefix all numbers with + or –.

Space

      Prefix all numbers with Space or –.

Prefix octal number with **0** when used with **o**.

      Prefix hexadecimal number with **0x** when used with **h** or **H**.

      Display radix point when used with **e**, **E**, **f**, **g**, or **G**.

      Display trailing zeroes when used with **g** or **G**.

      The behavior is ignored when used in any other conversion.

0   Pad field width with leading zeroes when used with **d**, **e**, **E**, **f**, **g**, **G**.

field_width is the minimum number of character positions displayed.
A number specifies a constant amount. The * character causes the value of the next *arg* to specify *field_width*.

precision takes one of the following forms:

.n   Specifies a constant width.

*.**   Specifies a variable width specified by the next *arg*.

.   Specifies a width of zero.

precision depends on the conversion type as follows:

d, o, u, x, X

      Prints specified minimum number of digits. The remaining precision width is padded with leading zeroes. The default precision is one.

e, E   Prints specified minimum number of digits. The remaining precision width is padded with zeroes after the decimal point. The default precision is ten digits after the decimal point. If the default is zero, then the decimal point is not printed.

f   Prints specified number of digits after the decimal point.

g, G   Prints specified maximum number of significant digits.

s, b, q   Prints specified maximum number of characters.

      The default is the number of characters in the string.

base can be specified with the **d** format conversion and is of the form *.n*, where *n* is the arithmetic base.

format is reused as often as necessary to satisfy the *arg* list. Any extra **c** or **s** conversion characters are evaluated as if a null string argument were supplied; other extra conversion characters are evaluated as if a zero argument were supplied.

Version: **printf** is available only on versions of **ksh** newer than the 11/16/88 version.

Examples
```
integer num=43
printf "%+d\n" num
+43
alphabet=abcdefghijklmnopqrstuvwxyz
printf "%.10s\n" $alphabet
abcdefghij
precision=5
printf "%10.*s\n" precision $alphabet
     abcde
printf "%s\n" 'hello world' 'hi again'
hello world
hi again
printf "%q\n" 'hello world' 'hi again'
'hello world'
'hi again'
printf "%P\n" '[0-9]*.L'
*([0-9])?L
printf "%s%n %d\n" foo bar bar
foo 3
```

read [**–Aprs**] [**–u** [*n*]] [**–d** *char*] [**–t** *sec*] [*name?prompt*] [*name...*]

Use **read** to read a line and split it into fields, using the characters in the **IFS** variable as delimiters. Ordinarily, a trailing \ at the end of a line causes the line to be continued onto the next line; **ksh** removes both the \ and the Newline.

Each *name* must be a valid *varname*. The first field is assigned to the first *name*, the second field to the second *name*, etc., with leftover fields assigned to the last *name*. The default *name* is **REPLY**.

If you specify *name?prompt*, then, when **ksh** is interactive, it displays *prompt* on standard error.

You can also specify:

–A **ksh** stores the fields in *name* as an indexed array starting at index 0.

–p **ksh** reads the input line from the co-process. An *End-of-file* causes **ksh** to disconnect the co-process so that you can create another co-process.

–r A \ at the end of a line does not signify line continuation.

–s **ksh** saves a copy of the input line as a command in the history file.

–u **ksh** reads from file descriptor *n*; default is 0. Before you specify **read** with a file descriptor other than 0 or 2, you must open a file on the descriptor, typically with **exec**.

–d *char*
> **ksh** terminates **read** at delimiter *char* rather than Newline.

–t *sec*
> **ksh** puts the limit *sec* on the user response time. *sec* is an integer in units of seconds.

Return value: True, unless an *End-of-file* or an error is encountered.

Version: The **–A**, **–d**, and **–t** options are available only on versions of **ksh** newer than the 11/16/88 version.

Example
```
while read -r
do    print -r "$REPLY"
done <<!
My Home directory is $HOME.
!
My Home directory is /usr/dgk.
```

OPERATING SYSTEM – ENVIRONMENT

cd [**–LP**] [*directory*]

Use **cd** to change the working directory.

If *directory* is:
- **–** (minus). **ksh** changes the working directory to the previous directory, and displays the new working directory name.
- **/***string* or **..**/*string* . **ksh** changes the working directory to **/***string* or **..**/*string* . The **CDPATH** variable is not used.
- Specified, but it does not begin with a **/** or **..**/ .
  - If **CDPATH** is set, and *directory* does not begin with a **./**, or **../**, **ksh** prepends, in turn, each directory in the **CDPATH** variable to *directory* to construct a directory name. **ksh** changes the working directory to the first constructed name, if any, that corresponds to a directory that you have permission to change to. **ksh** displays the directory name.
  - If **CDPATH** is not set, **ksh** changes the working directory to *directory*.
- Not specified. **ksh** changes the working directory to the value of the **HOME** variable.
- Non-existent, or you don't have appropriate permission. **ksh** displays an error message.

If you specify **–L**, **ksh** displays the logical name, and does not resolve symbolic links. **ksh** interprets the filename **..** (dot dot) as meaning move up one level towards **/**, even if the operating system doesn't. Thus, **cd ./foo** followed by **cd ..** changes the working directory to **foo** and then restores the working directory.

If you specify **–P**, **ksh** resolves all symbolic links and displays the resulting physical name.

If you specify both **–L** and **–P**, the last one on the line specifies the behavior that will be used. If neither is specified, **ksh** behaves as if the **–L** flag had been specified.

ksh sets the **PWD** variable to the working directory, and the **OLDPWD** variable to the previous working directory.

cd cannot be executed while the **restricted** option is set.

Version: The **–L** and **–P** options are available on versions of **ksh** newer than the 11/16/88 version and on some 11/16/88 versions.

Return value:
- If the change of the working directory was successful, True.
- Otherwise, False (1).

Example
```
pwd
/usr/src/cmd
cd;pwd
/usr/dgk
cd -
/usr/src/cmd
```

cd [*–LP*] *oldstring newstring*

ksh substitutes *newstring* for *oldstring* in the working directory name, **PWD**, and tries to change to this new directory. **ksh** displays the new working directory name.

Return value:
- If the change of the working directory was successful, True.
- Otherwise, False (1).

Example
```
cd /usr/foo/src/cmd
cd foo bar
/usr/bar/src/cmd
```

pwd [*–LP*]

Use **pwd** to display the working directory. **pwd** is equivalent to **print –r –** **$PWD** if you have not changed **PWD**.

If you specify **–L**, **ksh** displays the logical name, and does not resolve symbolic links.

If you specify **–P**, **ksh** displays the physical name, and resolves all symbolic links.

If you specify both **–L** and **–P**, the last one on the line specifies the behavior that will be used. If neither is specified, **ksh** behaves as if the **–L** flag had been specified.

Version: The **–L** and **–P** options are available on versions of **ksh** newer than the 11/16/88 version and on some 11/16/88 versions.

Return value: True.

Example
```
cd /usr/src/cmd
pwd
/usr/src/cmd
cd /bin
pwd
/bin
pwd -P
/usr/bin
cd -P /bin
pwd
/usr/bin
```

† times

Caution: **times** is obsolescent. The **times** built-in command has been removed in versions of **ksh** newer than the 11/16/88 version. A built-in alias for **times** will enable scripts using **times** to continue to run.

ulimit [–HSacdfmnstv] [*n*]

Use **ulimit** to set or display system resource limits. These limits apply to the current process and to each child process created after the resource limit has been specified. If you:
- Specify *n*. **ksh** sets the specified resource limit to *n*. *n* can be any arithmetic expression or **unlimited**.
- Do not specify *n*. **ksh** displays the specified resource limit.

Some systems allow you to lower resource limits and later increase them. These are called soft limits. Once a hard limit is set, the resource cannot be increased. If you specify:

–H   A hard limit is set or displayed.

–S   A soft limit is set or displayed if soft limits exist.

Neither –H nor –S
    Both hard and soft limits are set. Soft limits are displayed.

Different systems allow you to specify different resource limits. Some systems restrict how much you can raise the limit of a resource. Other systems do not allow you to raise limits for some or all of these resources at all. If your system has the capability, you can specify the following for **ksh** to set or display (–a displays only):

–a   All current resource limits.

–c   Size limit of *n* blocks on the size of core dumps. Each block is 512 bytes.

---

† See page 209

–d   Size limit of *n* kilobytes on the size of the data area.

–f   Size limit of *n* blocks on files written by child processes (files of any size may be read). Each block is 512 bytes.

–m   Limit of *n* kilobytes on the size of physical memory that this process or any of its children can use.

–n   The maximum number of file descriptors per process.

–s   Size limit of *n* kilobytes on the size of the stack area.

–t   Time limit of *n* seconds to be used by each process.

–v   Limit of *n* kilobytes on the size of virtual memory that this process or any of its children can use.

If you do not specify a resource, the default is the file size limit, **–f**.

Return value: True.

Example
```
ulimit -f 1000
ulimit -f
1000
```

umask [–S] [*mask*]

Use **umask** to set or display the file creation mask. If you:
- Specify *mask*, **ksh** sets the file creation mask to *mask*.
- Do not specify *mask*, **ksh** displays the file creation mask on standard output. If you specify **–S**, **ksh** displays the output in symbolic format, as described on page 34.

mask specifies what permissions the system should remove whenever **ksh** or any of its child processes create a file. See page 17 for an explanation of file permissions.

With **–S**, *mask* is a symbolic permission expression (described on page 34) that defines which permissions should ***not*** be removed. Otherwise, *mask* is a 3-digit octal number that specifies what permissions the system should remove. See page 17 for an explanation of file permissions.

Version: The **–S** option is available only on versions of **ksh** newer than the 11/16/88 version.

Return value: True.

Examples
```
umask 002   # Removes write permission for others.
umask
002
umask -S
=rx,ug+w
umask -S =rx,u+w
```

```
umask
022
```

OPERATING SYSTEM – JOB CONTROL

Note: When a command in this section takes an argument called *job*, *job* can be a process id. When the **interactive** option is on, *job* can also be specified as one of the following:

%number	To refer to the job by *number*.
%string	The job whose name begins with *string*.
%?string	The job whose name contains *string*.
%+ or *%%*	Current job.
%–	Previous job.

bg [*job...*]

fg [*job...*]

> *Implementation-dependent*: **bg** and **fg** are built-ins only on systems that support job control.

> Use **bg** to resume stopped jobs and run them in the background. Use **bg** without arguments to refer to the current job (the job that you most recently stopped). Use **bg** *job*s to refer to specific jobs.

> Use **fg** to move background jobs into the foreground one at a time. Use **fg** without arguments to refer to the current job (the job that you most recently stopped or started). Use **fg** *job*s to refer to specific jobs.

> *Return value*: If **monitor** option is:
> - On, True.
> - Off, False (1).

> *Examples*
> ```
> alias %=_fg
> function _fg
> {
>     fg %${1-%}
> }
> bg
> bg %2
> fg
> % 10
> bg %cc
> ```

disown [*job...*]

> Use **disown** to prevent **ksh** from sending a **HUP** signal to each of the given *job*s (or all active *job*s if *job* is omitted) when it terminates a login session.

Version: The **disown** command is available only on versions of **ksh** newer than the 11/16/88 version.

Return value: True.

jobs [**–lnp**] [*job...*]

Use **jobs** to display information about specified *job*s (or all active *jobs* if *job* is omitted) that the current **ksh** started. **ksh** displays:
- Job number, in [ ], with + in front of current job number, and – in front of previous job number.
- Status. **Running, Stopped, Done, Terminated**, etc.
- A number in ( ) after **Done** is the return value of that job. If there is no ( ) after **Done**, the return value is True.
- Command line. **ksh** obtains the command line from the history file. If **ksh** cannot access the history file, then it does not display the command line and displays <unknown job> instead.

If you specify **–l**, **ksh** displays process id's after the job number, in addition to the usual information.

If you specify **–n**, **ksh** displays only jobs whose status has changed since the last prompt and that have not as yet been reported.

If you specify **–p**, **ksh** displays only the process id's.

Return value: True.

Example
```
jobs -l
+[4] 139  Running            cc -c foo.c&
-[3] 465  Stopped            mail morris
 [2] 687  Done(1)            foo.bar&
jobs -p %m
465
```

kill [**–s** *signame*] *job...*
kill [**–n** *signum*] *job...*
kill [*–sig*] *job...*

Use **kill** to send a signal to the specified *job*s. This normally terminates processes that do not catch or ignore the signal.

Specify signal as one of the following:
signum   A signal number.
signame   A signal name (uppercase or lowercase). See **kill –l** (just below), to display the list of possible signal names.
sig   Either *signum* or *signame* with no space after the –.

If you do not specify **–s** *signame*, **–n** *signum*, or *–sig*, then **ksh** sends the **TERM** signal.

If the signal being sent is **TERM** (terminate) or **HUP** (hangup), then **ksh** first sends *job* a **CONT** (continue) signal if *job* is stopped.

Version: The **–n** and **–s** options are available only on versions of **ksh** newer than the 11/16/88 version.

Return value: Number of processes to which **kill** was unable to send the signal.

Example
```
kill -s HUP %cc
```

kill –l [*sig ...*]

Use **kill –l** without arguments to display signal names.

If you specify *sig* then, for each *sig* that is a:
- Name. **ksh** displays the respective signal number.
- Number. **ksh** displays the respective signal name. If *sig* > 255, then **ksh** displays the signal name corresponding to *sig* mod 256.

Version: *sig* arguments are available only on versions of **ksh** newer than the 11/16/88 version. Also, with the 11/16/88 version of **ksh**, signal numbers were also displayed.

Return value: False, if *sig* is an unrecognized signal name.

Example
```
kill -1        # Lists signals.
kill -1 HUP 1 257
1
HUP
HUP
```

wait [*job...*]

Use **wait** to have **ksh** wait for the specified *job*s to terminate.

ksh waits for the given process if you specify *job* as a number. Otherwise, **ksh** waits for all child processes of the specified *job* to terminate.

ksh waits for all currently active child processes to complete if you omit *job*.

Return value: Termination status of any previous background job waited for, not just the last one. *Version*: The termination status of the last process waited for was returned in older versions of **ksh**.

Examples
```
wait     # Waits for all background commands to complete.
wait %2  # Waits for job 2 to complete.  New version
```

```
            # only.
wait 346 # Waits for process 346 to complete.
wait $!  # Waits for last background process to complete.
```

MISCELLANEOUS

[†] : [*arg...*]   *Null Command*

Use : where you must have a command, as in the **then** condition of an **if** command, but you do not want the command to do anything.

The arguments to : are expanded. *Caution*: Parameter expansions can have side effects in the current environment.

Caution (Bourne shell): Some early versions of the Bourne shell did not have the comment syntax (**#**). Users therefore used this command to include a comment. However, unlike the real comment syntax, **ksh** splits the arguments of the : command into tokens, and expands them. Thus you should use the comment syntax for comments.

Return value: True.

Examples
```
: ${X=abc}
if    false
then  :
else  print $X
fi
abc
```

builtin [–ds] [–f *file*] [*pathname...*]

If *pathname* is not specified, and no **–f** option is specified, the built-ins are displayed on standard output. The **–s** option displays only the special built-ins.

Otherwise, the basename for each *pathname* determines the name of the built-in. For each *pathname*, **ksh** looks for a C language function that has been loaded into **ksh**, whose name is determined by prepending **b_** to the built-in name. If *pathname* contains a **/**, then the built-in is bound to this pathname. The built-in will only be executed if *pathname* is the first executable found during a path search.

[†] See page 209

On systems that support dynamic linking, the **–f** option names a shared library containing the code for built-ins. Once a library is loaded, its symbols become available for subsequent invocations of **builtin**. Multiple libraries can be specified with separate invocations of **builtin**. Libraries are searched in reverse of the order in which they are specified.

When a built-in command is invoked, the C language function **b_**$name$ is called with the same calling conventions as the C language **main** function, where *name* is the name of the built-in.

The **–d** option deletes each of the given built-ins. Special built-ins cannot be bound to a pathname or deleted.

Version: The **builtin** command is available only in versions of **ksh** newer than the 11/16/88 version.

Return value: True unless library cannot be loaded, a built-in *name* cannot be found, or you attempt to delete a special built-in.

Examples
```
type echo
echo is shell builtin
builtin -d echo
type echo
echo is a tracked alias for /bin/echo
```

false

Return value: False.

Version: The **false** command is a built-in only in versions of **ksh** newer than the 11/16/88 version. In older versions, **false** was an alias.

getconf [*name* [*pathname*]]

Without arguments, **getconf** prints a list of POSIX configuration parameters and their values. This list depends on the system that you are on. A pathname of **/** is used for any parameter that depends on the pathname.

If *name* is given, **getconf** prints the value of the given configuration parameter. The *pathname* argument is used for configuration parameters whose value depends on the path.

Version: The **getconf** command is available only in versions of **ksh** newer than the 11/16/88 version.

getopts [**–a** *name*] *optstring varname* [*arg...*]

getopts checks the argument list *arg* for legal options. If *arg* is omitted, **getopts** uses the positional parameters instead.

An option-argument begins with a –. An *arg* not beginning with a – indicates the end of options, as does the argument – –. If *optstring* begins with a + or :+, then **getopts** also recognizes option arguments that begin with a +.

optstring contains the option letters that **getopts** recognizes. If a letter is followed by a :, that option is expected to have an argument. The option can be separated from the argument by Spaces and/or Tabs. If a letter is followed by a #, that option is expected to have a numeric argument.

The : and # can be followed by a [*string*], which is used when generating a usage message. In addition, a Space terminates the option list and characters after the Space are appended in the usage message. If –**a** *name* is specified, it will be used in place of the function or script name in the usage message.

Each time you invoke **getopts**, it places the next option letter it finds in the variable *varname*. A + is prepended to *varname* if the option is found in an *arg* beginning with +. **ksh** stores the index of the next *arg* to be processed in the **OPTIND** variable. Whenever **ksh** or a script is invoked, **OPTIND** is initialized to 1. When an option requires an option-argument, **getopts** places it in the **OPTARG** variable.

A leading : in *optstring* affects the behavior of **getopts** when **getopts** encounters an option letter not in *optstring*. If *optstring* begins with :, **getopts** puts the letter in **OPTARG** and sets *varname* to ? for an unknown option, and sets *varname* to : when a required option argument is omitted. Otherwise, **getopts** displays an error message and sets *varname* to ?.

Version: The generation of usage messages, the –**a** option, the leading + in *optstring*, and the # for numeric option arguments are available only on versions of **ksh** newer than the 11/16/88 version. The 11/16/88 version of **ksh** behaved as if *optstring* began with +.

Return value: True until **getopts** encounters the end of options.

Examples
```
getopts -n foo 'ao:[outfile]n#[num]c [file]...' x '?'
Usage: foo [-ac] [-o outfile] [-n num] [file]...
while getopts "+abd:[delimiter] [file]" c
do  case $c in
    a)  aflag=1;;
    +a) aflag=;;
    b)  bflag=1;;
    +b) bflag=;;
    o)  oflag=$OPTARG;;
    esac
done
shift OPTIND-1
```

hist [−*e editor*] [−**nlr**] [*first* [*last*]]

hist provides access to your history file. Use **hist** to:
- Display commands from your history file; specify −l. An alternative is to use the preset alias **history** instead of **hist** −l.
- Edit and reexecute previous commands. Do not specify −l. **ksh** creates a file containing the commands that you specify, and invokes an editor on this file. **ksh** uses the editor as specified by the following sources, in the order listed:
  - *editor*
  - **HISTEDIT** variable
  - **FCEDIT** variable
  - **/bin/ed**

When you finish editing the commands, **ksh** reads, displays, and executes them.

first and *last* define the range of commands to which **hist** applies. **ksh** limits the number of previous commands that you can specify, to the value of the **HISTSIZE** variable. You can specify *first* and/or *last* as:
- Positive number, denotes command numbers.
- Negative number, is subtracted from current command number.
- String, denotes most recent command starting with specified string.
- *last* not specified. **ksh** defaults it to *first*.
- *first* and *last* not specified. **ksh** defaults as follows:
  first   −**16** if you specified −l. Otherwise, to −**1**.
  last   −**1** (the previous command).

You can also specify:
−**n** Suppresses command numbers when the commands are displayed.
−**r** Reverses order of the commands.

Version: The **hist** command is available only on versions of **ksh** newer than the 11/16/88 version. In older versions, the command was called **fc**.

Return value:
- Invalid arguments, False (1).
- Otherwise, if −l argument is specified, True. If not specified, value of last command is re-executed.

Examples
```
hist    # Invokes editor defined by HISTEDIT variable
        # (default /bin/ed) on the most recent command.
        # The command is executed when you finish editing.
hist -l # Lists the last 16 commands.
```

hist −**s** [*old=new*] [*command*]

Use this command to reexecute a previously entered command. **ksh** displays the command before reexecuting it.

Instead of this command, you can use the preset alias **r**, with or without *old=new* and *command*.

If you specify *old=new*, **ksh** replaces the string *old* with the string *new* before reexecuting it.

command specifies the command to be reexecuted. **ksh** limits the number of previous commands that you can specify, to the value of the **HISTSIZE** variable. You can specify *command* as:
- Positive number. Denotes command numbers.
- Negative number. Is subtracted from current command number.
- String. Denotes most recent command starting with specified string.
- Nothing. **ksh** defaults to the previous command.

Version: The **hist** command is available only on versions of **ksh** newer than the 11/16/88 version. In older versions, the command was called **fc**. The **–s** option is equivalent to **–e –** with the 11/16/88 version of **ksh**.

Return value: Return value of the re-executed command.

Examples
```
hist -s ${VISUAL-vi}
        # Same as above, except uses the editor defined
        # by the VISUAL variable, or defaults to vi.
r       # Displays and re-executes the most recent command.
r cc    # Displays and re-executes the most recent command
        # starting with cc.
r foo=bar cc
        # Finds the most recent command that starts with
        # cc, changes foo to bar, and displays and executes
        # the command.
```

let *arg...*

Use **let** to evaluate one or more arithmetic expressions.

ksh evaluates each *arg* as a separate arithmetic expression. Therefore, if you specify Spaces or Tabs within an arithmetic expression, you must quote them. Since many of the operators have special meaning to **ksh**, you must quote them.

You can use the command ((*arg* [,*arg*]...)) instead of **let** if you want to evaluate one or more expressions. When you use ((*arg* [,*arg*]...)) you do not have to quote the Spaces, Tabs, or any other special characters in *arg*. **ksh** processes them as if they were in grouping (double) quotes.

Return value:
- If value of last expression is non-zero, True.
- Otherwise, False (1).

Examples
```
let x=x+1 y=x%4+2
# The following script displays the first n lines of
# the standard input, where you can specify n as an
# optional argument whose default is 20.
typeset -i n=${1-20}              # Set n.
while let "--n >= 0" && read -r line # At most n lines.
do    print -r -- "$line"
done
```

† **newgrp** [*group*] [*arg...*]

newgrp is equivalent to **exec /bin/newgrp** *arg...*

Implementation-dependent: **newgrp** is only on systems that have a command **/bin/newgrp**. The command **/bin/newgrp** changes the group id of the process to the *group* that you specify.

Return value: This command does not return. If you specify an invalid group it may either cause the shell to terminate, or it will start ɩ new shell without changing the group.

Example
```
newgrp system     # Changes your group to system.
```

sleep *time*

Suspends execution for *time* seconds or fractions of seconds.

Examples
```
sleep 3600;date       # Runs date in an hour.
sleep .5              # Delay for a half second.
```

test [*expression*]

[[*expression*] **]**   ***Left Bracket Command***
Note: You must type the brackets shown in boldface.

Use **test** or [...] to check the type of a file, whether two pathnames are the same file, or permissions on files. Also use **test** or [...] to compare two files to see which is older or newer, to compare two strings, or to compare two arithmetic expressions.

test does not recognize the –– option to indicate the end of the option list.

Cautions:
- *expression* indicates all the arguments that together make up the *expression*. Each of the operators is a separate argument to **test** and [...].

----

† See page 209.

- **ksh** expands all of the words in the command before evaluating *expression*. Therefore you should use grouping quotes around words that are expanded. This will avoid errors due to words that expand to Null, due to words with embedded Spaces or Tabs, and due to words with embedded pathname expansion characters.
- The arguments to these commands can be ambiguous when an operand has the same representation as an operator, for example a file named =. Use the [[...]] command defined on page 167 to avoid these problems.
  Version: With versions of **ksh** newer than the 11/16/88 version, when expression contained three or fewer arguments (or four or fewer arguments when the first argument is !), the determination of which arguments are operators is based solely on the number of arguments.

Use any of the conditional expression primitives defined on page 139 to form *expression*. In addition, specify the following operators to combine these primitives within an *expression*:

!   Unary **negation** operator.
–a   Binary **and** operator.
–o   Binary **or** operator (**–a** has higher precedence than **–o**).
(*expression*)
        Parentheses for grouping. *Note*: Parentheses are **ksh** tokens. Therefore, you must quote them to use them as arguments to **test** or [...].

The [[...]] compound command makes **test** and [obsolescent.

Return value:

test evaluates *expression*. If the value is:
- True, returns True.
- Otherwise, returns False (1). **test** also returns False if you do not specify *expression*.

Examples
```
test -r "$x"      # Tests if value of x names a file that
                  # you can read.
if    [ -x "$file" -a ! -d "$file" ]
then  print "$file is an executable program"
fi
test x+1 -gt y  # True if x+1 is greater than y.
test X"$y" = X  # True if value of y is not set or is
                # Null. The reason for the X is that
                # the value of y might start with a -.
```

true

Use **true** where you must have a command, as in the **then** condition of an **if** command, but you do not want the command to do anything.

Version: The **true** command is a built-in only in versions of **ksh** newer than the 11/16/88 version. In older versions, **true** was an alias.

Return value: True.

whence [–afpv] *name*...

Use **whence** without –v to find the absolute pathname, if any, corresponding to each *name*. You can also use **whence** to find out what type of item each *name* is; specify –v (or use the preset alias **type**, which is defined as **whence –v**). For each *name* you specify, **ksh** displays a line that indicates if the *name* is:
- Reserved word
- Alias
- Built-in
- Undefined function
- Function
- Tracked alias
- Program
- Not found

If you specify –f, **ksh** does not check to see if *name* is a function.

If you specify –p, **ksh** does not check to see if *name* is a reserved word, a built-in, an alias, or a function.

If you specify –a, **ksh** displays all uses for *name*.

Version: The –a and –f options are available only in versions of **ksh** newer than the 11/16/88 version.

Return value: True if all *name*s are found, otherwise False.

Examples
```
whence vi      # Displays full pathname of vi.
/usr/bin/vi
whence -v vi
vi is a tracked alias for /usr/bin/vi
whence echo
echo
whence -v echo
echo is a shell builtin
whence -p echo
/bin/echo
type for
for is a reserved word
```

EXERCISES

1. What do each of the following built-in commands do?
   a. `print -r -- $PWD`
   b. `print "foo\tbar\c"`
   c. `kill -l`
   d. `kill -HUP %cc`
   e. `eval print \$$foo`
   f. `. foobar`
   g. `exec 3< foobar`
   h. `read -r -u3 foobar`
   i. `set -- "${a[@]}"`
   j. `set -s`
   k. `export foo`
   l. `typeset -Lu3 x=foobar`
   m. `alias foo`
   n. `unalias foo`
   o. `let x=x+1`
   p. `whence let`
   q. `test -r foobar`
   r. `[ X"$foo" = X"$bar" ]`
   s. `cd -`
   t. `cd foo bar`
   u. `umask`
   v. `umask 022`
   w. `shift 3`
   x. `set -x`
   y. `: ${foo?bar}`
   z. `jobs -l`

2. Write a built-in command to do each of the following:
   a. Display the current traps.
   b. Declare an integer variable.
   c. Declare a local variable in a function.
   d. Open a file to read on file descriptor 4.
   e. Read a line on file descriptor 4 and split it into three fields using **:** as a field delimiter.
   f. Cause a message to be displayed on standard error when a program is interrupted.
   g. Tell whether a pathname is a directory that you can write.
   h. Display all aliases.
   i. Unset all variables with the tagged attribute.
   j. Display the absolute pathname of the **date** command.
   k. Wait for the last background command to complete.
   l. Display the last positional parameter.
   m. Close file descriptor 4.
   n. Turn on execution tracing for a function named **foobar**.

3. Write an alias that repeats a range of commands stored in your history file. Hint: Use an "editor" that does nothing.

---

15   OTHER COMMANDS

The programs in this chapter are referred to elsewhere in this book, in the text, and/or in the examples. They exist on all UNIX systems and on many non-UNIX systems. If your system does not have any of them and you want to use them, you can write some of them in **ksh** language, and all of them in the C language.

Note: The descriptions here are not necessarily complete. They do, however, describe the features that are used by the examples in this book.

COMMANDS

cat [*file...*]

Concatenates one or more *file*(s) and writes their contents on standard output.

If you do not specify *file*, or if the argument – is encountered, **cat** reads from standard input.

Caution: Since **ksh** performs I/O redirection before **cat** is invoked, the command **cat** *file1 file2* > *file1* in the example below would not work as expected.

Example
```
cat file1              # Displays contents of file1.
cat file1 file2 > file3
                       # Concatenates file1 and file2,
                       # and places result in file3.
```

chmod *mode file...*

Changes file permissions according to *mode*. Only the owner of a file, or the superuser, may change its permissions.

Specify *mode* in the one of the following two formats:
• An octal number constructed from the bitwise or, of the following modes:
  4000   Set effective user id on execution.

2000   Set effective group id on execution. The group of
the file must correspond to your current group id,
in order for you to set the group id.

0400   Read by owner.

0200   Write by owner.

0100   Execute (search in directory) by owner.

0040   Read by group.

0020   Write by group.

0010   Execute (search in directory) by group.

0004   Read by others.

0002   Write by others.

0001   Execute (search in directory) by others.

- One or more of [*who*] *op* [*permission*] separated by a comma, where:

  who is a combination of the letters:

  u   User's permissions.

  g   Group permissions.

  o   Other permissions.

  a   Default if you do not specify *who*. Specifies user's, group, and other permissions.

  op is one of the following:

  +   Add *permission* to each *file*.

  −   Delete *permission* from each *file*.

  =   Assign *permission* to each *file*.

  permission can be any or all of:

  r   Read.

  w   Write.

  x   Execute.

  s   Set owner id and/or group id when used with **u** and/or **g**.

  Note: Omitting *permission* is useful only with **=**, to take away all permissions.

Examples

```
chmod o-w file1   # Denies write permission to others.
chmod +x file1    # Makes a file executable.
chmod 755 file1   # Sets permission on file1 to rwxr-xr-x.
```

cp *file... target*

Copies *file*(s) to *target*. *file* and *target* cannot refer to the same file.

If *target* is:

- Directory. *file*(s) are copied to that directory.
- File. Copying a file into *target* does not change the mode, owner, or group of the file. All links remain and the file is changed.
- Nonexistent. A new file is created with the same mode as *file*. The owner and group of *target* are those of the effective user and group.

Example
```
cp *.c newdir # Copies filenames in the current directory
              # ending in .c to directory newdir.
```

cut –f *list* [**–d** *delimiter*] [**–s**] [*file...*]

Concatenates only the specified list of fields from each line in one or more files with *delimiter*, and displays them on standard output.

list indicates the fields to be displayed. Specify *list* with field numbers or ranges (*low–high*) separated by commas. If *low* is omitted, then its default is field number 1. If *high* is omitted, then its default is the number of the last field.

options:
   –d *delimiter*
      The delimiter is the character that separates the fields.
      The default is Tab.
   –s   Lines with no delimiter characters are not displayed.

Example
```
ls -l | tr -s "\t" " " | cut -f1,9 -d" "
# Lists file permissions and files only.
```

cut –c *list* [*file...*]

Concatenates only the specified list of characters from each line in one or more files, and displays them on standard output.

list is specified the same way it is in **cut –f**.

Example
```
print "fools barter" > tempfile
cut -c 1-3,7,8,9 tempfile
foo bar
```

date [*+format*]

Displays date and time on standard output.

You can specify a *format* string preceded by a **+**, to display the date.
- All numeric output fields are of fixed size, zero-padded if needed.
- Each field descriptor is preceded by **%**, and is replaced in the output by its corresponding value. A single **%** is encoded by **% %**. All other characters are copied to the output without change.
- Some field descriptors:
   H   Hour   00 to 23
   M   Minute   00 to 59
   S   Second   00 to 59

Examples
```
date
Sat Aug 28 10:34:08 1993
date +%H:%M:%S
10:34:09
```

ed [–] [*file*]

ed is a line-oriented text editor for creating files consisting of any kind of alphanumeric text, adding or deleting text, locating a word or string of characters, moving lines of text around within a document or program, duplicating lines of text, and substituting words or strings of characters for other words or strings of characters.

ed operates on a copy of the file it is editing. Changes made to the copy have no effect on the file until a **w** (write) directive is given. The copy of the text being edited resides in a temporary file called the buffer. There is only one buffer.

file is the name of the file you wish to edit. If you do not specify *file*, **ed** will ask you to specify a pathname when you write the file.

Use – when the standard input is an editor script, to suppress the display of explanatory output.

Example
```
ed - foobar <<\!   # Prepends >> to each line of foobar.
1,$s/^/>> /
w
q
!
```

find *directory... expression*

Generates a list of all pathnames that are in each of the given *directory*(s), and applies *expression* to each of them.

expression indicates all of the arguments that together make up the expression. Each of the operators are separate arguments to **find**.

Some primitive *expression*(s):

–name *pattern*
> True if the last component of pathname matches the given *pattern*.

–perm *mode*
> True if the permission of the file matches *mode*.

–print Displays the pathname. Always True.

–type *t* True if the type of the file is *t*, where *t* is **d** for directory, or **f** for file.

–exec *command* [*arg*]... ;

>True if the executed command has a return value of zero.
Replaces *arg* {} with the current pathname.

–size [±] *n*

>True if file is size *n*.

–mtime [±] *n*

>True if file was modified in the last *n* days.

A + in front of a number means greater than. A − in front of a number means less than.

The following operators combine *expressions*:

! Unary **negation** operator.
–a Binary **and** operator.
–o Binary **or** operator (**–a** has higher precedence than **–o**).
(*expression*)

>Parentheses for grouping.

Quote *pattern*, ;, (, and) to prevent **ksh** from interpreting them.

Example
```
find / -type d -print   # Displays all directory names
                        # in the file system.
```

grep [*option...*] *pattern* [*file...*]

Searches the input *file*(s) (default is standard input), for lines matching regular expression *pattern*. Normally, each line found is copied to standard output. **grep** patterns are basic regular expressions by default, or extended regular expressions. *Caution*: Regular expressions use a different syntax than shell patterns. The **%P** format for **printf** converts an extended regular expression pattern to a shell pattern.

*option*s:

–E Pattern is an extended regular expression. Some systems have a separate command named **egrep** instead.

–c Prints a count of matching lines.

–e *pattern*

>Same as a simple *pattern*, but useful when the *pattern* begins with a −. Not available on all versions of **grep**.

–f *file*

>The *pattern* is taken from *file*. Not available on all versions of **grep**.

–i Ignores upper/lowercase distinction during comparisons.

–l Displays (once) only the names of files with matching lines, separated by Newlines.

–n Precedes each line by its relative line number in the file.

–s Suppresses error messages produced for nonexistent or unreadable files.

−v Displays all lines but those matching.

−x Displays only lines matched in their entirety. Not available on all versions of **grep**.

In all cases, the pathname is displayed if there is more than one input file. *Caution*: Take care when using characters that may also be meaningful to **ksh**. It is safest to enclose the entire *pattern* in literal (single) quotes.

Return value:
- True If any matches found.
- 1   If no matches found.
- 2   For syntax errors or inaccessible files (even if matches found).

Example
```
grep bar foobar
A foobar is defined as
law without the bar exam, therefore
```

ln [−s] *file... target*

Links *file*(s) to *target*. *file* and *target* cannot refer to the same file.

If *target* is a:
- Directory. For each *file* specified, a link, the name of which is the last component of *file*, is placed inside this directory.
- File. The file *target* must not exist and *file* must be a single argument.

On systems with symbolic links, −s indicates a symbolic link. In this case *file* represents the contents of the symbolic link to be created for *target*.

Example
```
ln $olddir/foobar $newdir
        # Creates filename foobar in $newdir that refers
        # to the same file as foobar in $olddir.
```

lp [*file...*]
lpr [*file...*]

Prints named *file*(s), or standard input if no file is specified, on a printer queue.

On some systems, this command is named **lp**. On other systems it is named **lpr**.

Example
```
lpr file1    # Prints file named file1.
```

ls [**–agltCF**] [*directory...*]

Displays the filenames in one or more *directories*, one filename per line. **ls** displays the contents of the current directory if you do not specify *directory*.

The meaning of the options is as follows:

–a Also displays filenames beginning with a . (dot).

–g Also displays the group ownership of the file.

–l Displays a longer listing that also shows its permission string, number of links, owner, group, size of the file, and the time that it was last modified.

–t Causes the filenames to be sorted by the time that they were last modified, most recent first.

–C Displays the filenames more than one to a line, using Tabs to separate the names. Some systems do this by default when displaying them to a terminal.

–F Displays directory names with a trailing /, executable files with a trailing *, and symbolic links with a trailing **@**.

Example
```
ls -l bin     # Displays a long listing for
              # files in bin.
```

mail [**–b**] [*user...*]

Sends or displays mail messages to and from users on your system or on other systems.

If you specify **–b**, the messages are displayed in a first-in, first-out order. ***Implementation-dependent***: Some systems use **–r** instead of **–b**.

Specify one or more *user*(s) if you want to send a message. The message will consist of all the characters on standard input until the end of file.

Example
```
mail morris <<!
We should finish the book and get it to the publisher ASAP.
!
```

mkdir [**–p**] [**–m** *mode*] *directory...*

Creates specified *directory*(s) with the permission specified by *mode*, or with permission 777 if *mode* is unspecified, less those permissions specified in the file creation mask.

mkdir requires write permission in the parent directory.

options:
   –m *mode*
      mode is specified by either a file permission mask or a file permission
      expression (see **chmod** command).
   –p   Creates any missing intermediate pathname components.

Return value:
- True, if all directories were successfully created.
- Otherwise, non-zero, and displays a diagnostic.

Example
```
mkdir -m g-r foobar
# Creates subdirectory foobar with read permission denied
# for the group in that subdirectory.
```

more [*file...*]

See **pg** on the next page.

mv [**–f**] *file... target*

Moves or renames *file*(s) to *target*. *file* and *target* cannot refer to the same file.

file may be a directory. On some systems the directories may be renamed
only if the two directories have the same parent, and *file* is renamed *target*.

If *target* is a directory, one or more *file*s are moved to that directory.

If *target* is a file, and if **mv** determines that the mode of *target* forbids writing,
it:
- Prints the file permissions. See **chmod**.
- Asks for a response.
- Reads standard input for one line. If the line begins with **y**, **mv** occurs if
  permissible. Otherwise, the command exits with a False return value. **mv**
  requires write permission in the directory to remove the old file. It does not
  require write permission for the file itself.
- Asks questions if standard input is a terminal and the **–f** option is not
  specified.

Example
```
mv /tmp/foo$$ savefile   # Moves /tmp/foo$$ to filename
                         # savefile in current directory.
```

paste [**–d** *list*] [**–s**] *file...*

Concatenates the corresponding lines of the input files, and then writes the
resulting lines to standard output.

options:

–d *list*
> Specifies zero or more characters with which to replace the Newline character. The default is the Tab character. When the list is exhausted, it is repeated in a circular manner.

–s   Concatenates the lines in command line order, and replaces the last line in each input file. If you specify **–d**, then the delimiter is reset to the first element of *list* after each file is processed.

file

The pathname of an input file. If no file operands are specified, or if a file operand is **–**, then standard input is used.

pg [*file...*]

Displays one or more files, a screenful at a time. If you do not specify *file*, **pg** displays its standard input. It normally pauses after each screenful, printing at the bottom of the screen. If you then press:

> ⌷RETURN⌷ Another screenful is displayed.
>
> **q**   **pg** exits.
>
> **h**   Displays help information.

Some systems use a command named **more** instead.

Example
```
ls -l | pg # Displays ls -l output a screenful at a time.
```

rm [**–f**] [**–r**] [**–i**] *file...*

Removes filename entries for *file*(s) from a directory. If an entry is the last link to the file, the file is destroyed. Removal of a filename requires write permission in its directory, but neither read nor write permission on the file itself.

If a file has no write permission and the standard input is a terminal, its permissions are displayed and a line is read from standard input. In the POSIX locale, if that line begins with **y**, the file is deleted. Otherwise, the file remains.

If standard input is a terminal and the **–f** option is not specified, **rm** asks questions.

file cannot refer to a directory unless you specify **–r**. **rm** recursively deletes the entire contents of the specified directory, and the directory itself.

If you specify **–i**, files are removed interactively. **rm** asks whether to delete each file and, under **–r**, whether to examine each directory.

It is forbidden to remove the filename **..** (dot dot) to avoid the consequences of inadvertently doing something like **rm –r .***.

Example
```
rm *.o  # Removes all files from current directory whose
        # names end with .o.
```

rmdir *directory...*

Removes one or more *directory*(s), which must be empty.

sort [*option...*] [*file...*]

Sorts lines in one or more file(s). If you do not specify *file*, **sort** uses its standard input.

*option*s:
- **+***n*   Skips the first *n* fields.
- **–b**   Ignores leading blanks.
- **–f**   Folds upper and lowercase letters.
- **–n**   Sorts by numeric value.
- **–o** *ofile*
  Puts output in *ofile*.
- **–t***c*   Uses *c* as the field delimiter character. Otherwise, fields are delimited by Spaces and Tabs.

Example
```
who | sort   # Sorts the output of the who command.
```

stty [**erase** *erase*]   [**kill** *kill*]   [**eof** *eof*]   [**int** *intr*]   [**quit** *quit*]

If you do not specify options, **stty** displays terminal settings. Otherwise, **stty** sets the characteristics that you specify. Different systems allow different settings to be specified.

There are many other terminal options and special characters that you can set with **stty**, for example, **tostop**.

Example
```
stty eof ^d # Sets the end-of-file character to ^d.
            # ^ indicates a control character.
```

tail [±*number*] [**–f**] [*file*]

Displays the last part of a file. Copies *file* to standard output, starting at a designated place. If *file* is not specified, standard input is used. Copying begins at distance +*number* of lines from the start, or –*number* from the end of the input. Specifying **–f** causes **tail** not to exit at the end of the file, but rather to wait and try to read repeatedly in case the file grows.

Example
```
ls -l | tail -3   # Displays last three lines of ls
                  # output.
```

tee [**–a**] *file...*

Reads standard input, and writes to standard output and *file*(s).

– a appends to *file*(s).

Example
```
date | tee file1 file2
# Writes date to standard output, file1, and file2.
```

tr [**–cds**]   [*string1* [*string2*]]

Transliterates characters in a file. Copies standard input to standard output, substituting or deleting characters based on *string1* and *string2*. Input characters in *string1* are mapped to corresponding characters in *string2*.

You can specify the following options:
–c   Complements the set of characters in *string1* with respect to the ASCII character set.
–d   Deletes input characters in *string1*.
–s   Squeezes multiple occurrences of characters in *string2*.

Example
```
tr "[a-z]" "[A-Z]" < filein > fileout
          # Changes characters in filein to uppercase.
          # Stores output in fileout.
```

tty

Displays the pathname of the terminal on standard output.

Example
```
tty
/dev/ttyp0
```

uniq [**–cdu**] [*input* [*output*]]

Copies lines from its input to its output, eliminating any adjacent lines that are duplicates.

You can specify the following options:
–c   Causes each line of the output to be preceded by the number of times that line appears. This option supersedes the **–d** and **–u** options.
–d   Displays duplicated line(s).
–u   Displays only lines that are not repeated.

Reads from standard input if you do not specify *input*.

Displays its output to standard output if you do not specify *output*.

wc [**–clw**] [*file...*]

Word count. Counts lines, words (a maximal string of characters delimited by Spaces, Tabs, or Newlines), and characters. It also keeps a total count for all named *file*(s).

–l, **–w**, **–c** causes only lines, words, and/or characters to be reported. Default is that all are reported.

file, if specified, causes pathnames to be printed along with the counts. Otherwise, count is taken from standard input.

Example
```
wc -l foobar   # Displays number of lines in foobar.
```

what *file...*

Looks for character strings in each of the *file*(s) prefixed by **@(#)** and displays them. **ksh** has a character string containing the version in this format.

Example
```
what $(whence ksh)
/bin/ksh:
     Version 12/28/93b
```

who [**am i**]

Displays the list of users who are currently logged onto your system, the filename of each terminal, and the time logged in. Use **am i** to restrict the listing to your own login.

Example
```
who am i
dgk     tty09     May 10 12:07
```

EXERCISES

1. Write a command that does each of the following:
    a. Displays the number of users currently logged onto the system.
    b. Displays all files in your home directory and subdirectories that have not been accessed in more than three days.
    c. Displays the last 10 lines in a file named **foo** that contains the string **bar**.
    d. Removes a file called **?*]**.
    e. Lists files in the working directory in order of increasing size.

2. What would be the effect of each of the following commands run in the order shown?

    a. `mkdir foobar`
    b. `date > foobar/foodate`
    c. `ln foobar/foodate foobar/bardate`
    d. `cat foobar/*date`
    e. `ls -1 foobar | tee foobar/out`
    f. `grep foo foo/*`
    g. `rm foobar/foodate`
    h. `chmod 600 foobar/out`
    i. `ls -lt foobar`
    j. `find foobar -type f -exec cat { } \;`
    k. `rm -f foobar`

16 INVOCATION AND ENVIRONMENT

This chapter specifies what **ksh** does when you invoke **ksh**, **ksh** scripts, and **ksh** functions. It also discusses what constitutes an environment for a **ksh** process, and how the **ksh** environment is shared or inherited across different types of invocations.

ENVIRONMENT

The environment of a **ksh** script or function is defined by:
- Open files.
- Access rights to files and processes.
- Working directory.
- Value of the file creation mask.
- Resources that you can set with **ulimit**.
- Current traps.
- Shell variables and attributes.
- Aliases.
- Functions.
- Option settings.

SHELL INVOCATION

ksh creates a new process each time that you invoke **ksh** explicitly, with or without arguments. You can also cause **ksh** to be invoked implicitly.

The items below are in the order that **ksh** sets up the environment.

Inheritance

A **ksh** child process inherits a copy of the environment of its parent process which includes:
- All the open files not set close-on-exec.

- Access rights to files and processes. **ksh** sets the effective user id of the process to the real user id of the process, and the effective group id of the process to the real group id of the process unless you invoke it with the **privileged** option (**–p**).
- The working directory.
- Value of the file creation mask.
- Values of resource limits.
- Signals that are ignored by the parent. **ksh** does not allow you to set traps for these signals.
- Signals not ignored by the parent process. **ksh** sets default actions for these, but they can be changed.
- Shell variables, with the exception of **IFS**, with the export attribute in the parent process, are inherited by the new **ksh** process. Other shell variables are not inherited. The attributes of the variables are also inherited.
- Alias definitions and function definitions are not inherited. You can put alias definitions in the environment file to cause interactive child processes to have access to them. Function definitions can be put in a directory defined in **FPATH** to make them accessible to child processes.
- Option settings are not directly inherited. However, option settings can be specified on the command line, and some option settings can be inherited indirectly through the value of exported variables.

Positional Parameters

ksh sets the positional parameters to the values of non-option arguments that you provide.

If you do not specify any non-option arguments to **ksh**, **ksh** sets parameter **0** to the name of **ksh**.

Otherwise, **ksh** sets parameter **0** to the first non-option argument, and the rest of the arguments become parameter **1**, **2**, **3**, etc.

Example
```
ksh -x -v prog abc
# Runs ksh with the x and v options.
# $0 is set to prog.
# $1 is set to abc.
```

Invocation Line Options

You can specify all of the options to the **set** command. You can also specify the following options at invocation:

–c *string*
> **ksh** reads commands from *string*.

–i   **ksh** runs as an interactive shell. In this case, the **QUIT** and **TERM** signals are ignored, and the **INT** signal is caught and causes the current command to be terminated and a new prompt to be issued.

–r   **ksh** runs as a restricted shell (see page 262).

–s   **ksh** reads commands from standard input. **ksh** automatically turns on the **–s** option if you do not specify the **–c** option, or any arguments to **ksh** other than options. **ksh** ignores the **–s** option if you specify **–c**.

–D   Displays the list of double quoted strings that are preceded by a **$** in the given script, but does not execute the script. *Version*: The **–D** option was not available with the 11/16/88 version of **ksh**.

ksh ignores an initial argument of **–** and since the **ksh** command follows the standard command conventions, **– –** terminates options and is otherwise ignored. Thus, you can use either **–** or **– –** to indicate an end of options to specify a first argument that begins with **–**.

ksh initially turns off all options that you do not specify, except that:

- **ksh** turns on the **interactive** option if you do not specify any non-option arguments to **ksh**, and standard input is directed from a terminal, and standard output is directed to a terminal.
- **ksh** turns on the **trackall** option.
- **ksh** turns on the **monitor** option if the **interactive** option is on, and if **ksh** can determine that the system can handle job control.
- **ksh** sets the **emacs**, **gmacs**, and/or **vi** options based on your settings of the **EDITOR** and **VISUAL** variables.
- **ksh** turns on the **bgnice** option. This is the default behavior when interactive.
- **ksh** sets the **restricted** option if the **SHELL** variable or the filename of the shell is **rsh**, **krsh**, or **rksh**.
- **ksh** turns on the **privileged** option if the effective user id of the process is not equal to the real user id of the process, or if the effective group id of the process is not equal to the real group id of the process.

Environment File

If the **privileged** (**–p**) option is:

- Off. If interactive, **ksh** expands the value of the **ENV** variable for parameter expansion. If the expansion yields the name of a file that you have permission to read, then **ksh** reads and executes each of the commands in this file in the current environment. *Version*: With the 11/16/88 version of **ksh**, the **ENV** file was also processed for non-interactive shells.
- On. If the file named **/etc/suid_profile** exists and **ksh** has permission to read this file, then **ksh** reads and executes each of the commands in this file in the current environment.

To cause alias definitions to be in effect for all interactive invocations of **ksh**, you must put them in your **ENV** file.

History File

For interactive shells, **ksh** opens or creates the history file at the earlier of:
• The first function definition it reads while the **nolog** option is off.
• After the environment file has been read and executed.

For non-interactive shells, **ksh** opens or creates the history file when it is first referenced, for example, with **read –s** or **print –s**.

LOGIN SHELLS

If the name of the **ksh** program starts with a – (minus), then **ksh** is a login shell. A login shell is the same as a regular **ksh** invocation except that:
• You cannot specify any non-option arguments.
• **ksh** reads and executes the file **/etc/profile** if it exists. This file is created by the system administrator.
• If the **privileged** option is off, then **ksh** reads and executes the commands from the file defined by expanding **${HOME:–.}/.profile**.

These profile files are read and executed one command at a time, so that aliases defined in these files affect subsequent commands in the same file.

RESTRICTED SHELLS

A restricted shell is an execution environment that is more controlled than that of the standard **ksh** shell. With a restricted shell you cannot:
• Change the working directory.
• Set the value or attributes of **SHELL**, **ENV**, or **PATH** variables.
• Specify the pathname of a command with a **/** in it.
• Redirect output of a command with **>** , **>|**, **<>**, or **>>**.
• Add built-in commands.

These restrictions do not apply when **ksh** processes the **.profile** file, and the file defined by the **ENV** variable.

If a restricted shell executes a shell script, **ksh** executes it in a non-restricted environment.

SHELL SCRIPTS

A script can be invoked by name or as the first argument to **ksh**. Except as listed in the next paragraph, invoking a script by name does not cause a separate invocation of **ksh** on most systems. Scripts invoked by name take less time to begin.

Shell scripts are carried out as a separate invocation of **ksh** when:
- The script has execute permission but does not have read permission.
- The script has the setuid or setgid permission set.
- *System-dependent*: On some systems, all shell scripts are carried out as a separate invocation of **ksh** for all scripts whose first line begins with the characters **#!** followed by the pathname for **ksh**. The characters after the **#!** define the interpreter to run to process the script.

When **ksh** executes a script without a separate **ksh** invocation:
- The history file is inherited.
- Exported arrays are inherited.

A script runs until it:
- Has no more commands left to run.
- Runs the **exit** command.
- Runs the **return** command when outside a function.
- Runs the **exec** command with an argument. In this case the script will be replaced by the program defined by the first argument to **exec**.
- Detects one of the errors listed on page 209 while processing a built-in command listed with a dagger.
- Receives a signal that is not being ignored, for which no trap has been set, and that normally causes a process to terminate.
- Exits from a command with a False return value while the **errexit** option is on and no **ERR** trap has been set.

SUBSHELLS

A subshell is a separate environment that is a copy of the parent shell environment. Changes made to the subshell environment do not affect the parent environment. A subshell environment need not be a separate process.

ksh creates subshells to carry out:
- (...) commands.
- Command substitution.
- Co-processes.
- Background processes.
- Each element of a pipeline except the last.

SHELL FUNCTIONS

Shell functions defined with the **function** reserved word share all of the environment with the calling process except:
- Variable assignments that are part of the call.
- Positional parameters.
- Option settings.
- Variables declared within the function with **typeset**.

DOT SCRIPTS

A dot script is a script that is specified with the **.** (dot) command. A dot script is read in its entirety and then expanded and executed in the current process environment. Thus, any aliases defined in such a script do not affect subsequent commands in the same script. A syntax error in a dot script causes the script that referenced it to terminate.

Arguments specified with the **.** (dot) command replace the positional parameters while executing the **.** script   *Version*: With the 11/16/88 version of **ksh**, the positional parameters were not restored after executing the **.** script.

POSIX FUNCTIONS

A function defined with the *name*( ) syntax, is expanded and executed in the current process environment just as a **.** (dot) script.

Arguments specified with the function replace the positional parameters while executing the function. *Version*: With the 11/16/88 version of **ksh**, functions with the *name*( ) syntax were executed in the same environment as functions defined with the **function** reserved word.

BUILT-IN COMMANDS

Each built-in is evaluated in the current process environment.

I/O redirection applied to built-ins other than **exec** do not affect the current environment.

Variable assignments for built-ins denoted by a † in the *Built-in Commands* chapter affect the current environment. Other assignments affect only the specific built-in.

PART V

APPLICATION
PROGRAMMING

17 SHELL FUNCTIONS AND PROGRAMS

This chapter contains several functions and programs written in the KornShell language. They are included here primarily for illustrative purposes. However, you may find some of these functions and/or programs useful.

SAMPLE LOGIN PROFILE

```
#
# This is a sample KornShell login profile
#

# First set and export the following:

set -o allexport
ENV=$HOME/.envfile
PATH=$HOME/bin:${PATH#:}:          FPATH=$HOME/fundir
HISTFILE=$HOME/sh_history          HISTSIZE=250
LOGNAME=${LOGNAME:-${HOME##*/}}
MAIL=/usr/spool/mail/$LOGNAME
MAILPATH=~uucp/$LOGNAME:$MAIL   MAILCHECK=60
EDITOR=$(whence vi)
PAGER=$(whence pg) || PAGER=$(whence more)
CDPATH=:$HOME:/usr
PWD=$HOME OLDPWD=$HOME
set +o allexport

# Put first character of hostname into prompt
# Different systems have different ways to get hostname
# Here we try them all
typeset -uxL1 HOSTCHAR=$( {
                    uname -n || hostname ||
                    cat /etc/whoami || print '?'
```

```
                              } 2>/dev/null
                      )

# Put first character of hostname and working directory into
# the prompt
PS1="$HOSTCHAR"':${PWD#$HOME/}:!$ '

# Initialize options
set -o ignoreeof

# Set the terminal the way I like it
stty intr '^?' erase '^h' kill '^x'

# Find out what terminal I am on
export COLUMNS=80 LINES=24 TERM TERMCAP
case $TERM in
""|dialup|network)
        if    [[ $(whence termid) != "" ]]
        then  TERM=$(termid)
        else  PS3='Please enter number or terminal name: '
              select TERM in hp2621 4014 vt100 \
                     ansi 630 vt52 xterm
              do  TERM=${TERM:-$REPLY}
                  break
              done
        fi
        ;;
esac

# Special terminal setups

case $TERM in
2621|hp*)
        stty cr0 nl0 tabs; tabs
        ;;
4014|tek)
        stty cr0 nl0 -tabs ff1
        print "\033;\c"
        ;;
630)    LINES=${LINES:-68} COLUMNS=${COLUMNS:-92}
        export DMD=/usr/add-on/630 DMDSGS
        ;;
esac
```

```
case $DMD in
"")     break;;
*)      DMDSGS=$DMD PATH=$PATH:$DMD/bin;;
esac
umask go-w    # Set file creation mask.
```

SAMPLE ENVIRONMENT FILE

```
#
# This is a sample ENV file
#

# set options
set -o trackall  # no longer necessary
# set up aliases and functions
alias  sh=${SHELL:-/bin/sh} \
       suspend='kill -STOP $$' \
       nmake=~gsf/bin/nmake
# Unnecessary to test for interactive with versions
# of ksh newer than 11/16/88.
case $- in
*i*)    # interactive
        alias cx='chmod +x' \
            h='fc -l'
        autoload 1 dirs _cd mcd
        alias cd=_cd;;
esac


# The following function allows you to list files in
# columns. It may be faster than ls.
# If you also want to make the function available to
# non-interactive shells, you must put it into a file
# named "l" in a directory that is in your FPATH list
# such as $HOME/fundir.

        function l   # list files in columns
        {
            set -o markdirs
            if    [[ $# = 1  &&  -d $1 ]]
            then  cd "$1"
                  trap 'cd $OLDPWD' EXIT
                  set --
            fi
            PS3=
            typeset i
```

```
            select i in ${@-*}
            do    :
            done < /dev/null
    }
```

pushd, popd, *AND* dirs

These functions show how you can define functions to provide the C shell directory management interface. Compare them to the directory manipulation functions in the next section.

Three **ksh** functions provide the C shell directory stack management interface. The function:

pushd   When you specify:
- A pathname, **pushd** changes the working directory to this pathname and pushes the previous working directory onto the stack.
- No argument, **pushd** exchanges the top two elements of the directory stack and changes back to the previous working directory.
- +*n*, **pushd** rotates the whole stack so that the *n*th argument of the directory stack becomes the top element and changes the working directory to it.

popd   When you specify:
- No argument, **popd** removes the previous working directory from the directory stack and changes the working directory to it.
- +*n*, **popd** deletes the *n*th previous working directory from the stack.

dirs   Displays the current directory stack starting from the working directory.

```
#
# DIRECTORY MANIPULATION FUNCTIONS pushd, popd AND dirs
#
# Uses global variables _push_max _push_top _push_stack
integer _push_max=100 _push_top=100
```

dirs

```
# Changes home directory to ~
# Shares variable dir with caller
function to_tilde
{
    case $dir in
    $HOME)
        dir=\~ ;;
    /*) ;;
```

```
        *)   dir=\~/$dir;;
        esac
}

# Display directory stack -- $HOME displayed as ~
function dirs
{
    typeset dir=${PWD#$HOME/}
    to_tilde
    print -r -- "$dir ${_push_stack[@]}"
}
```

pushd [*directory*]
pushd +*n*

```
# Change directory and put directory on front of stack
function pushd
{
    typeset dir= type=0
    integer i
    case $1 in
    "") # pushd
        if    ((_push_top >= _push_max))
        then  print -u2 pushd: No other directory.
              return 1
        fi
        type=1 dir=${_push_stack[_push_top]}
        ;;
    +[1-9]*([0-9])) # pushd +n
        integer i=_push_top$1-1  # Note, $1 contains +n
        if    ((i >= _push_max))
        then  print -u2 pushd: Directory stack not that deep
              return 1
        fi
        type=2 dir=${_push_stack[i]}
        ;;
    *)  if    ((_push_top <= 0))
        then  print -u2 pushd: Directory stack overflow.
              return 1
        fi;;
    esac
    case $dir in
    ~*)   dir=$HOME${dir#~};;
    esac
    cd "${dir:-$1}" || return 1
    dir=${OLDPWD#$HOME/}
    to_tilde
```

```
        case $type in
        0) # pushd name
            _push_stack[_push_top=_push_top-1]=$dir
            ;;
        1) # pushd
            _push_stack[_push_top]=$dir
            ;;
        2) # push +n
            type=${1#+} i=_push_top-1
            set -- "${_push_stack[@]}" "$dir" "${_push_stack[@]}"
            shift $type
            for dir
            do  (((i=i+1) < _push_max)) || break
                _push_stack[i]=$dir
            done;;
        esac
        dirs
    }
```

popd [+*n*]

```
# Pops the top directory
function popd
{
    typeset dir
    if    ((_push_top >= _push_max))
    then  print -u2 popd: Nothing to pop.
          return 1
    fi
    case $1 in
    "")
        dir=${_push_stack[_push_top]}
        case $dir in
        ~*)    dir=$HOME${dir#~}
        esac
        cd "$dir"
        ;;
    +[1-9]*([0-9]))
        integer i=_push_top$1-1
        if    ((i >= _push_max))
        then  print -u2 pushd: Directory stack not that deep
              return 1
        fi
        while ((i > _push_top))
        do _push_stack[i]=${_push_stack[i-1]}
              (( i -= 1 ))
```

```
        done
        ;;
    *)  print pushd: Bad directory.
        return 1;;
    esac
    unset _push_stack[_push_top]
    (( _push_top += 1))
    dirs
}
```

AN ENHANCED cd INTERFACE

These functions provide an alternative to the C shell directory stack interface routines. We use an alias to replace the **cd** command with an upward compatible function. Thus, you can continue to use **cd** and still benefit from the directory stack.

This directory stack management interface consists of three functions and an alias. The function:

_cd   When you specify:
- −*n*. **_cd** changes back to the *n*th previous working directory.
- *n*. Changes to the *n*th directory displayed with the **dirs** function.
- Anything else. **_cd** changes the working directory exactly the same as **cd** and saves the previous working directory onto a stack. If there are more directories than specified with the **CDSTACK** variable, the least recently referenced directory is removed from the list.

mcd   Displays a menu of the directories it has saved, each preceded by a number. You can then enter the number of a previous directory, or the name of a new directory to change the directory.

dirs   Displays the current directory stack, starting from the working directory.

The alias **cd** is defined to **_cd**.

To make these functions accessible, you must put them in the function path so that **autoload** can find them. You can put them in a file named "dirs" and then link the filenames "mcd" and "_cd" to that file. These filenames must be in a directory in your **FPATH** list, such as **$HOME/fundir**.

```
#
# DIRECTORY MANIPULATION FUNCTIONS, REPLACES CD
#
# Uses global variables _push_max _push_top _push_stack
integer _push_max=${CDSTACK:-32} _push_top=${CDSTACK:-32}
unalias cd
alias cd=_cd
# Display directory stack -- $HOME displayed as ~
```

```
function dirs
{
    typeset dir="${PWD#$HOME/}"
    case $dir in
    $HOME)
        dir=\~
        ;;
    /*) ;;
    *)  dir=\~/$dir;;
    esac
    PS3=
    select i in "$dir" "${_push_stack[@]}"
    do  :
    done < /dev/null
}

# Change directory and put directory on front of stack
function _cd
{
    typeset dir=
    integer n=0 type=4
    case $1 in
    -|-1|2) # cd -
        n=_push_top type=1
        ;;
    -[1-9]*([0-9])) # cd -n
        n=_push_top+${1#-}-1 type=2
        ;;
    1)  # keep present directory
        print -r -- "$PWD"
        return
        ;;
    [1-9]*([0-9])) # cd n
        n=_push_top+${1}-2 type=2
        ;;
    *)  if    ((_push_top <= 0))
        then  type=3 n=_push_max
        fi;;
    esac
    if    ((type <3 ))
    then  if    ((n >= _push_max))
          then  print cd: Directory stack not that deep.
                return 1
          else  dir=${_push_stack[n]}
          fi
```

```
        fi
        case $dir in
        ~*)    dir=$HOME${dir#~};;
        esac
        # \cd prevents alias substitution.
        # You can use command cd with 12/28/93 and newer.
        \cd "${dir:-$@}" > /dev/null || return 1
        dir=${OLDPWD#$HOME/}
        case $dir in
        $HOME)
            dir=\~
            ;;
        /*) ;;
        *)  dir=\~/$dir;;
        esac
        case $type in
        1)   # swap first two elements
            _push_stack[_push_top]=$dir
            ;;
        2|3)  # put $dir on top and shift down by one until top
            integer i=_push_top
            for dir in "$dir" "${_push_stack[@]}"
            do  ((i > n)) && break
                _push_stack[i]=$dir
                (( i += 1))
            done
            ;;
        4)   # push name
            _push_stack[_push_top=_push_top-1]=$dir
            ;;
        esac
        print -r -- "$PWD"
}


# Menu-driven change directory command
function mcd
{
        typeset dir="${PWD#$HOME/}"
        case $dir in
        $HOME)
            dir=\~
            ;;
        /*) ;;
        *)  dir=\~/$dir;;
        esac
```

```
        PS3='Select by number or enter a name: '
        select dir in "$dir" "${_push_stack[@]}"
        do  if     _cd $REPLY
            then   return
            fi
        done
}
```

SHELL VERSION OF cat *COMMAND*

```
#
#       SHELL VERSION OF cat COMMAND
#
alias open=exec                         # more descriptive
alias duplicate=exec                    # more descriptive
set -o noglob                           # no pathname expansion
for i                                   # do for each file
[[ -z $1 ]] && set -- -                 # use - if no arguments
do  if      [[ $i != - ]]               # - is standard input
        then    open 3< $i
        else    duplicate 3<&0          # use standard input
        fi
        IFS=
        while read -u3 -r line          # read in a line
        do      print -r -- "$line"     # print out the line
        done
done
exec 3<&-                               # close file
```

SHELL VERSION OF grep *COMMAND*

```
#
#       SHELL VERSION OF grep
#
USAGE="Usage: grep -vxcln [ -ef ] pattern file ..."

vflag= xflag= cflag= lflag= nflag=      # switch flags set off
set -f                                  # path expansion off

while getopts :vxclne:f: arg
do      case $arg in
```

```
            v)  vflag=on;;                  # lines not matched
            x)  xflag=on;;                  # exact match
            c)  cflag=on;;                  # count of matches
            l)  lflag=on;;                  # only file pathnames
            n)  nflag=on;;                  # print line number
            e)  expr=$OPTARG; arg=;;
            f)  expr=$(< $OPTARG); arg=;;   # get expr from file
            \?)print -u2 "${0##*/}: -$OPTARG: unknown option"
               print $USAGE; exit 1;;
         esac
done

shift $((OPTIND - 1))                    # get nonswitch args

if    [[ $expr = "" ]]
then  expr="$1"; shift
fi
[[ -n $xflag ]] || expr="*${expr}*"   # do if not exact match

noprint=$vflag$cflag$lflag             # don't print if set
integer n=0 c=0 tc=0 tn=0 nargs=$#     # initialize counters

# n  = current line number of text
# tn = total number of lines out of all files
# c  = counter of pattern matches for each file
# tc = total number of pattern matches

for i in "$@"''                        # all files until null
do     if    ((nargs <= 1))
       then  fname=''
       else  fname=$i:
       fi
       [[ -n $i ]] &&  exec 0< $i       # open file if needed
       while read -r line               # read line from file
       do    ((n = n + 1))
             case  $line in
             $expr)if    [[ $noprint = "" ]]
                   then  print -r "$fname${nflag:+$n:}$line"
                   fi
                   ((c = c + 1)) ;;   # line matches pattern

                *)if  [[ $vflag = on ]]
                  then if    [[ $cflag = "" ]]
                       then  print -r "$fname${nflag:+$n:}$line"
                       fi
```

```
                fi;;                # not a match
            esac
        done

        if      [[ $lflag = on ]] && ((c > 0))
        then    print -r "$i"       # print filename
        fi
        ((tc += c))                 # total # matches
        ((tn += n))                 # total # lines
        n=0 c=0                     # reinitialize counters
done

if      [[ $cflag = on ]]
then    [[ -n $vflag ]] && ((tc -= tn))
        print $tc                   # print total # matches
fi
let tc                              # set the return value
```

SHELL VERSION OF nohup COMMAND

```
#
#       SHELL VERSION OF nohup COMMAND
#
trap '' HUP                         # ignore hangup
set -o trackall
command=$(whence "$1")
oldmask=$(umask)
umask u=rw,og=                      # default mode for nohup.out
exec 0< /dev/null                   # disconnect input
if      [[ -t 1 ]]                  # redirect output if necessary
then    if      [[ -w . ]]          # file exists and is writable
        then    echo 'Sending output to nohup.out'
                exec >> nohup.out
        else    echo "Sending output to $HOME/nohup.out"
                exec >> $HOME/nohup.out
        fi
fi
umask "$oldmask"
if      [[ -t 2 ]]                  # direct unit 2 to a file
then    exec 2>&1
fi
```

```
# run the command
case $command in
*/*)   exec "$@"
       ;;
*)     "$@"
       ;;
esac
```

SHELL LINE COUNT PROFILER

The following script takes the name of a script and the arguments to the script.
It runs the script and then produces a report that shows how many times each line
in the script was executed.

It works by creating a script that sets a **DEBUG** trap for each line. The **DEBUG**
trap increments a count in an array indexed by **LINENO**.

```
# A shell line profiler
TMPFILE=${TMP-/tmp}/shprof$$
trap 'rm -f $TMPFILE' EXIT
function err_exit
{
      print -u2 "$@"
      exit 1
}
#create equivalent script with profiling enabled
cat > $TMPFILE <<- \EOF
      integer _line
      if    ( _line[4095]=0 ) 2> /dev/null
      then  _MAXARRAY=4095
      else  _MAXARRAY=1023
      fi
      readonly _MAXARRAY
      function _profend
      {
            integer i=1
            typeset file
            typeset -R7 count
            file=$(whence "$1")
            if    [[ $file = '' ]]
            then  file=$1
            fi
            print -u2 "*** line profile for $1 ***"
```

```
                  while  read -r -u4 && (( i < _MAXARRAY ))
                  do     if    ((count=_line[i]))
                         then    print -u2 "$count $i: $REPLY"
                         fi
                         i=i+1
                  done 4< $file
         }
         _command=$1
         shift
         integer i=1
         # could use arithmetic for loop with 12/28/93 version
         while (( i < _MAXARRAY ))
         do     _line[i]=0 i=i+1
         done
         unset i
         trap "_profend $_command" EXIT
         _line[1]=-1
         LINENO=0
         trap "((_line[LINENO]+=1))" DEBUG
EOF
file=$(whence "$1")
cat  "${file-$1}" >> $TMPFILE || err_exit "$1: cannot open"
chmod +x $TMPFILE
if     ( exec -a foo /bin/echo ) > /dev/null 2>&1
then   dollar0="-a $1"            # set $0 if possible
fi
exec $dollar0 $TMPFILE "$@"
```

EXERCISES

1. Modify the function **_cd** so that it executes a script named **.enter** when it enters a directory, and a script **.leave** when it leaves it.

2. Modify the new **cd** function so that it uses a circular stack instead of the downward growing stack. What advantages does this have?

3. Write the **wc** command as a shell function.

4. Suppose that you are on a system that does not have the **cp** command. It only has a command named **copy** that takes two arguments; a source file that must exist; and a destination file that must not exist. Write the **cp** command for this machine.

5. Write a command that generates all the pathnames of files starting from a specified directory, and executes a specified action for each pathname. The action can be specified as a function.

6. Write a function named **optparse** that takes an option string in the format used by **getopts**, the name of the command, and the arguments to the command, and does the option parsing. The routine should create an associative array named **.options** whose subscripts consist of any option that was specified, and whose values are the value of the option arguments given. The function should shift the arguments of the calling routine to eliminate option arguments.

7. Modify the **pushd**, **popd**, and **dirs** functions to use a single compound variable named **.push** for the global variables.

8. Write a command to compare two files and print out the first line of each where they differ.

9. Write a command that does arithmetic on roman numerals. The answer should also be in roman numerals.

10. Write a command that takes any number of single letters as arguments and displays all word combinations of these letters in alphabetic order, one per line. Do not use any of the commands in the *Other Commands* chapter.

11. Write a command that can quiz you on any number of subjects. Each subject is a file consisting of lines, where each line contains a question, followed by the number of the correct answer, followed by the list of choices, each separated by a **:**. All quizzes should be stored in the same directory.
    The command should take the subject to be quizzed on as an argument, and should then present each question and the choices to the user. After two tries, the user should be told the correct answer. At the end of the quiz the user should be given a score, both as a raw score and as a percent. The raw score is obtained by giving one point for each correct answer, and one-half point for each question answered correctly on the second try.

12. Write a command to display a list of files where each file begins on a separate page. Each page should have a heading that defaults to the name of the file left-justified on the left top of the page, and the date the file was last modified, right-justified on the right. Each line of each file should be numbered starting at 1. The command should allow option arguments:

−l *pagelength*	To specify the page length, default 60.
−w *pagewidth*	To specify the page width, default 80.
−h *string*	To specify the heading.

18 A COMPLETE APPLICATION

This chapter contains an example of how you can use **ksh** as a high-level programming language to program an application. The example that we use is a slightly modified version of the MH (Message Handling) system. MH was originally written at the Rand Corporation in the C language. It was later modified by the Department of Information and Computer Science at the University of California, Irvine. We have rewritten it in **ksh** for this book.

We chose MH because it is in the public domain, and because it illustrates many of the features of **ksh** as a high-level programming language. It is a useful system that you might want to adapt and install on your system for your actual use. Of course, this certainly is not necessary for you to understand and use **ksh**. MH is a moderately sized application; the source code for the MH system consists of tens of thousands of lines of C code. By comparison, the **ksh** implementation contains fewer than 800 lines of code.

Disclaimer: Although we believe that the MH code in this chapter should work if you correctly adapt and install it on your system, we make no claims for it, do not support it, and do not supply it in machine-readable form.

THE MH MESSAGE HANDLING SYSTEM

With MH you can send messages to other people on your system, and you can read messages that other people send to you. Depending on how things have been set up on your system, it may be possible for you to send messages to people on remote systems. You can also reply to messages that you have received, review them, organize them in folders, and delete them.

MH differs from other mail programs in that it is composed of many small programs instead of just one very large program. Among new users this sometimes causes some confusion along the lines of, What program do I run? With MH, you use **ksh** to invoke one command at a time. This means that when you handle mail, the entire power of **ksh** is at your disposal in addition to the facilities that MH provides.

Summary of Commands

The minimal list of MH commands that you can get by with (the complete list of commands in this book) is:

comp   Composes a new message to send.
folder   Tells you what the current folder is.
folders   Lists all folders.
inc   Incorporates mail (gets new mail).
next   Shows the next message.
prev   Shows the previous message.
refile   Files messages in folders.
repl   Replies to a received message.
rmm   Removes a message.
scan   Scans a folder and displays a summary of what is in it.
show   Shows the current message.

Messages and Folders

A message takes the form of a memorandum, and is composed of two major parts: A header, which contains information such as "To" and "From" addresses, "Subject," "Date," etc.; and the body, which is the actual text of the message. Each component in the header starts with a keyword followed by a **:** (colon) and additional information. If header lines continue past one line, then each subsequent line begins with one or more leading Spaces or Tabs. For example, in the message

```
Date: 12 Aug 92 11:21:34 EST (Wed)
To: ihnp4!ulysses!dgk
Subject: Software Development Environments
From: cbosgd!pds (Pat Sullivan)

This is the text.
```

There are four header items, and one line of text in the body. Note that a blank line separates the body from the headers.

MH stores a message as an ordinary file in a directory. This directory is called a folder. If you choose to keep and organize your messages, you may create as many folders as you wish. There is no limit to the number of messages in a folder. Typically, messages are numbered from 1 up.

All of your personal folders, along with some other information that MH needs to know, are kept in a special directory that you can specify, whose default is called **Mail** under your home directory. Normally, MH manages these files and directories automatically, so that you need not work with them directly unless you really want to.

Reading New Mail

When you are notified that you have mail (usually when you log in), perhaps with the message, "You have mail", then you know that messages are waiting in your system mailbox. To read these messages, you first have to incorporate the mail into your in-box by typing the command **inc**.

This incorporates the new mail from your system mailbox to your in-box, which is a folder named, naturally enough, **+inbox**.

As **inc** incorporates your new mail, it generates a scan listing of the mail. A scan list contains one line per message that consists of the message number, the month and day, the sender, and the first few characters of the message. The current message is indicated by a + after the message number.

```
Incorporating new mail into inbox...
2+  10/10 gsf               nmake <<A new version of nmak
3   10/10 ..!ulysses!dgk ksh <<I found a bug in the la
4   10/11 root             space << Please clean up any
```

Each time **inc** is invoked, any new messages are added to the end of your **+inbox** folder.

To read the first message, use the **show** command. This displays the current message. To read each subsequent message, use the **next** command.

If you want to back up, the **prev** command shows the previous message.

Another way to read your messages is to name them all at once with **show all**. This command displays them all, one after the other.

The **all** argument to **show,** above, might also be replaced with **next** or **prev**, as in **show next** or **show prev**, which are respectively equivalent to the **next** and **prev** commands.

If you have had occasion to type **inc** more than once, then you will find that **show all** is showing not only the new messages, but also the old messages that you have already seen. Therefore, you might find it better to use **show cur–last** instead. This command displays messages from the current message (**cur**), to the last message (**last**). Each time **inc** is invoked, it makes the first new message the current message.

It should be noted here that the name **all** given in a previous example, is equivalent to the message range **first–last**, where **first** is the name of the first message in **+inbox**. Also, **show** by itself is equivalent to **show cur**.

As mentioned earlier, with **ksh** as your interface to MH, it becomes easy to list a message on a line printer or to another file. For example, **show all | lpr** (or **show all | lp** on some systems) sends all the messages in the current folder to the line printer.

To summarize, the preceding discussion has introduced these important concepts:
- Folders (in particular, the **+inbox** folder).
- Messages.
- Message names (e.g., **prev**, **next**, **cur**, **first**, **last**).
- Message ranges (e.g., **cur–last**, **all**).

More will be said about folders and messages in following sections.

Originating Messages

To create a message draft from scratch, use the **comp** command. You will be placed in whatever editor you specify, with a default header template that you must fill in. If you make a mistake, you may correct it later with a text editor. The draft will be sent only if you give an explicit request before you exit this command, so you do not have to worry about the draft getting away from you prematurely.

To start, you simply type **comp**. The default draft template contains the following header fields:

To: Type the address of the person to whom you wish the message sent. If this person is on the same system as you, then that person's login id should serve as the address (e.g., **morris** or **dgk**). A discussion of addresses outside your system is beyond the scope of this book.

cc: "Carbon copy" (an archaism) address. It is customary, but not required, to put your own address here so that you get a copy of the message when it is sent. To put more than one address in the **To:** and/or **cc:** components, just use a **,** (comma) between each address on a line.

Subject:
A line of any descriptive text will do.

The subject line is followed by a dashed line, and you are then expected to type the body of the message. When you finish, just exit your editor in the customary fashion.

Caution:
- While in the editor, do not delete colons in the headers or change the spelling of **To:**, **cc:**, or **Subject:**, and do not leave blank lines between these lines.
- Feel free to change the addresses that you typed previously, or to add these lines if they are missing.
- Do not delete the dashes that separate the header lines from the text of the message.
- Do not add additional header lines unless you understand precisely what you are doing. This means particularly that you should not type or fill in a **From:** line. When the message is sent, the system automatically adds this line.
- Also, you should not type a **Date:** line in the header. When the message is sent, the system automatically adds the current date and time.

An example of a complete message draft, as it appears on your screen, might be:
```
To: morris
cc: gsf, ekrell
Subject: New KornShell Programming Language Talk
-------
A presentation on the ksh implementation of the Rand/UCI Mail
Handling System (MH), will be given in 1D-451 on April 1st at
1:30 PM. Refreshments will be served afterward.

David Korn
```

At this point, you are asked **What now?**. This is known as being at the "What now," level. For now, there are probably only four options that will interest you:

edit   Edit the draft.
list   List the draft on your screen.
quit   Quit, without sending the draft.
send   Send the draft, then quit.

edit   All of these options take various arguments. For example, the **edit** option will let you edit the draft before sending it. When you leave the editor, you will come back to the **What now?** level, where you can reedit the draft, send it, list it, or simply quit without sending the draft at all.

quit   If you **quit** without sending the draft, the draft is saved in a file whose default name is **Mail/draft** under your home directory. You can recall this file later using the **–use** argument to **comp**, **comp –use**. The **What now?** level permits you to do further editing and to send the final draft when you are ready.

send   When it is time to send the draft on its way, use the **send** option by itself. If there are any problems with the draft (for example, if one or more of the people whom you specified in the **To:** and **cc:** components do not exist), then you are notified at this time.

Replying to Messages

To reply to a message, use the **repl** command. For example, **repl** creates a reply to the current message. You may also reply to a specific message (other than the current one) by giving a message number (e.g., **1**, **4**), or a message name (e.g., **first**, **last**, **prev**); for example, **repl prev**.

We haven't really introduced message numbers yet. We discuss them in the next section.

The process of replying to a message is very similar to composing a message from scratch (see the previous section), but **repl** conveniently constructs and displays the header of the reply draft for you. You need only type in the text of the reply. The draft is sent only if you give an explicit **send** after you finish editing it, so you do not have to worry about the draft getting away from you prematurely. An example of a complete reply draft, as it appears on your screen, might be:

```
To: dgk
cc: morris
Subject: Re: New KornShell Programming Language Talk
In-reply-to: Your message of 27 Mar 93 18:15:08 EST.
------
     I'll be there.
gsf
```

At this point, you are asked **What now?**. Refer to the previous section regarding how to edit, display, or send the draft at this point.

As with **comp**, if you **quit** without sending the reply draft, the draft is saved in a file whose default name is **Mail/draft**, under your home directory. You can recall this file later using the **–use** argument to **comp**, **comp –use**.
The **What now?** level permits you to do further editing and to send the final draft when you are ready.

Scanning Messages

The scan listing created by **inc** shows the message number, the date on which the message was sent, the sender, and the subject of the message. If there is sufficient space remaining on the line, the beginning of the text of the message is displayed as well, preceded by **<<** (two left angle brackets). An example of a scan listing is:

```
1   10/10 attunix!crume  ksh in Japan << ksh is beginn
2+  10/10 gsf            nmake <<A new version of nmak
3   10/10 ..!ulysses!dgk ksh <<I found a bug in the la
4   10/11 root           space << Please clean up any
```

Note that all messages have message numbers.

To generate your own scan listing, use the **scan** command. Typing just **scan** will list all the messages in the current folder.

To scan a subset of these messages, you can specify the numbers of the messages that you consider interesting, e.g., **scan 2 3**.

You may display message names in addition to discrete message numbers.
The built-in message names recognized by MH are:

all All messages in the folder, **first–last**.

first First message in the folder.

last Last message in the folder.

prev Message immediately before the current message.

> **cur** Current message.
>
> **next** Message immediately after the current message.

You can specify message ranges in addition to discrete message numbers or names by separating the beginning and final message numbers with a – (minus). For example, **scan 5–10** scans messages 5 through 10 inclusive.

You can also specify a range of messages by separating a beginning message number and a relative number of messages with a **:**. For example:

> **scan last:3** scans the last three messages in the folder. Similarly, **scan first:3** scans the first three messages in the folder.
>
> **scan next:3** scans the next three messages.
>
> **scan cur:–3** scans backwards for three messages beginning from the current message.
>
> **scan 100:4** scans four messages beginning from message number 100.

To summarize, the important concepts discussed in this section are message ranges, message numbers, and message names. When an MH command is described as taking a *msg* argument, it accepts either a message name or a message number. Most MH commands are described as taking *msgs* arguments, meaning that more than one message or message range is accepted.

Deleting Messages

To delete a message, use the **rmm** command. By default, **rmm** deletes the current message, but you can give **rmm** a list of messages to be removed as well. There is no corresponding **unrmm** command. However, you can specify the command that removes the file and can therefore change the way **rmm** works so that it simply moves messages to another folder (say, **+wastebasket**).

Filing Messages

The possibility of having folders other than **+inbox** has been mentioned previously. The methods for moving messages between folders and manipulating folders are discussed here.

The **refile** command moves messages from a source folder to one or more destination folders.

By default, the current message is moved from the current folder (typically **+inbox**) to another folder specified as an argument to **refile**. For example, **refile +todo** moves the current message from the current folder to the folder **+todo**.

To move messages from a folder other than the current folder, use the
–src +folder switch, as in **refile –src +todo last +save +notes**
which moves the last message in the **+todo** folder to the folders **+save** and
+notes. Note that this operation is a move, not a copy. It removes the message
from the source folder. To keep a copy in the source folder as well, use the **link**
switch as in **refile –link –src +todo last +save +notes**.

Whenever you give a folder argument to an MH command, that folder becomes
the current folder. To find out which folder is current, use the **folder** command.
The **inc** command sets the current folder back to **+inbox** by default.

To find out about all of a user's folders, use the **folders** command. Since folders
can contain other folders, the **folders –recurse** command will recursively examine
each folder for you.

To set the current folder without doing anything else, use the **folder** command
with a folder argument. Hence, **folder +inbox** makes **+inbox** the current folder.

The Profile

The profile in this version of MH differs from the profile in the original MH
system both in the names of variables and in the syntax. In our implementation,
the profile file is in the format of a shell script.

You can customize the MH environment by creating and editing a profile file
named **.Mhprofile** in your home directory. Although there are lots of options,
here are the most useful:

MhPath   The pathname of the directory which includes all the folders.
The default is **$HOME/Mail**.

MhEditor

Lists the default editor that **comp** and **repl** should use. The default is
${VISUAL:–${EDITOR:–/bin/ed}}, but you might prefer another
editor.

MhMsg_protect

Whenever MH creates a message (for example, with **inc**), this is the
octal access permission that the message is created with; the default is
MhMsg_protect=644. This permission allows all other users on the
system to read your messages. Note that changing the mode in the
MH profile does not change the permission of messages that have
been created already; use **chmod** to change the modes of your existing
messages. *Caution*: To maintain privacy, use the access permission
600.

MhFolder_protect

Whenever MH creates a folder (for example, with **refile**), this is the access permission that the folder is created with. The default is **MhFolder_protect=751**. This permission allows other users on the system access to specific messages in your folders. *Caution*: To maintain stricter privacy, use the access permission 700.

MhSignature

When MH posts mail for you, it looks at this variable for your "real world" name. All the escape conventions understood by **print** get expanded. For example, **MhSignature='David Korn\nulysses!dgk'** causes a two-line signature to be appended to each message that you send.

MhAuditfile

A scan listing of each message that is placed in your **+inbox** folder will be appended to this file.

MhRm   The name of the command that removes message files. Default is **rm.**

MhList   The name of the command that displays messages to you. Default is **cat.**

MhStdform

The name of the default template that is used when you compose a message and when you reply to a message. Default is **$MhPath/.std_form**.

Use the alias feature of **ksh** to set your own default switch settings in your environment file. For example, if you want the default editor for **repl** to be **emacs**, the line **alias repl='repl –editor emacs'** is sufficient. Command line arguments tend to override alias settings. Given the environment file setting for **repl** above, if you invoked **repl** with **repl –editor vi**, **repl** would use the **vi** built-in editor instead of **emacs**.

Note that the **.Mhprofile** is a **ksh** script. Be sure that it is properly formatted.

Conventions

Now let's summarize the conventions that MH commands use:

- You can give any MH command that deals with messages a +*folder* argument to say which folder to use. However, you may give only one +*folder* argument per command in most cases.
- If an MH command accepts a *msgs* argument, then you can give any number of messages to the command. The MH command expands all the ranges and processes each message, starting with the lowest numbered message and working its way to the message with the highest number.
- If an MH command accepts a *msg* argument, then you can give at most one message.

- Switches to MH commands start with a **–**. Unlike the standard UNIX system convention, each switch consists of more than one character, for example, **–header**. To minimize typing, you need type only a unique abbreviation of the switch. Thus, for **–header**, **–hea** is probably sufficient, depending on the other switches accepted by the command.
- All MH commands have a **–help** switch, which you must spell out fully. When an MH command encounters the **–help** switch, it displays the syntax of the command and the switches that it accepts. In the list of switches, parentheses indicate required characters. For example, all **–help** switches will appear as **–(help)**, indicating that no abbreviation is accepted.
- Most MH switches have both on and off forms, such as **–format** and **–noformat**. In these cases, the last occurrence of the switch on the command line determines the setting of the switch.
- Since most switches have both on and off forms, it is easy to customize the default options for each MH command by defining aliases in your environment file, and to override those defaults on the command line.

DESIGN

The above description is not a complete specification. We fill in details as needed. We experimented with the original MH commands to determine their precise behavior. In most cases the format of the output is the same as the original MH system.

We will rely on the **mail** command for the posting and delivery of messages.

Folders and Messages

Folders are represented by directories. Messages are represented by files.

You always have a current folder, and each folder has a current message. We have chosen to use a file named:

    .current in each folder, to keep track of the current message.
    .master in the **Mail** directory, to keep track of the current folder.

We experimented with the original MH commands to discover how each command affected the current folder and the current message.

Architecture

We had to decide whether to write each command as a function or as a script. To make this decision you must be aware of the following tradeoffs:

- Scripts take longer to start executing because **ksh** must find the file that contains the shell script.
- Function definitions take time for **ksh** to read and process. They also use memory which causes **ksh** to take a little longer to invoke a process.

- You cannot use the *Suspend* character to stop a function even if your system has job control.

There are tradeoffs for each choice you make. You have to weigh the benefits and drawbacks to each approach. Since it is easy to change a function to and from a script, you can make this decision after you have written most of the code.

We have chosen to write each command as a separate shell script. Each script uses a common set of functions stored in a file named **mh_init**. When each command is invoked, it checks to see if the common set of functions are defined in the environment. If they are not, then each script causes **mh_init** to be read as a . (dot) script.

If you read the shell script containing the common function definitions with the . (dot) built-in, the MH commands will be executed faster. You would ordinarily put the . built-in in your login profile or your environment file.

Performance

Our objective was that the most frequently used commands (**show**, **next**, **refile**, and **scan**) respond without any noticeable delay. With the common functions pre-loaded, the response for **show** and **next** outperformed the C language versions. **scan** and **refile** were only slightly slower. Even without pre-loading the common functions, the performance was adequate.

Shared Functionality

The following functionality is shared by all the commands:
- Processing arguments. Each command must check for invalid switches, display help information, and decode message specifications.
- Keeping track of the current folder and message number.
- Displaying error messages.

The following functionality is shared by two or more of the commands:
- Reading a message header by **repl**, **scan**, and **inc**.
- Disposition of a draft by **comp** and **repl**.
- **What now?** is a portion of **comp** and **repl**.
- Reading a folder to determine its contents by **folder** and **folders**.
- Displaying a scan message by **inc** and **scan**.

Naming Convention

It is good practice to choose a naming convention for variables so that functions and shell scripts are easier to read, and to minimize the number of name conflicts that can arise.

We use the following conventions:

- Names with all uppercase letters are predefined by **ksh** or by the system.
- All variables shared by any shell script and one or more functions start with the prefix **Mh**.
- Local variables are used within functions whenever possible. Local variables are all lowercase.
- Variables that correspond to field names in the header portion of the header start with an uppercase letter.
- Each switch name is used to hold the switch setting.

IMPLEMENTATION

In this section we show and describe each of the functions and commands that we wrote to implement our modified version of the MH system.

Each of the following headings contains the name of a function or a command. Under the heading is a description of the code, and the code itself.

The code uses the following global variables in addition to the variables that you can specify in your MH profile file:

MhCommand
> The name for the current MH command. Each command sets this value from parameter **0** by stripping off any path prefix.

MhCurfolder
> Name of the current folder.

MhCurmsg
> Number of the current message.

MhFirst Message number corresponding to the first message in a range of messages.

MhFolder
> Name of the folder specified for this command.

MhLast Message number corresponding to the last message in a range of messages.

MhLastmsg
> Number of the last message in the current folder.

MhMany This variable is set to ... for each command that allows you to specify multiple folders.

MhMsg Message that is being processed by this command.

MhMsgs List of messages for this command.

MhSwitches
> List of legal switches for the command. Each switch is a separate argument. The value of **MhSwitches** is as follows:
> - Each switch that can take an argument is specified as
>   *−name=value.*

- Each switch that can have an optional **no** in front of it is specified as *–name–*.
- Each switch that can only be turned on is specified as *–name*.

The order of presentation of the **ksh** code is bottom up, with the shared functions first.

Note the use of quoting throughout the code. We try to protect against errors that occur if:
- A parameter is Null or unset.
- A parameter or folder name contains one or more Spaces or Tabs.
- A parameter or folder name contains the pathname expansion characters, [ ], ?, and/or *.
- A parameter or folder name contains a \.

err_exit [*message...*]

err_exit displays on standard error the command name, a **:**, and a brief description of the error as provided by *message*.

The command exits with a False (1) return value.

```
function err_exit # message
{
        print -u2 -r -- "$MhCommand: $@"
        exit 1
}
```

check_setup

Each command calls **check_setup** to read your **.Mhprofile** file and to read the **.master** file.

If you do not have a **.master** file then the current folder is set to **inbox**.

```
function check_setup
{
        set -o noglob
        MhPath=$HOME/Mail
        [[ -r $HOME/.Mhprofile ]]  && . $HOME/.Mhprofile
        if      [[ ! -d $MhPath ]]
        then    err_exit "$MhPath: not a directory"
        elif    [[ -r $MhPath/.master ]]
        then    . "$MhPath/.master"
        else    MhCurfolder=inbox MhCurmsg=0 MhLastmsg=1
        fi
}
```

check_args [*arg...*]

check_args checks each *arg* supplied with the command line and reports any syntax errors.

The outer **while** loop shifts through each *arg* and checks whether *arg* is a:
- Folder. It starts with a **+**. **check_args** sets the **MhFolder** variable, and checks to see if any other folder is specified.
- Message. It starts with a digit, or begins with one of the message names **all**, **cur**, **prev**, **next**, **first**, or **last**. **check_args** checks whether multiple messages are permitted.
- Help request. It is **–help**. **check_args** uses the **MhSwitches** variable to display the help message, and calls **exit**.
- A switch. It starts with a **–** and is followed by a lowercase letter. **check_args** checks that it matches one of the switches in **MhSwitches** and that the specification is not ambiguous, and it creates a variable whose name is the name of the switch.

```
function check_args # arg list
{
        # process the arguments
        typeset switch first=first val state
        while [[ $1 != "" ]]       # for each arg
        do      case $1 in
                +*)
                        case $first in
                        first)
                                MhFolder=${1#+} first=
                                ;;
                        "")
                                if      [[ $MhMany != "" ]]
                                then    err_exit "only one folder"\
                                "at a time!"
                                fi
                                MhFolder="$MhFolder ${1#+}";;
                        esac
                        ;;
                [0-9]*|all|cur*|prev*|next*|first*|last*)
                        if      [[ $MhMsg != "" ]]
                        then    MhMsgs="$MhMsgs $1"
                        else    err_exit "usage: [+folder]"\
                        "${MhMany+...} ${MhMsg+[msgs]} [switches]"
                        fi
```

```
                   ;;
        -help)print -nu2 "syntax: $MhCommand "
              print -nu2 "[+folder]${MhMany+...}"
              print -ru2 -- " ${MhMsg+[msgs]} [switches]"
              print -u2 '  switches are:'
              for i in ${MhSwitches}
              do      IFS==
                      case $i in
                      *-)
                              i=${i#-}
                              print -u2 "  -[no]${i%-}"
                              ;;
                      *)
                              print -u2 "  "$i;;
                      esac
              done
              print -u2 '  (-help)'
              exit 0
              ;;
        -[a-z]*[!-])
              val=$1 state=1
              if      [[ $val == -no* ]]
              then    val=-${1#-no} # strip off leading no
                      state=
              fi
              case $MhSwitches in
              *$val*)
                      switch=${val#-}${MhSwitches#*$val}
                      case $val in
                      if      [[ $val == ${switch} ]]
                      then    err_exit "$1: ambiguous"
                      fi
                      switch="${switch%% *}"
                      case $switch in
                      *=*)
                              shift
                              case $1 in
                              -*|"")err_exit "missing" \
                              "argument to -${switch%=*}"
                              ;;
                              esac
                              eval ${switch#*=}=$1
                              ;;
                      *)
                              eval ${switch%-}=$state
```

```
                                ;;
                        esac
                        ;;
                *)
                        err_exit "usage: [+folder]" \
                "${MhMany+...} ${MhMsg+[msgs]} [switches]"
                        ;;
                esac
                ;;
        *)
                err_exit "bad message list $1"
                ;;
        esac
        shift                           # get next arg
    done
}
```

check_folder

check_folder checks to see whether **MhFolder** exists. If it exists, **check_folder** returns True. If it does not exist, **check_folder** creates the folder, sets the protection mode, and returns False (1).

```
function check_folder
{
        typeset dir=$MhPath/$MhFolder \
                mode=${MhFolder_protect:-751}
        if      [[ ! -d $dir ]]
        then    read reply?"Create folder \"$dir\"? "
                case $reply in
                y|yes)
                        if      mkdir "$dir"
                        then    chmod $mode "$dir"
                                MhCurmsg=1
                                return 1
                        else    err_exit "cannot create folder" \
                                        "+$MhFolder"
                        fi
                        ;;
                *)      exit 1;;
                esac
        fi
        return 0
}
```

set_folder

set_folder changes to a new folder if **MhFolder** is not the current folder. It calls **check_folder** if the folder does not already exist. Otherwise it reads the **.current** file in the new folder. It does not update the **.master** file.

```
function set_folder
{
        typeset dir="$MhPath/$MhFolder"
        if      [[ $MhFolder != $MhCurfolder ]]
        then    MhCurfolder=$MhFolder
                if      check_folder && [[ -r $dir/.current ]]
                then    . "$dir/.current"
                fi
        fi
}
```

restore_env

restore_env updates the **.master** file with the current folder and the **.current** file in the current folder with the message range. Several commands specify this routine as a trap on **INT** and **EXIT**.

```
# this routine gets executed on EXIT
function restore_env
{
        print > $MhPath/.master "MhCurfolder=$MhCurfolder \
                MhCurmsg=$MhCurmsg MhLastmsg=$MhLastmsg"
        print > $MhPath/$MhCurfolder/.current \
                "MhCurmsg=$MhCurmsg MhLastmsg=$MhLastmsg"
        rm -f /tmp/Mh$$*
}
```

read_header *mfile*

read_header reads the header portion of the message file *mfile* and gives values to the global variables:

From   Second word on the first line beginning with **From** or **From:**.

Subject

        Remainder of the line starting with **Subject:**.

Cc   Remainder of the line starting with **cc:** or **Cc:** plus any continuation lines beginning with a Space or Tab.

To   Remainder of the line starting with **to:** or **To** plus any continuation lines beginning with a Space or Tab.

Message_id

> Remainder of the line starting with **Message-id:**.

Month and **Day**

> These are set from the first line that contains a time stamp of the form
> **HH:MM:SS.**

Mh_value

> Beginning of the body of the message. **read_header** uses the global
> variable **Mh_size** to determine how many bytes of the message body it
> should read.

```
function read_header # msg_file
{
      typeset field= IFS= from='From[: ]*' \
            date='[0-2][0-9]:[0-5][0-9]*'
      integer Jan=1 Feb=2 Mar=3 Apr=4 May=5 Jun=6 \
            Jul=7 Aug=8 Sep=9 Oct=10 Nov=11 Dec=12
      [[ -r $1 ]] || err_exit "no current message"
      exec 3< $1
      while read -u3  -r
      do      if      [[ $date != '' && $REPLY == *$date ]]
              then    IFS=' '; set -- ${REPLY%%$date}
                      if      (( $# >= 3 ))
                      then    shift $(($#-3))
                              Month=$2
                              if      [[ $1 == ?([0-3])[0-9] ]]
                              then    Day=$1 date=''
                              elif    [[ $3 == ?([0-3])[0-9] ]]
                              then    Day=$3 date=''
                              fi
                      fi
              fi
              case $REPLY in
              $from)          [[ $from != '' ]] || break
                      IFS=' '; set -- $REPLY
                      eval field=\${$#}
                      if      [[ $field == \<*\> ]]
                      then    field=${field#\<}
                      else    field=${2#\<}
                      fi
                      From=${field%\>}
                      if      [[ $From == *@* ]]
                      then    from=''
                      fi
                      ;;
```

```
                Subject:*)  Subject=${REPLY#Subject:}
                        field=subject
                        ;;
                Message-Id:*)  message_id=${REPLY#Message-Id:}
                        field=message
                        ;;
                [Cc]c:*)  Cc=${REPLY#[Cc]c:}  field=cc
                        ;;
                [Tt]o:*)  To=${REPLY#[Tt]o:}  field=to
                        ;;
                *:*)    field=${REPLY%%:*}
                        ;;
                [\ \     ]*)
                        if      [[ $field == cc ]]
                        then    Cc="$Cc $REPLY"
                        elif    [[ $field == to ]]
                        then    To="$To $REPLY"
                        fi
                        ;;
                *)      break;;
                esac
        done
        [[ "$Mh_size" != '' ]] || return
        # read size bytes of message
        ((Mh_size = Mh_size - ${#Subject} - 3))
        while read -u3  -r && ((Mh_size>0))
        do      ((Mh_size = Mh_size - ${#REPLY}))
                Mh_value="$Mh_value $REPLY"
        done
        exec 3<&-
}
```

scan_msg *mfile* [*auditfile*]

scan_msg formats and displays a one-line summary for the message file **mfile** that is specified. **scan** and **inc** call this function.

scan_msg uses **read_header** to extract the fields from the header portion of the message.

inc allows you to specify *auditfile*, where a log of these one-line messages is kept for all incoming mail.

```
function scan_msg # msg_file [auditfile]
{
        set -o noglob
```

```
      typeset label
      typeset -Z2 day mon
      typeset -R4 n
      typeset -L1 flag=' '
      typeset -L17 from
      Mh_size=${COLUMNS:-80}-31
      typeset -L$Mh_size message
      Subject= Mh_value=
      n=${1##*/}
      if     [[ $MhCurmsg == $n ]]
      then   flag=+
      fi
      read_header $1   # sets several values
      day=$Day From=$From
      message="$Subject   <<$Mh_value"
      print -nr -- "$n$flag ${mon:=$Month}/$day $From "
      print -r -- $message
      if     [[ $2 != "" ]]
      then   print -nr -- "$n  $Month/$day $From " >> $2
             print -r -- $message >> $2
      fi
}
```

back_to_prev [*n*]

back_to_prev is only called by the function **message_range**. It checks to see whether the message whose number is defined by the variable **MhFirst** exists. If it does, the function returns. If it does not, **ksh** keeps decrementing the **MhFirst** variable until a message by this number exists or it reaches the number 1.

back_to_prev assumes that you are in the correct folder when you call it.

```
function back_to_prev # n
{
      integer n=${1-1}
      while true
      do     until [[ -r $MhFirst ]] || ((MhFirst <= 1))
             do     ((MhFirst -= 1))
             done
             ((n -= 1)) || return
             ((MhFirst -= 1))
      done
}
```

skip_to_next [n]

skip_to_next is only called by the function **message_range**. It checks to see whether the message whose number is defined by the variable **MhFirst** exists. If it does, the function returns. If it does not, **ksh** keeps incrementing the **MhFirst** variable until a message by this number exists or it reaches the **MhLastmsg** value.

skip_to_next assumes that you are in the correct folder when you call it.

```
function skip_to_next # n
{
    integer n=${1-1}
    while true
    do     until [[ -r $MhFirst ]] ||
                  ((MhFirst >= MhLastmsg))
           do    ((MhFirst += 1))
           done
           ((n -= 1)) || return
           ((MhFirst += 1))
    done
}
```

set_message

set_message checks to see that only one message was specified and then sets **MhCurmsg** to the numeric value corresponding to this message.

```
function set_message
{
    case $MhMsgs in
    "")     ;;
    \ *\ *)err_exit 'only one (current) message' \
                'at a time!'
            ;;
    *)      if    [[ $MhMsgs != $MhCurmsg ]]
            then  message_list '' $MhMsgs
                  MhCurmsg=$MhFirst
            fi;;
    esac
}
```

message_list *action message...*

message_list sets the working directory to the current folder and then calls **message_range** for each *message* that is supplied.

action is the command or function to be executed for each message. *message* can be either a single message or a range.

```
function message_list # action messages
{
        typeset action=$1
        if      cd "$MhPath/$MhCurfolder" 2> /dev/null
        then    shift
                for i in "$@"
                do      message_range "$i" $action
                done
        else    err_exit "$MhCurfolder: no such folder"
        fi
}
```

message_range *message* [*command*]

message_range converts a message or a range of messages to numbers and sets the variables **MhFirst** and **MhLast**.

If *command* is specified, **message_range** calls *command* for each message from **MhFirst** to **MhLast**. **MhMsg** is set to the current message when *command* is called.

```
function message_range # message command
{
        integer last=0 skip=0
        typeset msg
        Mhmsg=$1
        case $1 in # check for : modifier
        *:-[0-9]*)   # check for msg:-number
              msg=${1%:-*} skip=${1##*:}
              ;;
        *:[0-9]*)    # check for msg:number
              msg=${1%:*} skip=${1##*:}
              ;;
        *)
              msg=$1;;
        esac
        case $msg in
        *-*)   # check for a range, no : modifier allowed
```

```
            (( skip )) && err_exit "bad message list $1"
            message_range ${msg#*-}
            last=MhFirst MhLast=MhFirst
            message_range ${msg%-*}
            ;;
all)    MhFirst=1 MhLast=MhLastmsg last=MhLastmsg
            ;;
last)
            MhFirst=MhLastmsg
            back_to_prev 1
            if     (( skip > 0 ))
            then   skip=-skip
            fi
            ;;
first)
            MhFirst=1
            skip_to_next
            ;;
next)   (( MhFirst == MhCurmsg + 1 ))
            skip_to_next
            ;;
prev)   (( MhFirst == MhCurmsg - 1 ))
            back_to_prev
            ;;
cur)    MhFirst=MhCurmsg
            ;;
[1-9]*)MhFirst=$msg
            ;;
*)      err_exit "bad message list $1";;
esac
if     (( skip > 0 ))
then   last=MhFirst
            skip_to_next $skip
            MhLast=MhFirst
            MhFirst=last
elif   (( skip < 0 ))
then   last=MhFirst MhLast=MhFirst skip=-skip
            back_to_prev $skip
fi
[[ $2 == "" ]] && return
set +o noglob
if     (( last>0 && MhLast != MhFirst )) # range of values
then   for i in [1-9] [1-9][0-9] [1-9][0-9][0-9]\
            [1-9][0-9][0-9][0-9] [1-9][0-9][0-9][0-9][0-9]
            do    case $i in
```

```
                    \[*|*-*)        ;;
                    *)      if      ((i>=MhFirst && i<=MhLast))
                            then    $2 $i
                                    last=$i
                            fi
                            ;;
                    esac
            done
            Mhlast=last
    else    $2 $MhFirst
            MhLast=MhFirst
    fi
}
```

folder_walk *folder*

folder_walk walks through *folder* and provides some statistics on messages in it. It is called by the **folder** and **folders** commands.

If the **pack** variable is set, then messages are renumbered sequentially from 1 up.

If the **recurse** variable is set, then **folder_walk** calls **folder_walk** for each directory in *folder*.

The working directory must be set to *folder* before this function is called.

folder_walk increments the variable **tfolder** and adds the number of messages in folder to variable **tmsg**.

```
function folder_walk # folder
{
        integer min=0 n=0 cur=0 max=0 newcurrent=0
        typeset -R4 nmsg first current last
        typeset -R22 folder=$1
        typeset other=
        typeset -L1 curf=' '
        if      [[ -r .current ]]
        then    . ./.current
                cur=MhCurmsg
        fi
        if      [[ $1 == $MhCurfolder ]]
        then    curf=+
        fi
        set +o noglob
        for i in ? ?? ??? ???? ????*
        do      case $i in
                [1-9]*(|[1-9]))
```

```
                    ((n += 1))
                    if    [[ $pack != "" ]] && ((i != n))
                    then  if    ((i == cur))
                          then  newcur=n
                          fi
                          mv $i $n
                    else  (( min )) || min=i
                          max=i
                    fi
                    ;;
        \*)         err_exit "$1 has no messages"
                    ;;
        ,*|'?'|'??'|'???'|'????'|'????*')
                    ;;
        *)          if    [[ $recurse != "" && -d $i ]]
                    then  cd "$i"
                          folder_walk "$1/$i"
                          cd ..
                    fi
                    other=';'
                    ;;
        esac
done
if    [[ $pack != "" ]]
then  max=n min=1 cur=newcur
fi
((cur <= max)) || cur=0
if    ((cur == 0)) && [[ -r .mh_sequences ]]
then  read -r i cur < .mh_sequences
fi
print "MhCurmsg=$cur\tMhLastmsg=$max" > .current
if    [[ $curf == + ]]
then  print > $MhPath/.master "MhCurfolder=$1 \
      MhCurmsg=$cur\tMhLastmsg=$max"
fi
print -rn -- "$folder$curf has "
if    ((min))
then  nmsg=$n last=$max first=$min curf=s
      ((n == 1)) && curf=' '
      print -rn -- "$nmsg message$curf ($first-$last)"
else  print -rn "  no messages${other:+                }"
fi
if    [[ $other != "" ]] || let cur
then  if    ((cur))
      then  current=$cur
```

```
                        print -rn -- "; cur=$current$other"
            else    print -rn -- "$other            "
            fi
            if      [[ $other != ""]]
            then    print -rn -- ' (others)'
            fi
        fi
        print .
        ((tmsg += n))
        ((tfolder += 1))
}
```

dispose_draft [*draft*]

dispose_draft is called by **comp** and **repl** when there is a draft that has not been sent.

dispose_draft uses a **select** list to present the user with the list of permitted responses. The user can reply by name or number.

```
function dispose_draft    #draft
{
        typeset disp draft=${1:-$MhPath/draft}
        print -rn "Draft \"$draft\" exists ("
        print -r -- $(wc -c < $draft) bytes\).
        select disp in quit replace use list refile
        do      case $REPLY in
                [a-z]*)
                        disp=$REPLY;;
                esac
                case $disp in
                q|quit)
                        exit
                        ;;
                rep|replace)
                        rm -f "$draft"
                        break
                        ;;
                u|use)
                        break
                        ;;
                l|list)
                        ${MhList:-/bin/cat} "$draft"
                        ;;
                ref|refile)
```

```
                        read -r "fold?MhFolder? "
                        if    refile "$draft" "+$fold"
                        then  break
                        fi
                        ;;
            r|re)
                        print -u2 -rn -- "$i: ambiguous. "
                        print -u2 "It matches\n\t-replace\n\t-refile"
                        ;;
            esac
      done
}
```

form_letter *template file*

form_letter uses the *template* file to construct *file*.

form_letter generates a script in a temporary file that uses the contents of template as a here-document to the **cat** command. After it executes the temporary script it removes it.

```
function form_letter      # infile outfile
{
      typeset temp=/tmp/Mh$$
      print -r "/bin/cat > $2 <<!EOF!" > $temp
      /bin/cat "$1" >> $temp
      print -r  '!EOF!' >> $temp
      . $temp
      rm -f $temp
}
```

what_now [*file*]

what_now presents the user with a choice of actions to take after the user has finished editing a draft.

```
function what_now  # [file]
{
      typeset i ifs file="${1:-$MhPath/draft}" \
            nomail="no mail sent"
      if    [[ ! -r $file ]]
      then  form_letter "$formfile" "$file"
      fi
      "${editor?No editor}" "$file"
```

```
       select i in edit list refile quit send
do     case  $REPLY in
       [a-z]*)
              i=$REPLY;;
       esac
       case $i in
       e|edit)
              "${editor}" "$file"
              ;;
       l|list)
              ${Mhlist:-/bin/cat} "$file"
              ;;
       r|ref|refile)
              read -r "i?MhFolder? "
              if    refile "$file" "+$i"
              then  break
              fi
              ;;
       q|quit)
              print -r "draft left in $file"
              return ;;
       s|send)
              Cc= To=
              read_header "$file"
              IFS='         ,:' ifs=$IFS
              set -- $To $Cc
              IFS=$ifs
              if    [[ $To == "" ]]
              then  err_exit "no addressees, $nomail"
              fi
              print -- "\n$MhSignature" >> $file
              if    /bin/mail $* < $file
              then  /bin/rm -f "$file"
                    break
              else  print -nu2 "$MhCommand: mail failed"
                    print -u2 ", $nomail"
              fi
              ;;
       *)     print -u2 -nr -- "$i unknown. Hit"
              print -u2 " <CR> for help."
              ;;
       esac
done
}
```

inc [+*folder*]   [**–audit** *auditfile*]

inc reads your **MAIL** file and creates a file for each message in an MH folder. If you do not specify +*folder*, then MH uses the **+inbox** folder.

If specified, **inc** will use the **MhFile_protect** variable to set the permission on each message. Otherwise, the MH default of 644 will be used.

If you specify *auditfile*, then **inc** appends a scan message to this file for each message. This is useful for keeping track of the volume and source of incoming mail.

The new messages being incorporated are assigned numbers starting with the next highest number in the folder. As the messages are processed, **inc** displays a scan listing (in the same format as **scan**) of the new mail.

```
# inc - incorporate new mail
set -o noglob
MhCommand=${0##*/}
. mh_init
trap  restore_env EXIT
check_setup
auditfile=$MhAuditfile MhFolder=inbox \
          MhSwitches='-audit=auditfile'
check_args "$@"
MAIL=${MAIL-/usr/spool/mail/${HOME##*/}}
# see if there is any mail to incorporate
if    [[ $MAIL == "" || ! -f $MAIL ]]
then  err_exit "no mail file"
fi
if    [[ ! -s $MAIL ]]
then  err_exit "no mail to incorporate"
fi
# check validity
dir=$MhPath/$MhFolder
# construct auditfile name
case $auditfile in
/*|"")        ;;
*)    auditfile=$MhPath/$auditfile
      ;;
esac
check_folder
set_folder
((MhCurmsg = MhLastmsg + 1))
# process each mail message
print -r "Incorporating mail into +$MhFolder"
while [[ -s $MAIL ]]
```

```
do      ((MhLastmsg += 1))
        mail -f $MAIL > /dev/null <<-!
        s $dir/$MhLastmsg
        d
        !
        chmod ${MhFile_protect:-644} "$dir/$MhLastmsg"
        scan_msg "$dir/$MhLastmsg" "$auditfile"
done
```

show [+*folder*] [*msgs*] [**–draft**]
prev [+*folder*] [*msgs*]
next [+*folder*] [*msgs*]

show displays each of the *msgs* you specify on standard output. The messages are displayed exactly as they are, with no reformatting. **show** displays the current message if you do not specify *msgs*.

If you specify the **MhList** variable in your Mh profile, it uses it instead of **cat** to display the messages.

prev is equivalent to **show prev**. **next** is equivalent to **show next**.

If you specify +*folder*, it displays messages from this folder and then makes this the current folder. The last message displayed becomes the current message.

If you specify **–draft** with **show**, then the current draft is displayed.

```
# show - show mail message
set -o noglob
MhCommand=${0##*/}
. mh_init
trap  restore_env EXIT
function print_msg # message
{
        if    [[ ! -r $1 ]]
        then  err_exit "$MhMsg: no such message"
        else  print "(Message $MhFolder:$1)"
              ${MhList-/bin/cat} $1
        fi
}
check_setup
MhFolder=${MhCurfolder:-inbox}
case $MhCommand in
prev|next)
        MhMsg=$MhCommand
        ;;
```

```
*)
        MhMsg=cur
esac
if      [[ $MhCommand == show ]]
then    MhSwitches='-draft'
fi
check_args "$@"
# check validity
if      [[ $MhList != "" && ! -x $(whence -p $MhList) ]]
then    err_exit "$MhList: No such executable"
fi
if      [[ $draft != "" ]]
then    if      [[ -r $MhPath/draft ]]
        then    ${MhList:-/bin/cat} "$MhPath/draft"
                exit 0
        else    err_exit "$MhPath/draft: No such file" \
                "or directory"
        fi
fi
set_folder
trap    restore_env INT
message_list print_msg ${MhMsgs-$MhMsg}
MhCurmsg=MhLast
```

scan [+*folder*] [*msgs*] [−[**no**]**header**]

scan displays a one-line-per-message listing of the specified messages. Each scan line contains the message number, the date, the "From" field, the "Subject" field, and, if room allows, some of the body of the message.

If you specify **−header**, then **scan** displays a header containing the names of each of the fields.

```
# scan - produce a one-line-per-message scan listing
set -o noglob
MhCommand=${0##*/}
. mh_init
trap    restore_env EXIT
check_setup
MhFolder=$MhCurfolder MhMsg=all MhSwitches=-header-
check_args "$@"
# check validity
set_folder
if      [[ $header != "" ]]
then    print "Folder $MhFolder\t\t\t\t\t$(date)\n"
```

```
fi
message_list scan_msg ${MhMsgs-all}
```

rmm [+*folder*] [*msgs*]

rmm removes the messages specified by *msgs*. **rmm** does not change the current message.

If you specify +*folder*, it removes messages from this folder and then makes this the current folder.

```
# rmm - remove messages
set -o noglob
MhCommand=${0##*/}
. mh_init
trap  restore_env EXIT
function rm_msg # message
{
        if      [[ ! -r $1 ]]
        then    err_exit "$MhMsg: no such message"
        else    ${MhRm:-/bin/rm} -f "$1"
        fi
}
check_setup
MhMsg=cur
check_args "$@"
# check validity
MhFolder=${MhCurfolder:-inbox}
set_folder
message_list rm_msg ${MhMsgs:-cur}
```

comp [−**editor** *editor*] [−**form** *formfile*] [−[**no**]**use**]

comp creates a new message to be mailed.

The file *formfile* can be used to override the default skeleton formfile **.std_form**. This also overrides the **MhStdform** variable, if any, in your MH profile file.

If a draft of the message already exists, **comp** asks if you want to delete it before continuing.

```
# comp - compose mail
set -o noglob
MhCommand=${0##*/}
. mh_init
trap  restore_env EXIT
```

```
check_setup
MhFolder=$MhCurfolder MhMsg=cur
formfile=${MhStdform:-$MhPath/.std_form}
editor=${MhEditor:-${VISUAL:-${EDITOR:-/bin/ed}}}
MhSwitches="-draft=folder -form=formfile \
            -editor=editor -use-"
check_args "$@"
# check validity
set_folder
set_message
draft=$MhPath/draft
PS3=Disposition?
if      [[ -r $draft && $use == "" ]]
then    dispose_draft "$draft"
fi
PS3="What now? "
what_now "$draft"
```

repl [+*folder*] [*msg*] [**–editor** *editor*]

repl aids a user in producing a reply to an existing message. If you do not specify
arguments, it sets up a message form skeleton in reply to the current message in
the current folder, invokes an editor on the message, and sends the composed
message if so directed.

If you specify +*folder*, it replies to a message from this folder and then makes this
the current folder.

If you specify *msg*, it replies to this message and then makes this the current
message.

```
# repl - reply to mail
set -o noglob
MhCommand=${0##*/}
. mh_init
trap  restore_env EXIT
check_setup
MhFolder=$MhCurfolder MhMsg=cur
formfile=${MhStdform:-$MhPath/.std_form}
editor=${MhEditor:-${VISUAL:-${EDITOR:-/bin/ed}}}
MhSwitches='-draft=folder -form=formfile -editor=editor'
check_args "$@"
# check validity
set_folder
set_message
print -r -- "$MhPath/$MhCurfolder/$MhCurmsg"
```

```
draft=$MhPath/draft
PS3=Disposition?
if      [[ -r $draft ]]
then    dispose_draft "$draft"
fi
PS3="What now? "
read_header "$MhPath/$MhCurfolder/$MhCurmsg"
what_now "$draft"
```

folder [+*folder*] [*msg*] [−[**no**]**pack**] [−[**no**]**header**]
folders [+*folder*] [*msg*] [−[**no**]**pack**] [−[**no**]**header**]

folder displays the current folder, the number of messages in it, the range of
messages (low-high), and the current message within the current folder.

If you specify +*folder* and/or *msg*, they become the current folder and/or message.

The **−pack** switch compresses the message numbers in a folder, removing holes
in the message numbering.

```
# folder - set or print information about folder
integer tfolder=0 tmsg=0
set -o noglob
MhCommand=${0##*/}
. mh_init
check_setup
MhFolder=$MhCurfolder MhMsg=$MhCurmsg
MhSwitches='-all -fast -header- -pack- -recurse'
# check validity
check_args "$@"
if      [[ $MhFolder != $MhCurfolder ]]
then    set_folder
fi
set_message
restore_env
if      [[ $MhCommand == folders || $header != "" ]]
then    print -n "\t\tFolder      # of messages "
        print "(  range  ); cur  msg  (other files)"
fi
if      [[ $MhCommand == folders ]]
then    cd "$MhPath" || err_exit "no $MhPath folder"
        set +o noglob
        for i in *
        do      if      [[ -d "$i" ]]
                then    cd "$i"
                        folder_walk "$i"
```

```
                       cd ..
              fi
       done
       print -n "\n\t\t    TOTAL= $tmsg messages "
       print -r "in $tfolder folders."
else   if     cd "$MhPath/$MhFolder"
       then   folder_walk "$MhCurfolder"
       else   err_exit "$MhFolder: no such folder"
       fi
fi
```

refile [−src +*folder*] +*folder*... [*msgs*] [−[no]link]

refile moves or copies messages from a source folder into one or more destination folders.

If the destination folder doesn't exist, **refile** asks you if you want to create one. **refile** exits if you specify a negative response.

If you specify −**src** +*folder*, then it becomes the current folder for future MH commands.

```
# refile - file messages
set -o noglob
MhCommand=${0##*/}
. mh_init
function file_msg # message
{
       if     [[ ! -r $1 ]]
       then   err_exit "$MhMsg: no such message"
       fi
       for MhFolder in $folders
       do     if     check_folder &&
                     [[ -r $MhPath/$MhFolder/.current ]]
              then   . "$MhPath/$MhFolder/.current"
                     ((MhLastmsg += 1))
              else   MhLastmsg=1
              fi
              fold=$MhPath/$MhFolder
              while [[ -f $fold/$MhLastmsg ]]
              do     ((MhLastmsg += 1))
              done
              print > $fold/.current \
                     "MhCurmsg=$MhCurmsg MhLastmsg=$MhLastmsg"
              ${MhLink:-ln} "$1" "$fold/$MhLastmsg" ||
                     cp "$1" "$fold/$MhLastmsg"
```

```
        done
        [[ $link == "" ]] && ${MhRm:-/bin/rm} -f "$1"
}
check_setup
MhMsg=cur MhMany=yes
MhSwitches='-src=folder -draft -link-'
check_args "$@"
folders=$MhFolder
[[ $folders ]] &&  err_exit "no folder specified"
if    [[ $folder != "" ]]
then  MhFolder=${folder#+}
      set_folder
fi
restore_env
check_folder
message_list file_msg ${MhMsgs:-cur}
```

.std_form

This is a copy of the form that is used with **comp** to compose mail, and with **repl**
to reply to messages. Note that this file is a form letter and is processed as a here-
document.

```
To: ${From}
cc: ${Cc}
Subject: ${Subject+Re: }${Subject}
--------
```

mh_init

The following code is in the common function file with the other function
definitions. It declares some global integer variables, and also declares all the
functions.

```
# This code gets executed first
integer MhCurmsg MhLastmsg MhFirst MhLast Mh_size Month
```

.Mhprofile

The following code is an example of an MH profile. It defines variables used by
the MH programs.

```
# profile for ksh version of MH
MhPath=$HOME/mailbag
MhFolder_protect=711
MhMessage_protect=600
```

```
MhSignature="David Korn\nulysses!dgk"
MhAuditfile=$MhPath/.auditfile
MhList=/usr/ucb/more
```

EXERCISES

1. Modify the MH application in each of the following ways:
    a. Allow message numbers greater than 9999.
    b. Change **rmm** so that it moves each message to a subdirectory named **.trashcan**. Add an **unrmm** command to restore messages from **.trashcan**. Add an option to **folders** to remove all messages in each **.trashcan** directory that is more than a day old.
    c. Allow the "To address" field to also be the name of a file containing a distribution list. Send the mail to everyone on the distribution list. Allow a distribution list to contain distribution lists.
    d. Add an option to include the original letter, without the header, as part of the reply template. The original message should have > prepended to each line.
    e. Add an option to **refile** that allows you to annotate a message, using your editor, before you file it. The annotation should be appended to the message.
    f. Write a script that produces a scan listing of all messages in a given folder, or all folders that contain a given keyword. The match for the keyword should be case insensitive.
    g. Add the ability to send form letters to a distribution list, with fields such as the user's name different for each letter.
    h. Use new features in the 12/28/93 version to simplify some of the code.
    i. Modify the code so that it will work in different locales. The mail header can contain keywords both in English and in the language defined by the locale. Error messages should be displayed in the language defined by the locale.

2. Write a program to archive files so that they can be restored or moved to a new location. The program should create a file that contains the contents of files in the specified directories and its subdirectories. The file should be in the format of a **ksh** script so that when the script is run, it recreates the directory hierarchy. The program should preserve the access permissions on all files. There should be an option to archive only those files newer than a specified file.

3. Write software to conduct an electronic survey. Assume that each recipient runs **ksh**. The program should take a file containing questions and choices for answers, and construct a **ksh** script and form letter to mail to each recipient. The form letter should instruct the recipient to run the generated script. The generated script should ask the user each of the questions, gather the results, and send the results back via mail. The generated script should allow the recipient to use the built-in editors while answering questions. It should also allow the user to add comments using the editor defined by the value of the user's **VISUAL** or **EDITOR** variable. Also, write a script that reads and processes the return mail and produces a summary of responses for each question.

4. Write a system for distributing software electronically with the following features:
    a. There is a database with an account for each potential recipient. The database should contain a variable amount of information about each user, including the user's name, electronic address, telephone number, etc. Write a program to add, delete, and change entries in this database.
    b. The software should bundle all the files, including a script that builds and installs the software, into a single file using the archive program of Exercise 2 above or a similar program.
    c. The program should generate a form letter to send to the recipient explaining the contents of the shipment and instructions for unbundling it.
    d. The software should run the script to build the software, and send a message back to the sender that indicates whether the software build was successful and that reports any problems it encountered.
    e. Include the program that bundles and sends the software as part of the distribution. Allow recipients to forward the software to other users. The program should send a carbon copy of the completion message to the originator of the software.

5. Write a program that plays draw poker. Your program must be able to shuffle cards, deal cards, handle betting, determine winning hands, and keep track of bets.

PART VI

APPENDIX

19 GLOSSARY

Alias. A name used as an abbreviation for one or more commands. An alias enables you to replace a command name with any desired character sequence.
- *Preset alias*. An alias that is already defined by **ksh** itself whenever it is invoked.
- *Tracked alias*. Not really an alias. Its value gets set to the pathname of a program the first time the program is run. It is used to reduce the time **ksh** spends locating a program on subsequent requests.

Array. A variable indexed by a subscript.

Attribute. Characteristics optionally associated with a variable, such as readonly or uppercase.

Backreference. Used within a pattern to refer to the string that matched an earlier sub-pattern. It is denoted by *digit*, where *digit* is the sub-pattern number.

Built-in command. A command processed by **ksh** itself. Its code is internal to **ksh**.

Built-in editor. Command line editors that are part of **ksh** itself. There are two of them, **emacs** and **vi**.

Command. An action for **ksh** to perform. A command can be a:
- *Simple command*.
  - Variable assignment.
  - I/O redirection.
  - Built-in command.
  - Arithmetic evaluation, ((...)).
  - Function.
  - Program.
- *Compound command*.
  - Pipeline.
  - Iteration command.
  - Conditional command.

Command substitution. A word or part of a word can be replaced by the output of a command.

Delimiter-word. The word that defines the string that ends a here-document.

Directive. A command processed by the **emacs** or **vi** built-in editor.

Directory. A file that contains filenames or directory names.
- Bin directory. A directory where programs are stored.
- Home directory. Your working directory when you log in.
- Root directory. The top level directory, named /.
- Subdirectory. A directory that exists in another directory.
- Working directory. Each pathname that does not begin with a / is defined relative to this directory. Each process has a working directory.

Environment. The state of a process, including such information as its open files, working directory, file creation mask, and local and global variables.
- *Child environment*. The environment of a child process.
- *Current environment*. The environment of the current process.
- *Parent environment*. The environment of the parent process.
- *Subshell environment*. The environment of a subshell.

Environment file. A script that gets read and executed whenever **ksh** begins an interactive execution.

Export. To pass a variable to a child process.

Field splitting. After parameter expansion and command substitution, **ksh** splits the resulting fields into command arguments.

File. An object that can be read from and/or written to, and/or executed.

File creation mask. A number that represents which permissions should be denied whenever a user creates a file.

File descriptor. A small number associated with an open file.

Filter. A command that reads from its standard input and writes to its standard output.

Flag. A command option, usually indicated by a single letter preceded by a –.

Function. A compound command that consists of a list of **ksh** commands. Once a function is defined, it is executed when its name is referenced. A function shares much of the environment with the script or function that invokes it.

Group id. Each user is a member of one or more groups, each of which is identified by a number called the group id.
- *Effective group id*. Each process has an id which defines its permissions with respect to group access of files.
- *Real group id*. Each process has the group id of the actual user.

Here-document. Lines of a script that represent the standard input of a command in the script itself.

History file. The file in which **ksh** saves each command that you enter interactively. You can edit and reenter commands in the history file.

Identifier. A string of characters starting with a letter or an underscore, and containing only letters, digits, or underscores.

Interpreter. A program that reads commands from a terminal or a file, and executes them.

Interrupt. A signal, typically generated by the keyboard. It causes the current executing process to terminate unless a trap was specified to handle the signal.

I/O redirection. The process of changing the file associated with one or more file descriptors.

Job. A synonym for a pipeline initiated by an interactive shell.
- *Background job*. A job running in a process group not associated with your terminal.
- *Foreground job*. A job running in the process group associated with your terminal.
- *Job control*. The ability to stop jobs and switch them from foreground to background and vice-versa.

Link. Each directory entry is called a link. A file may have several links to it.

Locale. Properties of strings and numbers that depend on language and cultural conventions such as collation order, character classes, and decimal point.

Option. A setting that affects the behavior of **ksh**.

Parameter. An entity that holds a value in the **ksh** language. Also see *variable*.
- *Named parameter*. A parameter denoted by an identifier. A shell variable.
- *Parameter expansion*. Replacing the parameter with its value.
- *Parameter modifier*. An operation which is applied while expanding a parameter.
- *Positional parameter*. A parameter designated by a number.
- *Special parameter*. A parameter whose name is $, #, @, !, –, or *.

Path search. The means of finding the pathname of a program that corresponds to the program name.

Pathname. A string that is used to identify a file.
- *Absolute Pathname*. A pathname beginning with /.
- *Pathname completion*. The means of generating all the pathnames that match a given pattern.
- *Pathname expansion*. The means of replacing a pattern with the list of pathnames that match the pattern.
- *Physical Pathname*. A pathname with all symbolic links resolved.

Pattern. A string of characters that consists of literal characters that match only themselves, and pattern characters that match one or more characters.
- *sub-pattern*. A part of a pattern that consists of a *pattern-list* enclosed in parentheses and preceded by one of the characters @, ?, *, +, or !.

- *pattern-list*. One or more patterns separated by | or **&**. A *pattern-list* must appear inside a *sub-pattern*.

Permission. The rights that you have to read, write, and/or execute a file, or to read, write, and/or search a directory.

Permission string. A string of 10 characters that is used to represent access permissions.

Pipe. A conduit by which a stream of characters can pass from one process to another. Each end of a pipe is associated with a file descriptor. A process will stop and wait if it reads from an empty pipe or writes to a full pipe.

Pipeline. One or more processes connected together by pipes.

Privileged mode. An option that is set when **ksh** runs with its real user id not equal to its effective user id, or with its real group id not equal to its effective group id.

Process. A single thread of execution that consists of a program and an execution environment.
- *Child process*. A new process created by a process.
- *Co-process*. A process created by **ksh** that has its input and output connected to **ksh** by pipes.
- *Parent process*. A process that creates a child process.
- *Process group*. Each active process is a member of a group identified by the process group id.
- *Process group id*. The process group id of the first process that starts a new process group.
- *Process id*. Each active process is uniquely identified with a positive integer called the process id.

Profile. A file containing shell commands. The file is executed when you log into the system.

Prompt. A message that an interactive **ksh** displays when it is ready to read input.

Quoting. A mechanism to enable special characters to take their literal meaning.

Reserved word. A word that is reserved as part of the **ksh** grammar. Reserved words are recognized as reserved words only in certain contexts.

Restricted shell. An option which, when set, limits the set of commands that can be executed.

Return value. A number from 0 to 255 that is returned by each command. A value of zero represents a True (successful) exit.

Script. A program written in the **ksh** language.
- *Dot script*. A script that is read and executed in the current environment.

Signal. An asynchronous message that consists of a number that can be sent from one process to another. It can also be sent from the operating system to a process when the user presses certain keys, or when an exceptional condition arises.

Standard error. The file associated with file descriptor 2. By convention, programs display all error messages on this descriptor.

Standard input. The file associated with file descriptor 0. Programs usually read their input from this descriptor.

Standard output. The file associated with file descriptor 1. Programs often write their output to this descriptor.

Subscript. A string or an arithmetic expression contained in brackets after a variable name. Each subscript of a variable can store a separate value.

Subshell. A child shell that initially contains a copy of the parent shell environment. A subshell does not have to be a separate process.

Superuser. A user id that is not restricted by file permissions.

Symbolic link. Some systems have a special file type called a symbolic link. A symbolic link is a special file whose contents is the pathname of a file. When referenced as part of a pathname, the contents of the symbolic link are used to locate the file.

Terminal control characters. Keyboard characters that are processed specially by the system to erase input, to stop and restart output, and to send signals. The terminal control characters and their defaults are listed on page 10.

Tilde expansion. **ksh** expands certain words that begin with a ~.

Token. **ksh** splits its input into units called tokens.

Trap. A specification for an action for **ksh** to perform when a given condition occurs. An example of a condition is the receipt of a signal.

User id. Each user is identified by an integer called the user id.
• *Effective user id*. Each process has a user id which defines its rights to access files and to send signals to other processes.
• *Real user id*. Each process remembers the user id of the actual user.

Variable. A shell parameter denoted by a dot-separated list of identifiers.
• *Array variable*. A variable that is indexed by a subscript.
• *Variable assignment*. A command that assigns a value to a variable.

Word. A word is any token that is not one of the operators defined on page 130, a here-document, or a Newline.

---

20   QUICK REFERENCE

Page references to the book are at the right.

Shaded areas indicate features available only on
versions of **ksh** newer than the 11/16/88 version.

QUICK REFERENCE INDEX

BUILT-IN COMMANDS   208

If return value is not shown, it is True.

† Dagger designates built-ins treated differently: **ksh** processes variable
  assignment lists specified with command before I/O redirection.
  Assignments remain in effect when the command completes. Errors in
  these built-ins cause the script that contains them to terminate.   209

Note: **bg**, **disown**, **fg**, **jobs**, **kill**, and **wait** take arguments called a *job*. *job* can be specified as a process id. When the **interactive** option is on, *job* can also be specified as one of the following:

%*number*	To refer to the job by *number*.
%% or %+	Current job.
%–	Previous job.
%*string*	Job whose name begins with *string*.
%?*string*	Job whose name contains *string*.

47

† **:** [*arg...*]   237
     Null Command. *args* are expanded.

† **.** *name* [*arg...*]   Dot Command   220
     If *name* is function defined by **function** *name*, executes *name*.
     Reads complete file *name* (dot script) and executes commands.
     Return value: Return value of last command executed.

† **alias** [**–pt**] [*name*[*=value*]...]   210
     –p   Causes word **alias** to precede each one.
     –t   Use to set and/or list tracked aliases.
     Return value: False if all *name*(s) not aliases.
     Value is the number of *name*s that are not aliases.

bg [*job...*]   234
     Runs *job* in background.
     Return value: False if **monitor** option is off.

† **break** [*n*]   220
     Exits smallest (or *n*th) enclosing **for, while, until, select** loop.

builtin [**–ds**] [**–f** *file*] [*name...*]   237
     Adds, deletes, or displays builtins.
     –d   Deletes builtin.
     –s   Special builtin.
     –f   Specifies library to link.

cd [**–LP**] [*directory*]   230
     Changes working directory.
     –L   Does not resolve symbolic links.
     –P   Resolves symbolic links.
     Return value: False if change not successful.

cd [**–LP**] *oldstring newstring*   231
     Substitutes *newstring* for *oldstring*.
     Return value: As above.

command [**–pvV**] *command* [*arg...*]   221
     Runs command without looking for functions.
     –p   Performs command search using the default value for **PATH**.
     –v   Equivalent to **whence**.
     –V   Equivalent to **whence –v**.
     Processes special built-ins like regular built-ins.

† **continue** [*n*]   221
     Continues smallest (or *n*th) enclosing **for, while, until,**
     or **select** loop.

disown [*job...*]   234
    HUP not sent when **ksh** terminates.

echo [*arg...*]   225
    Echoes *arg*(s) on standard output. Also see **print**, below.

† **eval** [*arg...*]   222
    Reads arguments and executes resulting commands.
    Return value: Value of command as determined by *arg*s.

† **exec** [**–c**] [**–a** *name*] [*command* [*arg...*]]   225
    If *command* omitted, opens, closes, and/or copies file descriptors.
    Replaces **ksh** with *command*, without creating a new process.
    arg(s) are arguments to *command*.

    –a   Causes command name passed to program to be *name*.
    –c   Clears the environment.
    Return value: If *command* specified, command does not return.
    Otherwise, True.

† **exit** [*n*]   222
    Exits. If this is the login shell, logs you out.
    Return value: *n*, if specified. Otherwise, value of preceding
    command.

† **export** [**–p**] [*name*[=*value*]]...   211
    Sets export attribute.

    –p displays list of variables in re-enterable format.

false   238
    Return value: False

fg [*job...*]   234
    Moves background *jobs* into foreground.
    Return value: False if **monitor** option off.

getconf [*name* [*pathname*]]   238
    Displays value of configuration parameter *name*, or all configuration
    parameters if *name* is not given, defined by the POSIX standard.
    Parameters whose value depends on path require *pathname*.

getopts [**–a** *name*] *optstring varname* [*arg...*]   238
    Checks *arg* for legal options as specified in *optstring*. Option letter
    is saved in *varname*. If no *arg*, processes positional parameters.
    –a *name*   Use *name* in usage messages instead of script name.
    Return value: True until **getopts** encounters the end of options.

hist [**–e** *editor*] [**–nlr**] [*first* [*last*]]   240
    Displays, edits, and/or re-executes commands from history file.
    –n   Suppresses command numbers when displayed.
    –l   Displays commands. Or use preset alias **history**.
    –r   Reverses order of commands.
    first   If *last* not specified, default is –16 if **–l**. Or –1 if no **–l**.
    last   Default is *first* if *first* specified. Otherwise, –1.
    Return value: False if invalid arguments. If **–l** not specified, value
    of last command re-executed.

Version: **hist** was named **fc** with the 11/16/88 version of **ksh**.

hist –**s** [*old=new*] [*command*]   240
Re-executes previous entered command. Or use preset alias **r**.
Return value: Value of re-executed command.

jobs [–**lnp**] [*job*...]   235
Displays *job*s (or all active jobs), with process id if –**l** specified.
Displays *job*s that have changed since last prompt if –**n** specified.
Displays only process ids if –**p** specified.

kill [–**s** *signame*] *job*...   235
kill [–**n** *signum*] *job*...
kill [–*sig*] *job*...
Sends signal to jobs or processes by name or number, default **KILL**.
Return value: Number of processes **kill** is unable to send the signal.

kill –**l** [*sig*...]   236
Displays signal names or numbers of given signals, *sig*. If *sig* not
specified, all signal names are displayed.
Return value: False if *sig* is the name of an unknown signal.

let *arg*...   241
Evaluates one or more arithmetic expressions.
Return value: False if value of last expression is zero.

†**newgrp** [*group*] [*arg*...]   242
Equivalent to **exec /bin/newgrp** *arg*....
Return value: None.

print [–**Rnprs**] [–**u** [*n*]] [–**f** *format*] [–] [*arg*...]   226
Displays *arg*(s) on standard output. Ignores optional arg –.
–**R**   Doesn't use \ conventions. Processes all but –**n** as *arg*.
–**f**   Does what **printf** command does.
–**n**   Doesn't add trailing Newline to output.
–**p**   Redirects output onto co-process.
–**r**   Doesn't use \ conventions.
–**s**   Redirects output to history file.
–**u**   Redirects output to file descriptor *n*. Default is 1.
Unless you specify –**r** or –**R** , **print** uses escapes:
\a   Alert character (bell).
\b   Backspace.
\c   Terminates *arg*(s) and displays line without adding Newline.
\f   Formfeed.
\n   Newline.
\r   Return.
\t   Tab.
\v   Vertical Tab.
\E   Escape.
\\   Backslash.
\0*x*   8-bit character, ASCII code is 1-, 2-, or 3-digit octal
       number *x*.

printf *format* [*arg...*]   227
 format:
    %[flags][field width][precision][base]conversion character
 flags:
  –   Left-justify arg within field.
  +   Prefix all numbers with + or –.
  Space Prefix all numbers with Space or –.
  #   Prefix octal with "0", hexadecimal with "0x".
  0   Pad field width with leading zeroes (**e**, **E**, **f**, **g**, or **G**).
 precision:
    A (.) character followed by an integer, or a * character for var.
 conversion character:
  b   String with **print** escape conventions followed for each argument.
  d, i Signed decimal.
  n   Number of bytes printed at this point is stored in variable whose
     name is next operand.
  o   Unsigned octal.
  P   Regular expression is printed as a shell pattern.
  u   Unsigned decimal.
  x, X Unsigned hexadecimal.
  f   Floating point.
  e, E Scientific notation.
  g, G Scientific notation with significant digits.
  c   Unsigned character.
  s   String.
  q   String with special characters quoted.
  %   % character.

pwd [**–LP**]   231
 Displays working directory.
 –L Displays logical name; does not resolve symbolic links.
 –P Resolves symbolic links.

read [**–Aprs**] [**–u**[*n*]] [**–d** *char*] [**–t** *timeout*] [*name?prompt*] [*name...*]
                               229

 –A Stores fields in *name* as indexed array starting at index 0.
 –d Terminates read at delimiter *char* rather than Newline.
 –p Reads input line from co-process.
 –r A \ at end of line doesn't signify line continuation.
 –s Saves copy of input line as command in history file.
 –t Sets limit *timeout* on user response time. *timeout* is floating point
    number in units of seconds.
 –u Reads from file descriptor *n*. Default is 0.

name
> If omitted, default is **REPLY**.

name?prompt
> If **interactive** on, displays *prompt* on standard error.
> Return value: True, unless an *End-of-file* or an error is encountered.

† **readonly** [**−p**] [[*name* [*=value*]]] ...   211
> Sets readonly attribute.
>
> **−p** displays list of variables in re-enterable format.

† **return** [*n*]   223
> Causes function to return to invoking shell script.
> Return value: *n*, if specified. Otherwise, value of preceding command.

† **set** [**±Cabefhkmnopstuvx−**] [**±o** *option*] ... [**±A** *name*] [**−**] [*arg...*]

                                                                                                                  216

> Set options. Specify **−** and option letter, or **−o** *option*.
> Unset options. Specify **+** and option letter, or **+o** *option*.
> Set positional parameters. Specify *arg*(s).
> Set array values. Specify **±A** *name* and *arg*(s).
> Sort positional parameters or *arg*. Specify **−s**.
> Unset positional parameters. Specify **−−** and do not specify *arg*.

allexport (**a**)	Sets export attribute for subsequent assignments.
(**b**)	See **notify**, below.
bgnice	Runs background jobs at lower priority.
(**C**)	See **noclobber**, below.
emacs	Puts you in **emacs** built-in editor.
errexit (**e**)	If False return value, executes **ERR** trap if set.
(**f**)	See **noglob**, below.
gmacs	Puts you in **gmacs** built-in editor.
(**h**)	See **trackall**, below.
ignoreeof	If **interactive** set, doesn't exit on *End-of-File*.
keyword (**k**)	Places words in variable assignment list.
markdirs	Appends **/** to directory names.
monitor (**m**)	Runs background job in separate process group.
noclobber (**C**)	Will not overwrite an existing file with **>** redirection operator. Specify **>|** to overwrite an existing file.
noexec (**n**)	Reads commands but doesn't execute them.
noglob (**f**)	Disables pathname expansion.
nolog	Doesn't store function definitions in history file.
notify (**b**)	Displays messages when background jobs complete.
nounset (**u**)	Error message when tries to expand unset variable.
privileged (**p**)	On when effective and real ids differ.
(**t**)	Reads and executes one command, then exits.
trackall (**h**)	Commands with alias name syntax become tracked.
(**u**)	See **nounset**, above.
verbose (**v**)	Displays input on standard error as it is read.

vi	Puts you in **vi** input mode.	
viraw	Specifies **vi** character-at-a-time input.	
xtrace (x)	Expands **PS4** and displays on standard error.	
--	No more option arguments.	

† **shift** [*n*]   219
    Shifts positional parameters left by *n*.

sleep *time*   242
    Suspends execution for *time* seconds.

test [*expression*]   139, 242
[[*expression*] **]** Left Bracket Command
    Note: The [[...]] command (page 167) makes **test** and **[** obsolescent.
    Checks type of a file, if two pathnames are same file, permissions, etc.
    Return value: False if value of *expression* is not True. Also False
    if *expression* is not specified.

† **trap** [*action condition...*]
† **trap −p** [*condition...*]   223
    Specifies action when *condition*(s) arise.
    Displays list of *action*(s) and *condition*(s) for trap settings.
    Return value: False if *condition* is unknown signal name or number.

true   243
    Use **true** where you must have a command, as in the **then**
    condition of an **if** command, but you do not want the command
    to do anything.
    Return value: True

† **typeset ±f** [**tu**] [*name...*]   212
    −t Turns on **xtrace** option for specified function(s).
    −u *name* refers to function that has not yet been defined.
    Return value: False if all *name*(s) not functions, unless **u**.
    Value is number of *name*s not functions.

† **typeset** [**±AHlnprtux**] [**±ELFRZi** [*n*]] [*name* [*=value*]] ...   213
    Turns on/off and displays attributes for variables.
    −p displays list of variables in re-enterable format.
    See **Attributes** on page 177.

ulimit [**−HSacdfmnstv**] [*n*]   232
    Sets or displays system resource limits on some systems.
    −a All current resource limits.
    −c Size limit of *n* blocks on size of core dumps.
    −d Size limit of *n* kilobytes on size of data area.
    −f Size limit of *n* blocks on files written by child processes.
    −m Size limit of *n* kilobytes on physical memory.
    −n Number of file descriptors.
    −s Size limit of *n* kilobytes on stack area.
    −t Time limit of *n* seconds to be used by each process.
    −v Size limit of *n* kilobytes on virtual memory.
    −H Hard Limit.

-**S**   Soft limit.

    n   Sets specified resource limit to *n*. Otherwise displays limit.

umask [–**S**] [*mask*]   233

    Sets or displays file creation mask.

    –**S** displays output in symbolic format

† **unalias** [–**a**] *name*...   215

    Removes each alias *name*. –**a** removes all aliases.

† **unset** [–**fnv**] *name*...   215

    Unsets value(s) and attributes.

    –**f**   Causes name to refer to a function instead of a variable.

    –**n**   If you specify –**n** and *name* is a name reference to another variable, *name* will be unset rather than the variable it refers to. Otherwise, –**n** is equivalent to –**v**.

    –**v**   If you specify –**v** or you do not specify –**f**, then *name* refers to a variable

    Return value: False if all *name*(s) not functions or variables.

    Value is number of *name*s not functions or variables.

wait [*job*...]   236

    Waits for *job*s (or all processes) to terminate.

    Return value: Termination status of last process waited for.

whence [–**afpv**] *name*...   244

    Finds absolute pathname of each *name* when *name* is a program.

    –**a**   Displays all uses for *name*.

    –**f**   Does not check if *name* is a function.

    –**p**   Finds absolute pathname for each *name*.

    –**v**   Finds type of item each name is. Or use preset alias **type**.

    Return value: False if any *name*(s) not found.

Use **whence** with –**p** to find the absolute pathname, if any, corresponding to each *name*. You can also use **whence** to find out what type of item each *name* is; specify –**v** (or use the preset alias **type**, which is defined as **whence** –**v**). For each *name* you specify, **ksh** displays a line that indicates what type of command *name* is.

---

emacs BUILT-IN EDITOR   99

√ means directive can be preceded by ESCAPE *n*, where *n* is a number.

Moving the Cursor   100

√ CONTROL **f**   (forward) Moves cursor right 1 (*n*) character(s).

√ CONTROL **b**   (back) Moves cursor left 1 (*n*) character(s).

√ ESCAPE **f**   (forward) Moves cursor right to 1st character past end of current (*n*th) word.

√ ESCAPE **b**   (back) Moves cursor left to start of (*n*th) word.

    CONTROL **a**   Moves cursor to start of line.

    CONTROL **e**   (end) Moves cursor to end of line.

√ CONTROL]*c*   Moves cursor to next (*n*th) character *c* on current line.

Deleting

√ *Erase*   Deletes preceding 1 (*n*) character(s).

  Kill   Deletes entire line. Consecutive *Kill*s toggle paper terminal mode.

`CONTROL` **k**   (**k**ill) Deletes from cursor to end of current line.

`ESCAPE` *n* `CONTROL` **k**

      (**k**ill) Deletes if *n* is to left or right of cursor:
Left, from *n* up to, but not including, cursor.
Right, from cursor up to, but not including, *n*.

√ `CONTROL` **d**   (**d**elete) Deletes 1 (*n*) character(s).

√ `ESCAPE` **d**   (**d**elete) Deletes from cursor to end of current (to right) 1 (*n*) word(s).

√ `ESCAPE` `CONTROL` **h** or `ESCAPE` `CONTROL` **?** or `ESCAPE` **h**

      Deletes from current cursor back to start of current (to left) 1 (*n*) word(s).

`CONTROL` **w**   (**w**ipe out) Deletes characters, from cursor to mark.

Marking, Yanking, and Putting

## 103

`ESCAPE` `SPACE`

      Sets mark at location of cursor.

`ESCAPE` **p**   (**p**ush) Saves region from cursor to mark, and "pushes" into buffer for use with `CONTROL` **y**.

`CONTROL` **y**   Restores last text deleted from line at cursor.

`CONTROL` **x** `CONTROL` **x**

      (exchange) Interchanges cursor and mark.

Miscellaneous

`CONTROL` **t**   (**t**ranspose) **emacs** transposes current with previous character; **gmacs** transposes previous 2 characters.   104

√ `CONTROL` **c**   (**c**hange) Changes current (*n*) character(s) to uppercase; moves cursor to right 1 (*n*) characters.

√ `ESCAPE` **c**   Changes from current cursor to end of current (*n*th) word to uppercase. Moves cursor to next (*n*th) word.

√ `ESCAPE` **l**   (**l**owercase) Changes from cursor to end of current (*n*th) word to lowercase. Moves cursor to next (*n*th) word.

`CONTROL` **l**   (**l**ine redraw) Moves to next line; displays current line. Use to redraw current line if screen garbled.   105

End-of-file   End of file only if 1st character on line.

`CONTROL` **j** or `CONTROL` **m**

      Executes current line.

`ESCAPE` **=**   Lists commands or pathnames matching current word as if ∗ appended to current word.

`ESCAPE` **∗**   Command or pathname expansion.   106

`ESCAPE` `ESCAPE`

      Command or pathname completion.

`CONTROL` **u**	Multiplies count of next directive by **4**.	106
\	Escapes next character.	
`CONTROL` **v**	(version) Displays version date of **ksh**. Press any key to resume entering commands.	
`ESCAPE` *letter*	(macro expander) Searches alias list for alias *_letter*. *letter* must not be **f, b, d, p, l, c,** or **h**.	107
√ `ESCAPE` **.** or `ESCAPE` **_**	(dot or underscore). Inserts on line, last (*n*th) word of previous **ksh** command.	
`ESCAPE` **#**	Inserts **#** and enters command as a comment.	

History Directives
108

√ `CONTROL` **p**	(previous) Fetches (*n*th) previous line back in history file. Each time you press `CONTROL` **p**, the previous line is accessed.	
`CONTROL` **o**	(operate) Processes current line; fetches next line from history file. Repeat for multiline commands.	
`ESCAPE` **<**	Fetches least recent (oldest) history file line. Cannot go back more commands than defined by **HISTSIZE**.	
`ESCAPE` **>**	Fetches most recent (one you input last) line.	
√ `CONTROL` **n**	(next) Fetches next 1 (*n*th) line forward from most recent line fetched.	
√ `CONTROL` **r** [[**^**] *string*] `RETURN`	(reverse) Searches backwards in history file for 1st occurrence of command line with *string*. Specifying **^** requires command line to begin with *string*. If *string* is omitted, fetches next command line with most recent *string*. Specifying *n* reverses the direction of the search.	

vi BUILT-IN EDITOR
110

√ means directive can be preceded by an integer *n*, *n*>0.

Input Mode
112

Erase	Deletes preceding character.
Kill	Deletes line.
`CONTROL` **v**	Next character processed with literal meaning.
\	*Erase* and *Kill* processed with literal meaning.
`CONTROL` **w**	(word) Deletes previous input vi-word.
End-of-file	Returns end of file only if 1st character on line.
`ESCAPE`	Switches to control mode.
`RETURN`	Executes **ksh** current line.

Control Directives
113

`RETURN`	Executes **ksh** current line.
`CONTROL` **l**	(line redraw) Moves to next line. Displays current line.

CONTROL v	Displays version of **ksh**.	
#	Inserts # and enters command as a comment.	
=	Lists commands or pathnames that match current word.	
\	Command or pathname completion.	
*	Command or pathname expansion.	
@letter	Macro substitution of alias named _ *letter*.	
√ ~	Upper/lowercase. Moves 1 (*n*) character(s) right.	
√ .	Repeats 1 (*n*) time(s), most recent **vi** directive that changed current or previous command.	
√ **v**	Invokes **vi** program with designated command.	

Control Mode – Moving the Cursor 116

√ **l** or SPACE	Moves right 1 (*n*) character(s).	
√ **w**	(**w**ord) Moves right to start of next (*n*th) vi-word.	
√ **W**	(**W**ord) Moves right to start of next (*n*th) vi-WORD.	
√ **e**	(**e**nd) Moves right to next (*n*th) end of vi-word.	
√ **E**	(**E**nd) Moves right to next (*n*th) end of vi-WORD.	
√ **h** CONTROL **h**	Moves left 1 (*n*) character(s).	
√ **b**	(**b**ack) Moves left to preceding (*n*th) start of vi-word.	
√ **B**	(**B**ack) Moves left to preceding (*n*th) start of vi-WORD.	
^	Moves left to 1st character on line not Space or Tab.	
0	(zero) Moves left to 1st character on line.	
$	Moves right to last character on line.	
√ **|**	Moves to next (*n*th) character on line. Default is 1.	

Control Mode – Moving to Character 118

√ **f***c*	(**f**ind) Moves right to next (*n*th) *c*.	
√ **F***c*	(**F**ind) Moves left to preceding (*n*th) *c*.	
√ **t***c*	(**t**o) Moves right to character before next (*n*th next) *c*.	
√ **T***c*	(Back **T**o) Moves left to character after preceding (*n*th preceding) *c*.	
√ **;**	Repeats most recent **f**, **F**, **t**, or **T** directive once (or *n* times).	
√ **,**	As above, but reverses direction to original directive.	
%	Moves to balancing (,), {, }, [, or].	

Control Mode – Adding and Changing Text 120

Type directive (puts you into input mode) and type text to append or insert. Press ESCAPE to return to control mode or RETURN to execute command. *motion* consists of the text from the current cursor position to the cursor position defined by ***Moving the Cursor*** or ***Moving to Character*** directives.

a	(**a**ppend) Appends to right of cursor.	
A	(**A**ppend) Appends to end of current line.	
i	(**i**nsert) Inserts to left of cursor.	
I	(**I**nsert) Inserts to left of 1st character not Space or Tab.	

√ **c***motion* (**c**hange) Changes to the text you type, characters
            starting at cursor up to other end of specified *motion*.
            You can put *n* before or after **c**.

   C   (**C**hange) Deletes current character through end
            of line, and enters input mode. Same as **c$**.

   S or **cc** (**S**ubstitute) Deletes entire line and enters input mode.

√ **s**   (**s**ubstitute) Deletes 1 (*n*) characters from current
            character and enters input mode.

Control Mode – Replace   122

√ **r***c*   (**r**eplace) Replaces with *c*, 1 (*n*) character(s) starting at
            cursor. Cursor positioned on last character changed.

√ **_**   (underscore) Appends last word (or *n*th) vi-WORD from
            previous command, and enters input mode.

   R   (**R**eplace) Replaces.

Control Mode – X/Delete   122

motion consists of the text from the current cursor position to the cursor position
defined by **Moving the Cursor** or **Moving to Character** directives.

√ **x**   (**x**-ing out) Deletes 1 (*n*) character(s) at cursor.

√ **X**   (**X**-ing out) Deletes 1 (*n*) character(s) to left of cursor.

√ **d***motion* (**d**elete) Deletes 1 (*n*) character starting at cursor up to
            and including other end specified by *motion*. Saves
            characters in buffer. Retrieve with **u**ndo or **p**ut.
            You can put *n* before or after **d**.

   D   (**D**elete) Deletes from cursor to end of line. Same as **d$**.

   dd   (**d**elete) Deletes entire command, no matter where
            cursor is on line.

Control Mode – Yank/Put   123

motion consists of the text from the current cursor position to the cursor position
defined by **Moving the Cursor** or **Moving to Character** directives.

√ **y***motion* (**y**ank) Yanks current character through character that
            n motion would move cursor to; stores characters in
            buffer for subsequent use with **p** or **P**. Text and cursor
            not changed. You can put *n* before or after **y**.

   Y   (**Y**ank) Yanks from cursor to end of line. Same as **y$**.

   yy   (**y**ank) Yanks (copies) entire current line into buffer,
            no matter where cursor is on line.

√ **p**   (**p**ut) Puts previously yanked or deleted text
            (or *n* copies of yanked text) to right of cursor.

√ **P**   (**P**ut) Same as above, but to left.

Control Mode – Undo   124

   u   (**u**ndo) Undoes preceding text-modifying directive.

   U   (**U**ndo line) Undoes all text modifying directives made on current line. Use **u** to undo **U**.

Fetching Previous Commands 125

√ **k** or **−** (minus) Moves up (back) to fetch (*n*th) preceding command. Each time you enter **k**, preceding command back is fetched.

√ **j** or **+** (plus) Moves down (forward) to fetch (*n*th) next command. Each time you enter **j**, next command forward is fetched.

√ **G** (**G**o back) Fetches oldest accessible command, or command *n* from start of history file.

/ [^] *string* RETURN
Moves left and up (back) through history file to search for most recent occurrence of *string*. Specifying ^ requires command line to begin with *string*. Null *string*: Previous string specified is used.

? [^] *string* RETURN
Same as above, but searches in reverse direction, right and down (forward).

n Repeats most recent / or ? directive.

N As above, but in reverse direction.

SPECIAL CHARACTERS 129

| & ; < > ( ) $ ` \ " ' Space Tab Newline
When patterns are processed * ? [ ]
When they begin a new word # ~
When variable assignments are processed = [ ]

COMMENTS 129

Begin with unquoted # sign, and go to next Newline.
Legal anywhere token may begin.

IDENTIFIERS 132

[:alpha:] **0-9** _ (underscore)
First character cannot be a digit.
No limit on number of characters.
Uppercase and lowercase characters are distinct.
In POSIX locale, character class **alpha** consists of A-Z and a-z.

VARIABLE NAMES 132

Simple variable name is an identifier.
Compound variable name is:
- Identifier preceded by . (dot).
- More than one identifier, separated by . (dot) and optionally preceded by . (dot).

ALIAS NAMES 131

First character is any non-special printable character.
Other characters are same as for identifiers (see above).
Aliases whose names are of form *_letter* define macros for **emacs** and **vi** built-in editors.
See aliases, and **alias**.

SIMPLE VARIABLE ASSIGNMENTS 132

varname=value
varname[string]=value
varname[expression]=value

OPERATORS 130

I/O redirection operators: > >> >& >| < << <<− <& <>
Control operators: | & ; ( ) || && ;; (( )) |& ;&

RESERVED WORDS 130

{ } case do done elif else esac fi for function if in select then time until while [[ ]] !
Version: ! is a reserved word only on versions of **ksh** newer than 11/16/88.
ksh recognizes only:
- As first word on line.
- After operators ; | || & && |& ( ).
- As 1st word after reserved word, except after **case**, **for**, **in**, **select**, [[.
- As second word after **case**, **for**, **select**. However, **in** is the only legal reserved word in this case.

PATTERNS	133

A *pattern-list* is one or more patterns separated by | or **&**.

Regular Characters

Regular characters are all those characters that are not pattern characters.
Regular characters match themselves.
Quote with a \ any special characters to use them as regular characters.

Pattern Characters

[...] Delimits set of characters. Inside [...] :   133
    – (minus) indicates range of characters.
    ! Immediately after opening [, reverses the match.
    ] Stands for itself after opening [, or after ! following opening [.
    \ Removes special meaning of –,], !, and \.
    [:*class*:] indicates characters in the same class, where
        class is one of **alnum alpha blank cntrl digit graph lower print punct space upper xdigit**
    [=*c*=] indicates characters with same primary weight as *c*.
    [.*symbol*.] indicates the collating element symbol.

? Matches any single character.   134
* Matches zero or more occurrences of any and all characters.
?(*pattern-list*)   135
    Optionally matches *pattern-list*.
*(*pattern-list*)
    Matches zero or more occurrences of *pattern-list*.
+(*pattern-list*)
    Matches one or more occurrences of *pattern-list*.
@(*pattern-list*)
    Matches exactly one occurrence of *pattern-list*.
!(*pattern-list*)
    Matches everything except *pattern-list*.
n A backreference. Matches same string as the *n*-th parenthesis group in the pattern. The group must precede this backreference.   136

QUOTING/GROUPING	141

\	Escape character	141
\Newline	Line continuation	
'...'	Literal (single) quotes	142
$'...'	ANSI C string	
"..."	Grouping (double) quotes	
$"..."	Message grouping (double) quotes	143
`` `...` ``	Old command substitution	
$(...)	New command substitution	144

${...}	Parameter expansion	144
((...))	Arithmetic evaluation	
$((...))	Arithmetic expansion	
varname[...]=	Array variable assignment	

I/O REDIRECTION   145

Operator can be preceded by 0-9, with no intervening Space or Tab.

Standard input   File descriptor 0 open for reading.
Standard output   File descriptor 1 open for writing.
Standard error   File descriptor 2 open for reading or writing.   23

< *word*		Reading
> *word*	>| *word*	Writing
<< *word*	<<– *word*	Here-Document
<& *word*	>& *word*	Duplicating Input/Output
<&*digit*–	>&*digit*–	Moving Input/Output
<&–	>&–	Closing
<> *word*		Reading/Writing
>> *word*		Appending

SIGNALS   21

Always needed:
  Interrupt (**INT**)
  Hangup (**HUP**)
  Termination (**TERM**)
  Kill (**KILL**)

Required for job control:
  Keyboard stop (**TSTP**)
  Tty input (**TTIN**)
  Continue (**CONT**)
  Stop (**STOP**)

PERMISSIONS   34

File can have these permissions:
  Read, Write, and/or Execute, by owner, group, and/or others.
  Setuid and/or setgid
Specify with 4-digit octal number:
  1st: Setuid and/or setgid
  2nd: Owner
  3rd: Group
  4th: Other
Each octal digit is sum of values corresponding to permissions of owner, group, and/or others:
  Read: 4
  Write: 2
  Execute or Search: 1

Permission string is 10 characters. First is **d** for directory; – for file. Other 9, in groups of 3, are owner, group, and other: **r** read; **w** write; **s** setuid or setgid; **x** execute/search. – in any location indicates it lacks that permission.

CONDITIONAL EXPRESSION PRIMITIVES 139

Conditional expressions are used with [[..]], [...], and **test**.
Primitive can be any of the following unary *file* expressions:

–a *file*	True if *file* exists. *Caution*: **–e** is preferred.
–b *file*	True if *file* is a block special file.
–c *file*	True if *file* is a character special file.
–d *file*	True if *file* is a directory.
–e *file*	True if *file* exists.
–f *file*	True if *file* is a regular file.
–g *file*	True if *file* has its set-group-id bit set.
–k *file*	True if *file* has its sticky bit set.
–p *file*	True if *file* is a named pipe (fifo).
–r *file*	True if *file* is readable.
–s *file*	True if *file* has a size greater than zero.
–u *file*	True if *file* has its set-user-id bit set.
–w *file*	True if *file* is writable.
–x *file*	True if *file* is executable.
–G *file*	True if the group of *file* is the effective group id of the process.
–L *file*	True if *file* is a symbolic link. (You can also use **–h** *file*.)
–O *file*	True if the owner of *file* is the effective user id of the process.
–S *file*	True if *file* is a special file of type socket.

Primitive can be any of following unary expressions:

–t *fildes*	True if file whose file descriptor number is *fildes* is open and is associated with a terminal device.
–o *option*	True if *option* is on.
–z *string*	True if length of *string* is zero.
–n *string*	True if length of *string* is non-zero.

With **test** and [, primitive can be any of these binary string expressions:

string1 = *string2*	True if *string1* is equal to *string2*.
string1 != *string2*	True if *string1* is not equal to *string2*.

With [[...]], primitive can be any of these binary string expressions:

string = *pattern*	True if *string* matches pattern *pattern*. (Obsolete)
string == *pattern*	True if *string* matches pattern *pattern*.
string != *pattern*	True if *string* does not match pattern *pattern*.
string1 < *string2*	True if *string1* comes before *string2* .
string1 > *string2*	True if *string1* comes after *string2*.

Primitive can be any of these binary file expressions:

file1 **–nt** *file2*	True if file *file1* is newer than file *file2*.
file1 **–ot** *file2*	True if file *file1* is older than file *file2*.
file1 **–ef** *file2*	True if *file1* is another name for file *file2*.

Primitive can be any of these expressions comparing 2 arithmetic expressions:

exp1 **–eq** *exp2* True if value of *exp1* and *exp2* are equal.
exp1 **–ne** *exp2* True if value of *exp1* and *exp2* are not equal.
exp1 **–gt** *exp2* True if value of *exp1* is greater than value of *exp2*.
exp1 **–ge** *exp2* True if value of *exp1* is greater than or equal to value of *exp2*.
exp1 **–lt** *exp2* True if value of *exp1* is less than value of *exp2*.
exp1 **–le** *exp2* True if value of *exp1* is less than or equal to value of *exp2*.

Primitive can be a string by itself. In this case the primary is True if the string is not Null.

ARITHMETIC EXPRESSIONS 136

Use arithmetic expressions:
- As indexed array subscript.
- For each argument in **let**.
- Inside ((...)). ((...)) is same as **let** "...".
- Inside $((...)).
- Inside **for** ((...;...;...)).
- As shift count in **shift**.
- For arithmetic comparison operators of **test**, [, or [[...]].
- As resource limits in **ulimit**.
- As right-hand side of variable assignment to an integer or floating point variable.
- As operands to arithmetic formats with **print** or **printf**.

Calculations use the double precision floating point arithmetic type.
Associativity is left to right, except = and *op=* are right to left.
Precedence:

  Operators at top are highest precedence.
  Operators of the same precedence are listed under the same bullet.

• (*expression*)	Overrides precedence rules	138
• *varname*++	Post increment	
varname––	Post decrement	
+*expression*	Unary plus	
++*varname*	Pre-increment	
––*varname*	Pre-decrement	
–*expression*	Unary minus	
!*expression*	Logical negation	
~*expression*	Bitwise negation	
• *	Multiplication	
/	Division	
%	Remainder of 1st expression modulo 2nd expression	
• +	Addition	
–	Subtraction	
• <<	Left shift	
>>	Right shift	

- <=   Less than or equal to
  >=   Greater than or equal to
  <   Less than
  >   Greater than
- ==   Equal to
  !=   Not equal to
- &   Bitwise and
- ^   Bitwise exclusive or
- | Bitwise or
- &&   Logical and
- || Logical or
- ?:   Conditional operator
- =   Assignment
  op=   Compound arithmetic assignment
- ,   Comma operator

Integer constant	*[base#] number*	
base	Decimal integer 2-64. Default base 10.	
number	Any non-negative number	
Floating constant	*number[.number] [exponent]*	
number	Any non-negative decimal number.	
exponent	**E** or **e** optionally followed by + or – and a non-negative decimal number.	
varname	Variable	

An arithmetic function is denoted by *function(expression)*, where *function* is one of the following:

abs	Absolute value
acos	Arc cosine of angle in radians
asin	Arc sine
atan	Arc tangent
cos	Cosine
cosh	Hyperbolic cosine
exp	Exponential with base *e* where $e \approx 2.718$
int	Greatest integer less than or equal to value of *expression*
log	Logarithm
sin	Sine
sinh	Hyperbolic sine
sqrt	Square root
tan	Tangent
tanh	Hyperbolic tangent

PARAMETER EXPANSION 183

Note: You can use * in place of @ in each of the following expansions that uses @. When the expansion is inside double quotes, * versions expand to a single argument whereas @ expands to the number of arguments defined by the positional parameters or the array.

Basic 184

${*parameter*}

Modifiers 185

${*parameter*:–*word*}	Using default values
${*parameter*:=*word*}	Assigning default values
${*parameter*:?*word*}	Displaying error if Null or unset
${*parameter*:+*word*}	Using alternate value

Substrings 186

${*parameter*#*pattern*}	Remove small left *pattern*
${*parameter*##*pattern*}	Remove large left *pattern*
${*parameter*%*pattern*}	Remove small right *pattern*
${*parameter*%%*pattern*}	Remove large right *pattern*
${*parameter*:*offset*:*length*}	Substring of length *length* starting at *offset*
${*parameter*:*offset*}	Substring starting at *offset*
${*parameter*/*pattern*/*string*}	Substitute first *pattern* with *string*
${*parameter*/#*pattern*/*string*}	Substitute left anchored *pattern* with *string*
${*parameter*/%*pattern*/*string*}	Substitute right anchored *pattern* with *string*
${*parameter*//*pattern*/*string*}	Substitute each occurrence of *pattern* with *string*

Subarrays 190

${@:*offset*}	Positional parameters starting at *offset*
${@:*offset*:*n*}	At most *n* positional parameters starting at *offset*
${*varname*[@]:*offset*}	Subarray starting at *offset*
${*varname*[@]:*offset*:*n*}	Subarray of at most *n* elements starting at *offset*

Other 188

${#*parameter*}	String length
${#*varname*[@]}	Number of elements of an array
${!*varname*}	Name of variable
${!*prefix*@}	Names of variables starting with *prefix*
${!*varname*[@]}	Names of indices of an array

ATTRIBUTES	177

PARAMETERS AND VARIABLES	190

.sh.edchar	Character that caused **KEYBD** trap	196
.sh.edcol	Cursor position before **KEYBD** trap	
.sh.edmode	Escape when **KEYBD** trap invoked in **vi** input mode	
.sh.edtext	Contents of input buffer before **KEYBD** trap	
.sh.name	Name of variable that invoked discipline function	197
.sh.subscript	Subscript for variable that invoked discipline function	
.sh.value	Value of variable that invoked discipline function	
.sh.version	Version of shell	198

Variables Used by ksh

198

		Default	
CDPATH	Search path for **cd** built-in	None	198
COLUMNS	Number of columns on terminal	Implicit: 80	199
EDITOR	Pathname for your editor	Implicit: **/bin/ed**	
ENV	User environment file	None	
FCEDIT	Editor for **hist** built-in	Implicit: **/bin/ed**	
FIGNORE	Ignore filenames	None	
FPATH	Search path for auto-load functions	None	200
HISTEDIT	Editor for **hist** built-in	Implicit: **/bin/ed**	
HISTFILE	History pathname	Note 1	
HISTSIZE	Number of history commands	Implicit: 128	201
HOME	Your home directory	Note 2	
IFS	Internal field separators	Space-Tab-Newline	
LANG	Language locale	Implicit: POSIX	202
LC_ALL	Locale settings	None	
LC_COLLATE	Locale collation	None	
LC_CTYPE	Locale character classes	None	
LC_NUMERIC	Locale decimal	None	203
LINES	Number of lines on terminal	Implicit: 24	
MAIL	Name of your mail file	Note 2	
MAILCHECK	Frequency of mail check	600	
MAILPATH	List of mail files	None	
PATH	Path search directories	**/bin:/usr/bin:**	204
PS1	Primary prompt string	$Space	
PS2	Secondary prompt string	>Space	205
PS3	Command prompt for **select**	#?	
PS4	Debug prompt string	+	
SHELL	Pathname of the shell	Note 3	206
TERM	Terminal type	None	
TMOUT	Timeout variable	Note 4	
VISUAL	Visual editor, overrides **EDITOR**	None	

Note 1: Implicit: **$HOME/.sh_history**
Note 2: Set by system administrator.
Note 3: May be set to pathname for **ksh** during login.
Note 4: Zero (unlimited), or set by system administrator.

KornShell LANGUAGE GRAMMAR

newline	Newline character.	
identifier	Syntax of an identifier.	132
varname	Syntax of a variable name.	132
test-primitive	Conditional test expression.	139
string	Any sequence of non-special characters.	23
typeset-opts	Any **typeset** options except **–f**, **–p**, or **–x**.	213
digit	0–9	
expression	Syntax of an arithmetic expression.	136

complete-command

        list newline

list

        term...

        [*term...*] *and-or*   166

term

        and-or newline

        and-or ;   166

        and-or **&**   167

        and-or **|&**   167

and-or

        pipe   164

        pipe **&&** [*newline...*] *pipe*   166

        pipe **||** [*newline...*] *pipe*   166

pipe

        [**time**] *pipeline*   165

        [**!**] *pipeline*   165

pipeline

        command

        pipeline **|** [*newline...*] *command*   164

command

        simple-command   154

        compound-command [*io-redirect...*]   164

compound-command

        (*compound-list*)   173

        { *brace-group* }   173

        [[*test-expr*]]   167

        ((*expression*))   173

        for *varname* [**in** *word...*] *separator group*   171

        for (([*expression*];[*expression*];[*expression*])) *do-group*   171

        select *varname* [**in** *word...*] *separator group*   169

        while *compound-list separator do-group*   172

        until *compound-list separator do-group*   172

        if *compound-list* **then** *compound-list else-part* **fi**   168

        case *word* **in** [*case-body*] **esac**   168

| | function-def [newline...] brace-group [io-redirect] | 174 |

compound-list
          [newline...] list [newline... list]... [newline...]

group
          brace-group
          do-group

brace-group
          { compound-list }

do-group
          do compound-list **done**

else-part
          [**elif** compound-list]... [**else** compound-list]

case-body
          case-item... [newline...]

case-item
          [newline...] [(] pattern) [compound-list] **;;**
          [newline...] [(] pattern) [compound-list] **;&**

pattern
          word [| word]...

function-def
          [varname.]identifier ( )
          function [varname.]identifier

simple-command
          cmd-word...

cmd-word
          assignment
          io-redirect
          word

assignment
          simple-assignment
          varname= (word ...)
          varname= ([word]=word ...)
          varname= (assignment-list [separator assignment-list]...)

| varname= (assignment) | 154 |

simple-assignment

| varname [[word]]=word | 132 |

assignment-list

| [**typeset** typeset-opts] simple-assignment ... | 154 |

io-redirect

| [digit]io-operator word | 145 |

io-operator
          < or **<<** or **<<-** or **<&** or **<>**
          > or **>|** or **>>** or **>&**

word
          string
          varname

separator

> ;
> *newline*...

test-expr

> *test-primary*
> (*test-expr*)
> **!** *test-expr*
> *test-expr* **| |** *test-primary*
> *test-expr* **&&** *test-primary*

PRESET ALIASES 156

```
autoload='typeset –fu'
command='command '
fc=hist
float='typeset –E'
functions='typeset –f'
hash='alias –t – –'
history='hist –l'
integer='typeset –i'
nameref='typeset –n'
nohup='nohup '
r='hist –s'
redirect='command exec'
stop='kill –s STOP'
times='{ {time;}2>&1;}'
type='whence –v'
```

OTHER COMMANDS 246

cat [*file*...]	Concatenates *file*(s); writes on standard output.	246
chmod *mode file*...	Changes file permissions.	
cp *file*... *target*	Copies *file*(s) to *target*.	247
cut –f *list* [**–d** *delimiter*] [**–s**] [*file*...]		248
	Cuts *delimiter* separated fields specified by *list* to output. Default delimiter is Tab.	
cut –c *list* [*file*...]	Cuts columns specified by *list* to output.	
date [+*format*]	Displays date and time on standard output.	
ed [–] [*file*]	Text editor.	249
find *directory*... *expression*		
	Generates list of pathnames; applies *expression*.	
grep [*option*...] *pattern* [*file*...]		250
	Searches *file*(s) for lines matching *pattern*.	
ln [**–s**] *file*... *target*	Links *file*(s) to *target*.	251

lp [*file...*]	Prints *file*(s) on standard input.	
lpr [*file...*]	Name of **lp** (above) on some systems.	
ls [**–agltCF**] [*directory*]	Displays filename(s).	252
mail [**–b**] [*user...*]	Sends or displays mail messages.	
mkdir [**–p**] [**–m** *mode*] *directory...*		
	Creates *directory*(s).	
more [*file...*]	Name of **pg** (below) on some systems.	253
mv [**–f**] *file... target*	Moves or renames *file*(s) to *target*.	
paste [**–d** *list*] [**–s**] *file...*		
	Concatenates corresponding lines of input files, then writes resulting lines to standard output.	
pg [*file...*]	Displays *file*(s).	254
rm [**–fri**] *file...*	Removes filename entries for *file*(s).	
rmdir *directory...*	Removes *directory*(s), which must be empty.	255
sort [*option...*] [*file...*]	Sorts lines in *file*(s).	
stty [**erase** *erase*] [**kill** *kill*] [**eof** *eof*] [**int** *int*] [**quit** *quit*]		
	Displays or changes terminal settings.	
tail [±*number*] [**–f**] [*file*]		
	Displays last part of *file*.	
tee [**–a**] *file...*	Reads standard input, and writes.	256
tr [**–cds**] [*string1* [*string2*]]		
	Transliterates characters in a file.	
tty	Displays pathname of terminal on standard output.	
uniq [**–cdu**] [*input* [*output*]]		
	Copies lines from *input* to *output* eliminating and/or counting duplicates.	
wc [**–clw**] [*file...*]	Counts characters, lines, and words.	257
what *file...*	Looks for character strings.	
who [**am i**]	Displays users currently logged in.	

21 PORTABILITY

This chapter summarizes the differences between versions of the Bourne shell and versions of **ksh** that you need to know if you plan to write scripts that run with more than one shell and/or on more than one system.

One aspect of portability is the ability to write scripts that run on different systems. Shell scripts rely on commands that are built into the language and on programs that are available on the operating system. While some programs may not be present on all systems, the command language and built-in commands of a given shell will always behave the same no matter what system the shell is running on. Because so many of the features of **ksh** are built in, it is possible to write **ksh** programs that do not rely heavily on the underlying operating system. This makes them easy to port to other systems running the same version of **ksh**.

The other aspect of writing portable scripts is writing them to run on systems that do not have **ksh**, or that don't have the latest version. In this case you have to restrict the features you use to those found in all versions of the shell you wish to run it with. However, scripts will not be completely portable if they rely on other programs.

This chapter summarizes most of the differences between the original version of the Bourne shell, the System V Release 4 Bourne shell, the POSIX shell, the 11/16/88 version of **ksh**, and the 12/28/93 version of **ksh**.

FEATURES OF ksh NOT IN BOURNE SHELL

The following features are not in the early version of the Bourne shell. Therefore, for maximal portability, avoid using these **ksh** features:
- # for comment. (Use : instead.)
- ! for negation within a character class.
- : within parameter expansions.
- Redirection with built-in commands.
- Shell functions.

test and **echo** were not built-ins on early versions of the Bourne shell and thus their behavior is system dependent.

ksh *FEATURES IN POSIX NOT IN SYSTEM V*

The following are features defined by the POSIX 1003.2 shell standard that are not in the System V Release 4 shell:

- Substring expansions ${*name#pattern*} ${*name%pattern*}
- Substring expansions ${*name##pattern*} ${*name%%pattern*}
- String length expansion ${#*name*}.
- Expansion of positional parameters greater than 9, ${*digits*}.
- Assigning **values** with **readonly** and **export**.
- Symbolic names for signals and traps.
- Command substitution syntax $(*command*).
- Arithmetic expansion syntax $((*expression*)).
- Aliases, tilde expansion, command line editing, and history.
- Built-in commands **alias, command, fc, getconf, printf, umask,** and **unalias**.
- [=*character*=], [:*class*:], and [.*symbol*.] inside shell pattern character classes.
- The variables **ENV, FCEDIT, HISTFILE, HISTSIZE, LANG, LC_*, LINENO,** and **PPID**.
- Redirection operators >| and <>.
- Compound command **!**.

FEATURES OF ksh *NOT IN POSIX SHELL*

This section lists features that are part of **ksh,** but are not required by the POSIX shell standard. This list is not complete. There are additions to some built-in commands that are not noted.

The following are features of the 12/28/93 version of **ksh** not specified in the POSIX 1003.2 shell standard:

- Attributes other than readonly and export for variables, array variables, compound variables, and compound assignment.
- Floating point arithmetic, the ((...)) arithmetic command, and the use of variables within arithmetic expressions. The arithmetic **for** command.
- Operators **;&** and **|&** (coprocesses).
- Reserved words **function, time, select,** [[and]].
- Pattern matching *(*pattern-list*)   ?(*pattern-list*)   +(*pattern-list*)   !(*pattern-list*) @(*pattern-list*).
- Variables **_, FIGNORE, FPATH, HISTCMD, HISTEDIT, OLDPWD, PS3, RANDOM, REPLY, SECONDS, TMOUT,** and **.sh.***.
- Built-in commands **builtin, disown, hist, let, print, typeset,** and **whence**.
- **test** operators **–nt, –ot, –ef, –O, –G,** and **–S**.
- **cd –** and **cd** with two arguments.
- Names for options and **set –o**.
- Traps **DEBUG, ERR,** and **KEYBD**.
- Autoload functions and discipline functions.
- Fine granularity **sleep**.

COMPATIBILITY OF ksh *WITH SYSTEM V SHELL*

This section lists the incompatibilities known to exist between the 12/28/93 version of **ksh** and the System V Release 4 version of the Bourne shell. It also lists the requirements for the POSIX shell standard. *Note*: For conciseness, we refer to the System V Release 4 version of the Bourne shell here as **bsh**, and the POSIX shell standard as **psh**.

In addition to the incompatibilities listed here, the output of built-in commands and error messages differs between **ksh** and **bsh** in a few cases. For instance, **times** produces two lines of output in **ksh** and only one line in **bsh**.

Character ^:
  ksh Is not special.
  bsh Is an archaic synonym for |.
  psh Is not special.

IFS variable:
  ksh Is only effective for **read**, and the results of parameter expansion and command substitution. **ksh** always initializes **IFS**.
  bsh Is effective for all words. Thus, for instance, **IFS=x; exit** executes **e** with argument **it**.
  psh Is only effective for **read**, and the results of parameter expansion and command substitution.

If an environment variable is modified:
  ksh New value is passed to the child processes.
  bsh You must export the variable for this to happen.
  psh New value is passed to the child processes.

time:
  ksh Is a reserved word. Thus **time a | b** times the pipeline in **ksh**, while only **a** is timed in **bsh**. You can also **time** built-in commands and functions.
  bsh Is not a reserved word. You cannot **time** built-in commands or functions.
  psh The behavior is unspecified when **time** is used in a pipeline command.

select and **function**:
  ksh Are reserved words.
  bsh Are not reserved words.
  psh POSIX standard allows **select** and **function** to be added.

Scope of variable assignments on command lines:
  ksh Except for a subset of built-in commands, denoted with † in the *Built-In Commands* chapter, the scope of variable assignments is only for the command or function they precede.
  bsh All built-in commands and functions treat variable assignments as globals.
  psh Same as **ksh**.

for, while, and **until** loops with I/O redirection:
    ksh Are executed in the current process environment. Assignments made within loops remain in effect after the loop completes.
    bsh Executes in a separate process environment. No side effects are possible.
    psh Same as **ksh**.

Semantics of functions:
    ksh Functions defined with *name*( ) syntax behave the same as **psh**. With functions defined with **function** *name*, you can specify local variables, and you can write recursive functions. Errors in functions abort the function, but not the script that they are in. Parameter **0** expands to the function name. Traps defined in functions are local. **ksh** allows function names to be the same as variable names; therefore, **unset** requires you to specify **–f** when the name refers to a function.
    bsh All variables are global. You cannot write recursive functions. Errors in functions abort the script that calls them. Parameter **0** is unchanged inside a function. Traps are global. Functions and variables must have distinct names.
    psh Same as **bsh** except that a variable and a function can have the same name.

Words that begin with **~**:
    ksh May be expanded by tilde expansion.
    bsh Does not have this feature.
    psh May be expanded by tilde expansion.

When '((' occurs where a command name is valid:
    ksh Assumes that an arithmetic expression follows.
    bsh Means nested (...).
    psh Behavior is unspecified.

Two adjacent **IFS** delimiters, other than Space or Tab, used with **read**:
    ksh Generates a Null input argument. Therefore, you can use **IFS=:** and correctly read the **/etc/passwd** file even when fields are omitted.
    bsh Multiple delimiters count as a single delimiter.
    psh Same as **ksh**.

Arithmetic test comparison operators (**–gt, –eq, –lt,** ...):
    ksh Allows any arithmetic expressions as operands.
    bsh Allows only constants.
    Note: If you say **test x –eq 0** in **bsh** (which is meaningless), it returns True. In **ksh**, it depends on the value of the variable **x**. If there is no variable **x** or if **x** does not evaluate to a number, then **ksh** produces an error message.
    psh The result when operands are not numbers is not specified.

Environment handed down to a program:
    ksh Is not sorted.
    bsh Is sorted.
    Note: No program should ever rely on the environment variables being sorted since any program can modify the environment.
    psh Not specified.

hash command:
> **ksh** Has a preset alias **hash** that does most of what the **bsh** built-in **hash** command does, except for the **–r** option. In **ksh**, you must specify **PATH=$PATH** to achieve the same result as **–r** in **bsh**.
> **bsh** Has a built-in **hash** command.
> **psh** Not specified.

set – – with no arguments:
> **ksh** Unsets the positional parameter list.
> **bsh** Sets parameter **1** to Null, and unsets the other positional parameters.
> **psh** Unsets the positional parameter list.

Specification of command line options:
> **ksh** Accepts options of the form **–x –v** as well as **–xv** both for invocation and for **set**.
> **bsh** Only allows one option argument.
> **psh** Same as **ksh**.

Unbalanced quotes:
> **ksh** Does not allow unbalanced quotes with any script. *Note*: **ksh** behaves like **bsh** for **eval** statements.
> **bsh** If the end-of-file is reached before a balancing quote in **bsh**, it quietly inserts the balancing quote.
> **psh** Not specified.

Failures of any built-in command:
> **ksh** Except for built-ins denoted with † in the **Built-In Commands** chapter, failures cause a return value of False, but do not cause the script that contains them to abort. In this respect, **ksh** treats most built-in commands semantically the same as non-built-in commands.
> **bsh** Causes a script that contains the built-in to abort.
> **psh** Same as **ksh**.

Sequence **$(**:
> **ksh** Is special. When used within grouping (double) quotes, **$(** must be preceded by \ to remove its special meaning.
> **bsh** Sequence is illegal outside of grouping (double) quotes. Processed literally inside grouping quotes.
> **psh** Same as **ksh**.

exec, when used without arguments (for I/O redirection):
> **ksh** Sets close-on-exec on each file descriptor greater than 2.
> **bsh** Does not set close-on-exec on any files.
> **psh** Allows either behavior.

When the real user id is not equal to the effective user id, or the real group id is not equal to the effective group id:
> **ksh** Resets the effective user and group ids to the real user and group ids unless the **privileged** option (**–p**) is on.

bsh Does not do this.
psh Not specified.

NEW FEATURES IN 12/28/93 VERSION OF ksh

Enlarged Name Space

The name space for shell variables is a hierarchy of identifiers with **.** (dot) as the delimiter. A variable with a **.** (dot) in the name is called a compound variable.

Associative Arrays

The new version of **ksh** supports both indexed arrays and associative arrays. Indexed arrays are arrays whose subscript is an arithmetic expression; indexed arrays were available in earlier versions of **ksh**. Associative arrays are arrays whose subscripts are strings. The **–A** attribute of **typeset** specifies that a variable is an associative array. The indices of an array are generated with the expansion ${!*varname*[**@**]}.

Compound Assignments

Compound assignments can be used to assign values to an indexed or associative array, and to assign values to related compound variables.

Name References

The **–n** attribute of **typeset** specifies that a variable is a reference to another variable. The name for a name reference variable must be an identifier. Once a name reference is created, each reference to this variable causes the variable named by the name reference to be used. The first identifier in a *varname* is replaced by the contents of a matching name reference.

Discipline Functions

Each variable can have one or more functions associated with it by defining functions whose names are of the form *varname.action*, where *varname* is the name of the variable and *action* is the name of the discipline function.
The discipline functions named **get**, **set**, and **unset** can be set for any variable. Other discipline functions can be used for application-specific variables created by user-defined built-in commands.

Changes and Additions to Arithmetic

ksh now supports floating point arithmetic. The **typeset** attributes exponential (**–E**) and float (**–F**) are used to specify real valued variables. Each can be specified with a number that specifies:

–E The number of significant figures to use when the number is expanded.
–F The number of places after the decimal when the number is expanded.

The following operators have been added:
- The conditional operator **?:** .
- The comma operator **,**.
- The postfix and prefix operators **++** and **– –**.
- The unary **+**.

You can use functions from the ANSI C math library within arithmetic expressions.

For integer constants, you can specify arithmetic bases up to base 64.

Arithmetic expansion (**$((...))**) is now documented.

New Parameter Expansions

The following parameter expansions have been added.
- **${!*varname*}** Name of the variable defined by *varname*.
- **${!*varname*[@]}** Name of the indices for the array variable *varname*.
- **${*param*:*offset*}** Substring starting at *offset*.
- **${*param*:*offset*:*length*}** Up to *length* characters of *varname* starting at *offset*.
- **${@:*offset*}** Positional parameters starting at *offset*.
- **${@:*offset*:*length*}** Up to *length* positional parameters starting at *offset*.
- **${*varname*[@]:*offset*}** Array elements of *varname* starting at *offset*.
- **${*varname*[@]:*offset*:*length*}** Up to *length* array elements of *varname* starting at *offset*.
- **${*param*/*pattern*/*string*}** Value of *param* with the first occurrence of *pattern* replaced by *string*.
- **${*param*/#*pattern*/*string*}** If *param* begins with *pattern*, *pattern* is replaced by *string*.
- **${*param*/%*pattern*/*string*}** If *param* ends with *pattern*, *pattern* is replaced by *string*.
- **${*param*//*pattern*/*string*}** Value of *param* with each occurrence of *pattern* replaced by *string*.

You can use ***** in place of **@** in each of the above expansions that uses **@**. When the expansion is inside double quotes, ***** versions expand to a single argument whereas **@** expands to the number of arguments defined by the positional parameters or the array.

ksh applies pattern operations to each element separately when applied to positional parameters and to arrays.

ksh performs tilde expansion when a **~** is found in a parameter expansion modifier.

New Quoting Mechanisms

ksh processes a single quoted string preceded by a $, $'...', using ANSI C string conventions.

ksh processes a double quoted string preceded by a $, $"...", as a string that needs to be translated when the locale is not C or POSIX. The $ is ignored in the C or POSIX locale.

Input/Output Additions

The redirection operators **>&** *digit* and **<&** *digit* can be followed by a – to cause a given file descriptor to be moved rather than duplicated.

The **printf** built-in command and the **–f** *format* option to **print** can be used to produce formatted output using ANSI C formatting conventions. In addition to the format conversions defined by ANSI C, the *format* argument to **print** and **printf** can contain:
- **%b**   Expand escape sequences in each argument
- **%q**   Quote strings that contain special characters.
- **%P**   Treat argument as regular expression and convert it to a shell pattern.

The **alias**, **export**, **readonly**, **set**, **trap**, and **typeset** commands produce output with strings quoted so that they can be used as input to the shell. The output for an execution trace has strings with special characters quoted.

The **read** built-in command has options to specify a timeout and to specify the line delimiter character. In addition, you can specify that **read** split fields into an indexed array.

The character escape sequence **\E** (page 226) has been added to all ANSI C strings, and to the **echo** and **print** built-in commands. The sequence **\E** expands to the Escape character.

New Behavior for Functions

If you declare a function with the **function** *varname* format, then **ksh** executes the function in a separate function environment described on page 174.

If you declare a function in *varname*( ) format, then **ksh** executes the function in the current environment, like a dot script. This is the behavior of the System V shell and is required by the POSIX shell standard.

New Pattern Matching Capabilities

The pattern matching construct [:*character_class*:] inside [ ], matches the specified set of characters. The following character classes are available:

[:alnum:] [:alpha:] [:blank:] [:cntrl:] [:digit:] [:graph:]
[:lower:] [:print:] [:punct:] [:space:] [:upper:] [:xdigit:]

The pattern matching construct [=*character*=] inside [ ], matches all characters whose primary collation weight is the same as that of *character*.

The pattern matching construct [.*element*.] inside [ ], matches the collating element given by *element*.

A pattern can contain backreferences to earlier sub-patterns using the notation *digit*, where *digit* is the sub-pattern number.

The use of **&** inside pattern lists has been documented.

Editing Changes and Additions

The following changes have been made to the built-in editors:

- A new **KEYBD** trap which is triggered each time you enter a key from the terminal can be used to provide alternate key bindings.
- When completion, listing, or expansion directives are applied on the first word of a command that does not contain a **/**, built-ins, functions, and all files on the **PATH** are considered for matching in all the edit modes.
- The new **vi** directive **%** (page 120) moves the cursor to the balancing (,), {, }, [, or] character.
- The **vi** directive **s** (page 121) deletes characters starting at the current cursor position up to *n* characters to the right, and enters input mode.
- In **emacs** mode, successive kills and deletes are appended to the buffer.
- The CONTROL **t** directive in **emacs** now transposes the current character and the previous character.

Changes to Variables

Sixteen new variables have been added:

.sh.edchar	(page 196) is Character that caused **KEYBD** trap.
.sh.edcol	(page 196) is Cursor position before **KEYBD** trap.
.sh.edmode	(page 196) is Escape character for **vi** input mode **KEYBD** trap.
.sh.edtext	(page 196) is Contents of input buffer before **KEYBD** trap.
.sh.name	(page 197) is Name of variable that invoked discipline function.
.sh.subscript	(page 197) is Subscript that invoked discipline function.
.sh.value	(page 197) is Value of variable that invoked function.
.sh.version	(page 198) is Version of shell.
FIGNORE	(page 199) is Ignore filenames.
HISTCMD	(page 193) is History command number.
HISTEDIT	(page 200) is Editor to use with **hist** command.
LANG	(page 202) is Language locale.
LC_ALL	(page 202) is Locale settings.
LC_COLLATE	(page 202) is Locale collation.

LC_CTYPE   (page 202) is Locale character classes.
LC_NUMERIC   (page 203) is Locale decimal.

The **ERRNO** variable has been deleted. Error messages produced by **ksh** give the reason for system failures in most cases.

The **ENV** variable is now effective only for interactive shells.

The **SECONDS** variable has a granularity of milliseconds rather than seconds.

The **TMOUT** variable also sets the timeout for the **select** command.

If a character in the **space** class is repeated consecutively in the value of **IFS**, then each occurrence of this character delimits a field.

New Compound Commands

The new negation compound command (reserved word **!**) negates the return value of an expression.

The new arithmetic **for** compound command is very similar to the ANSI C language **for** command.

New PATH Search Rules

The following changes have been made to the way **ksh** searches for commands:
- Only special built-ins are searched for first. All built-ins were searched for first in earlier versions.
- Functions are searched before other built-ins.
- When searching **PATH**, **ksh** treats directories that are also in **FPATH** as function directories. In earlier versions of **ksh**, functions found in **FPATH** were found only after searching **PATH**.
- Built-ins can be associated with a pathname. In this case the built-in is only used when the **PATH** search would yield this **PATH**.
- **ksh** turns the **trackall** option on by default.

Changes to Return Values

The return value has been changed as follows:
- Commands that are not found, return 127.
- Commands that are found but cannot execute, return 126.
- Commands that terminate because of a signal, return 256 plus the signal number. You can use **kill –l** to get the name of the signal given the return value.

Additions and Changes to Traps

The **DEBUG** trap is now executed before each command.

The **KEYBD** trap has been added to make it possible to bind editing keys.

Additions and Changes to Built-in Commands

The **–?** option has been added to all regular built-in commands and all other commands that have been implemented. It displays a list of options available for the command.

The following built-ins have been added:
- **builtin** can be used to list built-in commands or to add dynamically linked libraries and new built-in commands.
- **command** eliminates functions from the search order. In front of a special built-in command, **command** causes the special built-in to behave like a regular built-in command.
- **disown** causes **ksh** not to send a **HUP** signal to the specified jobs.
- **false** has a False return value. It was an alias in the 11/16/88 version of **ksh**.
- **getconf** displays the value of system configuration parameters.
- **hist** is the same as **fc** with the 11/16/88 version of **ksh**. **fc** is now an alias.
- **printf** is nearly the same as the ANSI C Programming Language **printf** function.
- **true** has a True return value. It was an alias in the 11/16/88 version of **ksh**.

The **–L** and **–P** options to **cd** have been documented.

The **alias** command and the **typeset** command with the **–f** option ignore the **–x** option since aliases and functions are no longer exported to scripts.

The following options have been added to **exec**:
- **–a** *name* to specify the command name argument.
- **–c** to clear the environment first.

The following changes have been made to **getopts**:
- Usage messages can be automatically generated.
- **#** can be used in place of **:** to specify a numeric option argument.
- To recognize option arguments beginning with **+**, **getopts** requires a **+** at the beginning of the option specification argument.
- **–a** file option has been added to specify the script or function name that will be used in usage messages.

The **–n** option to **jobs** has been documented.

The following options have been added to **kill** or have changed:
- **–n** to specify the signal by signal number.
- **–s** to specify the signal by signal name.
- **–l** without arguments lists only the signal names, not their numbers. **–l** can be used to convert a signal name to and from a signal number.

The **–L** and **–P** options to **pwd** have been documented.

The following options have been added to **set**:
- **notify** to display job completion messages as soon as jobs complete.
- **–C** as a synonym to the **noclobber** option.

The following options have been added to **test** and [:
- A –**e** option has been added to test whether a specified file exists or not. The –**e** option also applies to the [[...]] conditional command.
- The operand for the –**t** option is no longer optional.
- The string equality operator == has been added.
- When four or fewer arguments are given, the interpretation of the arguments is determined by the number of arguments rather than their contents.

The –**S** option has been added to **umask** to specify a symbolic format for output.

The following options have been added to **unset**:
- The –**n** option unsets a name reference variable.
- The –**v** option specifies that only variables will be unset.

The following options have been added to **whence**:
- The –**a** option displays all matches for each name.
- The –**f** option skips the search for functions.
- The –**p** option has been documented.

The built-in dot (.) command now executes functions as well as files. **ksh** executes the specified function in the current environment. **ksh** uses the search path specified by the **FPATH** variable to find the function. In addition, arguments given to . (dot) are restored when the . (dot) script or function completes.

New ksh *Invocation Options*

The following invocation options to **ksh** have been added or modified:
–**n** displays many warning messages.
–**D** generates a dictionary for strings that need translation.

OBSOLESCENT FEATURES

Caution: The following features are currently supported by **ksh** for backward compatibility only. Their use is strongly discouraged. These features may be removed from **ksh** at some point in the future.
- The –**k** and –**t** options to **set**.
- **echo** as a built-in command. (Use **print** instead.)
- **test** and [as built -in commands. (Use [[...]] instead.)
- – to end the list of options for a command. (Use – – instead.)
- = inside [[...]] to compare two strings. (Use == instead.)
- The –**a** option to the **test** command. (Use –**e** instead.)
- The `...` command substitution. (Use $(...) instead.)
- The **times** command. (Use **time** instead.)
- The **trackall** option and tracked aliases.
- The –**x** options to **alias** and **typeset** with the –**f** option.
- **!** as command number in prompt. Use **$HISTCMD** instead.

POSSIBLE EXTENSIONS

Process Substitution

This is available only on versions of the UNIX system that support the **/dev/fd** directory for naming open files. Each command argument of the form <(*list*) or >(*list*) runs process *list* asynchronously connected to some file in the **/dev/fd** directory. The name of this file becomes the argument to the command. If the form with > is selected, then writing on this file provides input for *list*. If < is used, then the file passed as an argument will receive the output of the *list* process.

The following example cuts fields 1 and 3 from files **fi1** and **fi2**, respectively, pastes the results together, and sends the results to the processes **pro1** and **pro2**, as well as putting them onto standard output. Note that the file that is passed as an argument to the command is a UNIX system pipe, so that the programs that expect to seek on the file will not work.

Example
```
paste <(cut -f1 fi1) <(cut -f3 fi2) | tee >(pro1) >(pro2)
```

Brace Group Expansion

Any word that is subject to pathname expansion handles a comma-separated list of words enclosed in { and } specially. After field splitting, and before pathname expansion, **ksh** forms fields for each word with { and } by prefixing each word in the list to anything that comes before the { and appending anything that follows the }.

Examples
```
print foo{xxx,yyy}bar
fooxxxbar fooyyybar
print {foo,bar}.{c,o,h}
foo.c foo.o foo.h bar.c bar.o bar.h
```

Reference Database

With this extension, **ksh** will generate a cross-reference entity-relation database for a given script that provides information about where functions and variables are defined and used. Invoke **ksh** with the **–R** *filename* option to generate the reference database in *filename*. The format of this database is beyond the scope of this book.

Object Oriented

The **–C** option to **typeset** can be used to associate a class name to any variable.

A class name is the name of a variable and can be used like any other variable.

Discipline functions are inherited by variables that are members of a class. Thus, if **foo** belongs to class **bar**, then any discipline function defined for **bar** will be executed in place of the corresponding function for **foo** if the **foo** discipline function does not exist.

HINTS FOR csh USERS CONVERTING TO ksh

Here is a list of items to help the large number of users who switch from **csh** or **tcsh** to **ksh**.

To assign values to variables, use *name=value* rather than **set** *name=value*. With **ksh** no space is allowed before or after the =, and values that have special values or spaces need to be quoted. Use *name=(value...)* to create an array variable.

Aliases cannot take arguments with **ksh**. You need to define a function to get the equivalent of aliases with arguments.

The variable qualifiers do not exist. You must use the substring operators or use quoting to get the equivalent behavior.

With **ksh** you can redirect each file descriptor from 0-9 individually. To redirect both standard output and standard error use > *file* **2>&1**. The override for the **noclobber** option is >| in **ksh**, not >!.

There is no *logout* file in **ksh**. To get equivalent behavior, you have to set an **EXIT** trap in your **.profile** file.

The equivalent of the **source** command in **csh**, is the **.** (dot) command in **ksh**.

Compound commands have a different syntax, and there is no **goto** command in **ksh**. Conditions for **if** and **while** commands are expressions in **csh**, but are commands in **ksh**.

There is a separate command for arithmetic expressions and for all other tests. Arithmetic expressions must be enclosed in ((...)), and variables do not need to be quoted. Assignment is legal.

ksh uses the value of the special variable, **$?**, to hold the exit status of a command rather than **$status**.

Array variables in **ksh** are slightly different than in **csh**. Each element of an array in **ksh** can be a string. In **csh**, each element is a word. If you do not use a subscript, you get the first element (element 0) in **ksh**, and you get the complete array in **csh**. You need to use a subscript of **@** or * to get all the elements of an array in **ksh**.

22 CHARACTER SET

This table may be useful when you specify ranges of characters in character classes, or when you read a printout that shows non-printing characters in their octal representation, or when you use **print** or **echo** with the \n option, etc.

ksh displays letters, digits, and punctuation characters as you would expect. For instance, **ksh** displays control characters as **^A** (octal 001), **^B** (octal 002), etc.

The character set shown here may differ slightly on different terminals and different systems.

√ indicates that this character is included in the minimum character set required by the IEEE POSIX standard.

The numeric Decimal, Octal, and Hexadecimal values are for the ASCII encoding of the character shown in the *Glyph* column. Note: *Glyph* is a graphic symbol.

The *Class* column indicates the character class or classes to which the given character belongs in the C or POSIX locale. It is indicated using the following:
[:alnum:] is **d** or **l** or **u**
[:alpha:] is **l** or **u**
[:blank:] is **b**
[:cntrl:] is **c**
[:digit:] is **d**
[:graph:] is **d** or **l** or **p** or **u**
[:lower:] is **l**
[:print:] is **d** or **l** or **p** or **u** or the Space character
[:punct:] is **p**
[:space:] is **s**
[:upper:] is **u**
[:xdigit:] is **x**

CONTROL CHARACTERS

	Dec	Octal	Hex	Glyph	Class	Explanation
√	0	000	00	^@	c	NUL (Null)
	1	001	01	^A	c	SOH (Start of heading)
	2	002	02	^B	c	STX (Start text)
	3	003	03	^C	c	ETX (End text)
	4	004	04	^D	c	EOT (End of transmission)
	5	005	05	^E	c	ENQ (Enquiry)
	6	006	06	^F	c	ACK (Acknowledge)
√	7	007	07	^G	c	BEL (Bell)
√	8	010	08	^H	c	BS (Backspace)
√	9	011	09	^I	b c s	TAB (Tab)
√	10	012	0A	^J	c s	LF (Linefeed, Newline)
√	11	013	0B	^K	c s	VT (Vertical Tab)
√	12	014	0C	^L	c s	FF (Formfeed)
√	13	015	0D	^M	c s	CR (Carriage return)
	14	016	0E	^N	c	SO (Shift out)
	15	017	0F	^O	c	SI (Shift in)
	16	020	10	^P	c	DLE (Data link escape)
	17	021	11	^Q	c	DC1 (X-ON)
	18	022	12	^R	c	DC2
	19	023	13	^S	c	DC3 (X-OFF)
	20	024	14	^T	c	DC4
	21	025	15	^U	c	NAK (Negative acknowledge)
	22	026	16	^V	c	SYN (Synchronous idle)
	23	027	17	^W	c	ETB (End transmission blocks)
	24	030	18	^X	c	CAN (Cancel)
	25	031	19	^Y	c	EM (End of medium)
	26	032	1A	^Z	c	SUB (Substitute)
	27	033	1B	^[	c	ESC (Escape)
	28	034	1C	^\	c	FS (IS4) (File separator)
	29	035	1D	^]	c	GS (IS3) (Group separator)
	30	036	1E	^^	c	RS (IS2) (Record separator)
	31	037	1F	^_	c	US (IS1) (Unit separator)

SPACE

	Dec	Octal	Hex	Glyph	Class	Explanation
√	32	040	20		b s	SPACEBAR SP (Space)

PRINTING CHARACTERS

Dec	Octal	Hex	Glyph	Class	Explanation
√ 33	041	21	!	p	Negation operator
√ 34	042	22	"	p	Grouping quoting
√ 35	043	23	#	p	Comment character
					Substring operator, left truncate
					Default primary prompt
					for superuser
√ 36	044	24	$	p	Default prompt
					Parameter expansion
					Special parameter
√ 37	045	25	%	p	Substring operator, right truncate
					Job identifier
√ 38	046	26	&	p	Asynchronous execution
√ 39	047	27	'	p	Single quote
					Literal quoting
√ 40	050	28	(	p	Subshell grouping
√ 41	051	29	)	p	
√ 42	052	2A	*	p	Wildcard match in patterns
√ 43	053	2B	+	p	
√ 44	054	2C	,	p	
√ 45	055	2D	−	p	
√ 46	056	2E	.	p	(dot) Working directory
					Built-in command
√ 47	057	2F	/	p	Name of root directory
					Pathname delimiter
√ 48	060	30	0	d x	
√ 49	061	31	1	d x	
√ 50	062	32	2	d x	
√ 51	063	33	3	d x	
√ 52	064	34	4	d x	
√ 53	065	35	5	d x	
√ 54	066	36	6	d x	
√ 55	067	37	7	d x	
√ 56	070	38	8	d x	
√ 57	071	39	9	d x	
√ 58	072	3A	:	p	Null built-in command
√ 59	073	3B	;	p	Command delimiter
√ 60	074	3C	<	p	Redirects command input

	Dec	*Octal*	*Hex*	*Glyph*	*Class*	*Explanation*
√	61	075	3D	=	p	Used in variable assignments
√	62	076	3E	>	p	Redirects command output
√	63	077	3F	?	p	Default secondary prompt Single character match in patterns
√	64	100	40	@	p	
√	65	101	41	A	u x	
√	66	102	42	B	u x	
√	67	103	43	C	u x	
√	68	104	44	D	u x	
√	69	105	45	E	u x	
√	70	106	46	F	u x	
√	71	107	47	G	u	
√	72	110	48	H	u	
√	73	111	49	I	u	
√	74	112	4A	J	u	
√	75	113	4B	K	u	
√	76	114	4C	L	u	
√	77	115	4D	M	u	
√	78	116	4E	N	u	
√	79	117	4F	O	u	
√	80	120	50	P	u	
√	81	121	51	Q	u	
√	82	122	52	R	u	
√	83	123	53	S	u	
√	84	124	54	T	u	
√	85	125	55	U	u	
√	86	126	56	V	u	
√	87	127	57	W	u	
√	88	130	58	X	u	
√	89	131	59	Y	u	
√	90	132	5A	Z	u	
√	91	133	5B	[	p	
√	92	134	5C	\	p	Escape quoting
√	93	135	5D	]	p	
√	94	136	5E	^	p	
√	95	137	5F	_	p	(underscore)

	Dec	Octal	Hex	Glyph	Class	Explanation
√	96	140	60		p	Backquote (grave accent) Used for old command substitution
√	97	141	61	a	l x	
√	98	142	62	b	l x	
√	99	143	63	c	l x	
√	100	144	64	d	l x	
√	101	145	65	e	l x	
√	102	146	66	f	l x	
√	103	147	67	g	l	
√	104	150	68	h	l	
√	105	151	69	i	l	
√	106	152	6A	j	l	
√	107	153	6B	k	l	
√	108	154	6C	l	l	
√	109	155	6D	m	l	
√	110	156	6E	n	l	
√	111	157	6F	o	l	
√	112	160	70	p	l	
√	113	161	71	q	l	
√	114	162	72	r	l	
√	115	163	73	s	l	
√	116	164	74	t	l	
√	117	165	75	u	l	
√	118	166	76	v	l	
√	119	167	77	w	l	
√	120	170	78	x	l	
√	121	171	79	y	l	
√	122	172	7A	z	l	
√	123	173	7B	{	p	Command grouping
√	124	174	7C	|	p	Pipe command output
√	125	175	7D	}	p	
√	126	176	7E	~	p	Tilde substitution

DELETE, RUBOUT

Dec	Octal	Hex	Glyph	Class	Explanation
127	177	7F		c	DEL, RUB (Delete, rubout)

INDEX

Symbols